PLANTING THE WORD

ERIN CRIDER

PLANTING THE WORD

Missional Ecclesiology in Twenty-First-Century America

BAYLOR UNIVERSITY PRESS

Cover and book design by Elyxandra Encarnación
Cover image: "Rehabilitation client and county supervisor discuss planting problems. Cherokee County, Kansas." The Miriam and Ira D. Wallach Division of Art, Prints and Photographs: Photography Collection, New York Public Library Digital Collections.

Library of Congress Cataloging-in-Publication Data

Names: Crider, Erin, author.
Title: Planting the word: missional ecclesiology in twenty-first-century America / Erin Crider.
Description: Waco, Texas: Baylor University Press, [2025] | Includes bibliographical references and index. | Summary: "Surveys the history, culture, and theology of contemporary American church planting movements and explores practical implications for church planting ministries"—Provided by publisher.
Identifiers: LCCN 2024056188 (print) | LCCN 2024056189 (ebook) | ISBN 9781481322874 (paperback) | ISBN 9781481324229 (library binding) | ISBN 9781481322904 (adobe pdf) | ISBN 9781481322898 (epub)
Subjects: LCSH: Church development, New—United States—History—21st century. | Evangelistic work—United States—History—21st century. | United States—Church history—21st century.
Classification: LCC BV652.24.C75 2025 (print) | LCC BV652.24 (ebook) | DDC 254/.1—dc23/eng/20250721
LC record available at https://lccn.loc.gov/2024056188
LC ebook record available at https://lccn.loc.gov/2024056189

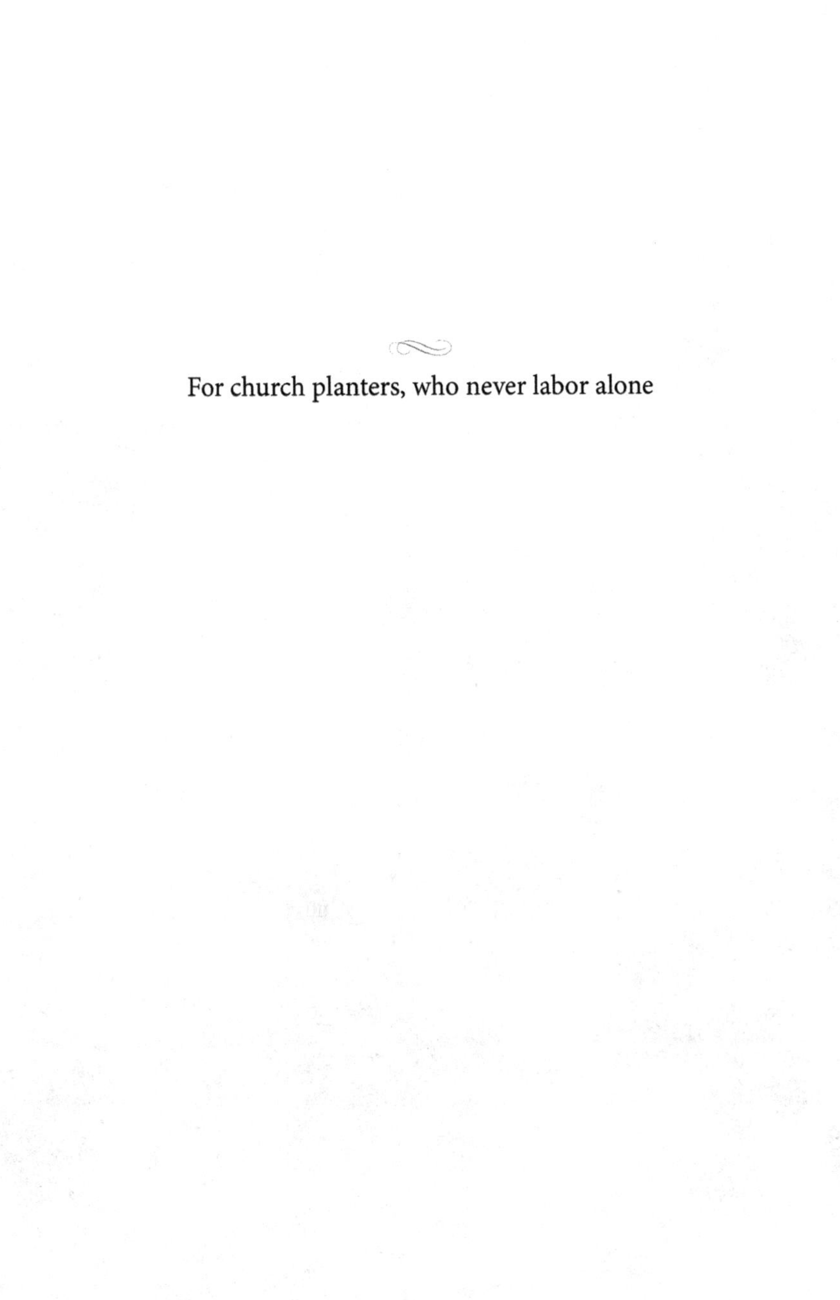

For church planters, who never labor alone

Contents

Acknowledgments

The research behind this project has been a labor of love over many years, during which time a variety of generous and thoughtful scholars enriched my thinking. Particular thanks go to Dr. Nathan Eubank, Dr. Matthew Kirkpatrick, Dr. Benjamin Johnson, Rev. Dr. Liz Hoare, and Dr. Cathy Ross for challenging me to reexamine my understandings of church and reflect more deeply on key biblical texts. I owe deep appreciation to three different mentors: Rev. Dr. Michael Lloyd, Rev. Dr. Michael Moynagh, and the late Rev. Dr. Michael Green. Each of these men graciously offered wise advice, thoughtful questions, a listening ear, and patient encouragement, and my life has been richer for it. Professors in the University of Aberdeen's Divinity Faculty were thoughtful and inspiring conversation partners. Particular thanks go to my patient PhD supervisors, Rev. Dr. Kenneth Jeffrey and Dr. Tom Greggs, but I also owe a debt of gratitude to Dr. Philip Ziegler, Dr. Léon van Ommen, and Dr. Katie Cross. Colleagues at Gordon-Conwell Theological Seminary offered me the most precious gifts a budding scholar could hope to receive: teaching experience, library resources, and opportunities to discuss my work in formal and informal settings. Special thanks to Dr. Scott Sunquist, Dr. Justin Young, Dr. Bradley Howell, and Dr. Gerry Wheaton. Many thanks as well to the dedicated team at Baylor University Press, especially Dave Nelson and Jenny Hunt.

The prayers and encouragement of my church, my Bible study friends, and my prayer partners have been deeply felt. The faithful friendship of pastors and Christian leaders serving throughout the United States and United Kingdom, too many to name here, have inspired me to keep my academic musings grounded in the beautiful, messy realities of church life. I am forever grateful to Ned and Donna Hastings, whose longtime friendship first inspired me to get involved in church planting.

This project would never have come to life without the love and support of my brother, Matt, and my mother, Janet. Matt, thank you for your gentle spirit, encouraging perspective, and abiding confidence in me. Mom, thank you for always believing in me, for letting me ramble about ideas during many long walks, for listening patiently while I read draft chapters aloud, and for countless large and small acts of kindness whenever I needed them most. May this book reflect your love, grace, and wisdom, just as you've reflected God's unfailing love to me. To God be the glory.

Introduction

Church Planting in Twenty-First-Century America

In many American communities, people need not look far before finding a freshly planted congregation. Movie theaters, shopping malls, and schools throughout the United States have hosted new church fellowships, and new church buildings dot many communities. One study found that between 1990 and 2000, the United States saw 3600 new churches planted annually, a figure that increased by 10 percent between 2000 and 2005.[1] This trend shows few signs of slowing. According to one recent report, the Southern Baptist Convention (SBC) alone planted 588 new congregations in the United States in 2020, slightly more than in 2019, despite the Covid-19 pandemic.[2] Furthermore, the influence of American church planting movements extends well beyond their immediate congregations. Pastors like Rick Warren and Bill Hybels have written internationally best-selling books on the subject, and training conferences focused on missional church praxis have proliferated.[3] Consequently, there is widespread interest in understanding planted churches. Many church leaders and lay Christians hope to understand their ministries or replicate their successes. Church planting has become a highly visible expression of American evangelical Christianity.

At the same time, troubling questions and disturbing scandals have also arisen within church planting movements. *Christianity Today*'s podcast *The Rise and Fall of Mars Hill* documented the troubled history of one high-profile planted church in Seattle, WA.[4] Shortly after its initial release,

The Rise and Fall of Mars Hill was the third most downloaded podcast on Apple's iTunes platform; several months later, it remained comfortably within the top ten most downloaded religious podcasts.[5] Unfortunately, Mars Hill was not alone in either troubles or media attention. In 2022, Hillsong's Australian founder resigned in disgrace, and a series of disturbing allegations arose within Hillsong's American congregations that were later featured in two separate documentary series.[6] Away from the national media glare, other planted churches have faced similarly troubling scandals. Less dramatically, the best estimates indicate that roughly 30 percent of planted American congregations close within five years of opening, leaving untold questions, confusion, and disappointment in their wake.[7] Many are also seeking to understand this side of America's church planting movements in order to avoid or heal from tragic missteps.

Despite widespread interest in church planting, contemporary academic literature has yet to offer a comprehensive account of the history or theology of church planting movements in twentieth- and twenty-first-century American contexts. Some church planters have written about their personal experiences and observations. While their accounts tend to be impressionistic, highly pragmatic, and/or written with non-US contexts in mind,[8] they often include valuable local histories of planted churches and descriptions of their aims, practices, and beliefs.[9] Qualitative researchers have published studies of specific planted congregations, which offer a wealth of helpful material.[10] Nonetheless, their focus is generally local, and their methodological approach does not naturally offer a comprehensive understanding of wider patterns in operant theology or praxis. As a result, significant, urgent, fundamental questions about the culture of American church planting remain unanswered. What exactly do American church planters understand themselves to be planting? How has the practice of planting churches impacted beliefs about church and mission?

This book aims to answer these two questions by identifying and examining patterns in the operant missional ecclesiology of planted American churches. As we will see, there are clear and significant patterns in the practices of many congregations that engage in church planting, and these practices both shape and reflect shared understandings of church and mission. Planted American congregations embody an understanding of "mission" as offering compelling, contextualized services with an eye to people who are not currently church members. Their missional vision often aligns reasonably well with Donald McGavran's Church Growth

Theory.[11] Operant understandings of "church" are less clear. Many planted congregations embody a strong understanding of "church" as local. In some, "church" becomes a platform for a gifted preacher to proclaim the gospel to Christians and unbelievers alike. As we will also see, patterns of missional ecclesial praxis drawn from America's revivalist history, entertainment industries, and sociopolitical culture have weakened rather than strengthened operant understandings of church as community. When congregations become consumerist and individualized, undue pressure easily mounts on church leaders. Nonetheless, planted churches have a rich heritage of Protestant theology that offers resources to clarify their identity as missional churches. Since many value the Word highly, theologians who describe the church as a creature of the Word and the body of Christ offer planted churches helpful tools to frame their ecclesial identity and missional callings. Drawing on such resources, this book will not only trace the history and theology behind present practices, but will also offer clear, theologically grounded guidance for planted churches seeking sustainable, faithful ways forward.

Aims and Scope of the Research

It is important to state at the outset that the aim of this study is not to offer the final word on contemporary American church planting. The aim is to begin a conversation. There is far more that can and should be said about the subject than one book could possibly articulate. Within the present literature, there are many important observations to be made about American church planting, and there are also many significant gaps in the current research. For example, church planting literature often favors larger churches with high-profile leaders. As we will see in chapter 2, the literature reflects the reality that large, attractional churches have been "influencers," shaping both popular perceptions and common practices well beyond their immediate fold. One Faith Communities Today (FACT) study from early 2020 found that roughly 70 percent of Americans attended congregations of 251 or more people, and larger congregations were growing more rapidly than smaller congregations.[12] Americans are clearly drawn to larger churches, and many have had personal experience with growing churches like those that are prominent in the present literature. These trends make it appropriate to begin a conversation about church planting by unpacking the influence of larger, high-profile congregations and megachurches. At the same time, important questions about planted house churches and microchurches bear more focused attention from subsequent studies. Similarly, this book will describe the rise of structural entities like church planting networks and multisite churches, but a full examination of their considerable variety requires further research. Finally, and perhaps most importantly, church planting beyond white-majority congregations has been widely neglected in current literature, for reasons we will only begin to explore in chapter 3. Multiethnic and monoracial congregations are poised to make substantial contributions to America's next generation of planted churches, and their missional visions merit fuller articulation. By defining the broader strokes of American church planting movements and creating a framework for researchers, this book will equip subsequent studies to add important detail, nuance, and complexity to the picture painted here.

This book examines church planting ministries that originated in the United States and launched from the mid-1960s to the present day, a span of approximately sixty years. As chapter 2 details, common patterns of praxis that have had a lasting influence on the operant missional ecclesiology of American church planting movements first appeared in the 1960s, creating a natural starting point for this study. The choice to focus on American congregations presents some challenges. For example, the Acts 29 Network began through the ministry of Mars Hill Church in Seattle, but today it partners with many churches around the world.[13] Similarly, the Hillsong movement originated in Australia, but planted a handful of congregations within the United States and produced worship music used in many American congregations.[14] This book will occasionally mention international church planting networks and partnerships, but the focus will remain congregations and church planting networks that originated within the United States. This focus will allow a clearer articulation of important connections between church planting and threads of American cultural life. Further studies will be needed to articulate the influence of international partnerships on American church planting ministries.

In spite of these parameters, some might be concerned that the scope of this project remains too broad. After all, the United States is a large nation which enjoys considerable cultural, theological, and geographic diversity. America's long-standing commitment to freedom of worship has resulted in a wide variety of Christian confessions and expressions, which are broadly concentrated in different geographic regions.[15] Furthermore, the growing missiological emphasis on contextualization has created an expectation that missional congregations will necessarily differ from one another as they work to reach people within their own local cultures.[16]

For this reason, Dana Robert even called contextualization a kind of "radical localism."[17] It is therefore important to clarify that this project will argue that common patterns exist within the operant theology and praxis of many planted American churches, but not that all planted American churches are entirely uniform in their operant theology, nor that they have all adopted completely identical praxes. With so much thoughtful scholarly attention already devoted to the uniqueness of specific planted churches, it is now worth exploring the shared culture that shapes their theology and practices.

As we will see, churches from different American regions and confessional traditions can be more similar than they might initially appear. A century ago, Dietrich Bonhoeffer observed that confessional statements were not particularly prominent in American churches; as a result, he argued, substantive theological differences between congregations often seemed less visible and less significant to American worshipers.[18] Recent studies of American megachurches have reached similar conclusions. As Scott Thumma recently wrote, "The most important differences [between megachurches] are in aesthetic and organizational style. By contrast, the theological differences are minimal."[19] Thumma adds that the common "Big Box" style of church architecture bespeaks broader similarities, which, like the design of shopping malls, transcend regional differences.[20] Sung worship patterns suggest further similarities. In 2020, one researcher estimated that as many as fifty million Christians globally sang Hillsong music during gathered worship each week.[21] Shared worship music suggests deeper similarities, as both the style and theological content of selections must be consistent with the culture of churches where they are sung. More substantial commonalities unite American churches than one might initially assume.

Within the narrower context of planted American congregations, it is even easier to overlook significant but meaningful patterns that unite congregations. This happens in part because the founding narratives of planted congregations tend to emphasize the pioneering ministries of entrepreneurial leaders and downplay the influence of other churches or ecclesial structures.[22] If one judges churches solely by these narratives, planted churches often seem to be largely independent entities. In reality, a surprising range of formal and informal ties connects seemingly disparate congregations. Church planting networks like the SBC's Send Network, the Acts 29 Network, and many other less formal networks provide some of the same support that denominations traditionally offered, uniting congregations across different regions.[23] Some congregations are even affiliated with more than one church planting network; for example, the SBC and Acts 29 have jointly supported many churches.[24] Ideas and practices can thus be shared far beyond even a single church planting network.[25] The extent of cross-pollination can be significant. Mark Driscoll, whose church in Seattle, WA, founded Acts 29, spoke about church planting at one annual meeting of the SBC and guest preached at SBC-affiliated Saddleback Church in Lake Forest, CA.[26] In turn, Saddleback's pastor, Rick Warren, preached the final sermon at Driscoll's Mars Hill Church.[27] Furthermore, church staff have moved widely among planted churches. One of the first Emerging churches was founded in Southern California, near Saddleback Church, by a pastor who had previously worked at Chicago-area Willow Creek Church.[28] Interconnections are even more evident in the literature, where church planting practitioners frequently cite one another's work approvingly. Acts 29, for example, cites Tim Keller's essay "Why Plant Churches?" on its website as part of its own statement of faith, even though Keller ministered within a more traditionally Reformed church planting network based in New York City.[29] Keller's "Why Plant Churches?" in turn cited studies by C. Peter Wagner, a California-based charismatic church planting scholar, and Lyle Schaller, a Midwestern United Methodist Church (UMC) pastor and church planting consultant, as well as "denominational studies" of church planting conducted by the SBC.[30] There is thus a remarkable kind of ecumenism among church planting practitioners, who eagerly reach across geographic and confessional boundaries in search of helpful new insights. The common project of planting churches has created a national subculture within contemporary American Christianity, making it both appropriate and essential to examine the operant missional ecclesiology evident within this subculture.

Working Definitions: Church Planting Movement, Planted Church, Operant Missional Ecclesiology

Three terms are important to clarify at the outset. First, the term "church planting movement," which in this book describes a formal or informal network of planted churches which remain committed to starting new congregations for missional purposes. This definition of "church planting" represents a departure from older Christian understandings of the same term. Pre-Reformation Christians generally used the term "church planting" to describe the process of introducing or "planting" the one Catholic Church into new areas where Christianity had no visible expression.[31]

Some advocates still hold to this definition of "church planting" and question whether the term should apply to those starting new American churches.[32] By contrast, references to the practice of "church planting" in twentieth- and twenty-first-century American contexts generally describe efforts to plant new local congregations within any community, even those where many Christian churches may already exist.[33] This newer understanding of "church planting" is well suited to American culture, where the apparent diversity of local churches at times obscures visions of one Church universal.[34] In general, contemporary American church planting movements primarily engage in what Stuart Murray called "saturation planting": starting new congregations in areas where churches already exist in order to "enhance the ability of . . . churches to engage in mission."[35] Planting churches in contemporary American communities thus remains a missional act, now intended to enhance or complement the missional witness of existing churches within a local community. The plural form, "church planting movements," will be used where appropriate to acknowledge formal, structural distinctions between different church planting networks.

This book will also prefer the term "planted church" over the more common expression "church plant." This phrasing renders "church" the noun and "planted" the modifier, in deference to Roland Allen's insistence that planted churches are first and foremost "churches."[36] This move also reflects the approach commonly taken to planting new churches in the United States, which differs from that seen elsewhere. In the United Kingdom, for example, planted churches commonly begin as community outreach activities or social meetings which only gradually start to offer gathered worship services.[37] By contrast, planted American churches typically start by creating space for gathered worship services, making the distinctions between planted churches and other missional projects, social groups, and community networks much clearer.[38] Planted American churches quickly meet the Reformers' definition of church as a site where the Word is rightly proclaimed and the sacraments rightly administered.[39] The churches examined in this book all profess Trinitarian Christianity and offer regular, gathered worship.[40] Planted churches in America are therefore rightly understood as churches.

In one sense, every church could be considered a "planted church," as all were founded at some point. The term "church planting," though, has become associated with specific operant understandings of church and mission, which chapters 1 and 2 will detail more fully. The churches described in this book which self-identify as "planted" generally began as entirely new congregations, not as existing churches relaunching under a new name.[41] Many American churches that self-identify as "planted" also began recently enough that their founding act remains comfortably within the congregation's living memory. In these churches, the founding pastor often continues to serve as the primary teaching pastor.[42] These churches frequently engage with church planting movements, supporting and sponsoring other planted congregations once their own has become established. Ongoing involvement in church planting networks encourages a congregation to keep their founding narrative alive. Churches that identify as "planted" thus maintain a strong connection to their original missional vision and to the broader culture of contemporary American church planting.

A third term in need of clarification is "operant missional ecclesiology." This is a more specific form of "operant theology," which Helen Cameron and her coauthors succinctly define as "the theology embedded within the actual practices of a group."[43] The distinction between "operant" and "espoused" theology is particularly important because it highlights the possibility of substantive differences between lived theological understandings, which are embedded within practices, and official theological statements, which a church and its members sincerely profess.[44] For example, a congregation that espouses faith in the power of prayer might spend little time in gathered services actually praying, or might use corporate prayer only to mark transitional moments in the service. As John Swinton and Harriet Mowat observed, "what people say, what people do and what people say about what they do are entirely different things."[45] Operant theology is therefore deeply tied to observable praxis. Nonetheless, beliefs and practices still relate to each other. As Cameron and her coauthors also explain, operant theology "is not external to faith or superimposed on it," but it is embodied in the "faith-carrying words and actions of believers."[46] As will be demonstrated, practices in the context of planted American churches stem from and express sincere theological convictions, even when those convictions are not fully articulated. Swinton and Mowat rightly explain that practices "contain values, beliefs, theologies and other assumptions which, for the most part, go unnoticed until they are complexified and brought to our notice through the process of theological reflection."[47] The theological reflection in this book will therefore explore ways that church planting practices both illustrate and complicate common espoused beliefs about church and mission.

A few counterexamples will further clarify the concept of "operant theology." "Operant theology" does not necessarily imply "subterranean theology," a term "employed by sociologists, phenomenologists and historians of religion to describe common or popular religiosity that is not controlled either by the church or (in its more theological expression) by the academy."[48] "Subterranean theology" draws helpful distinctions between popular theological expressions and formal understandings of theology that leaders or academics articulate, but it also implies that some beliefs are "deliberately hidden, secret or even subversive, or . . . unconventional and experimental (as in the phrase 'the underground press')."[49] "Operant" theology is therefore a more helpful category for describing beliefs embedded within church planting practices because these beliefs are not intentionally hidden, nor are they subversive or necessarily opposed to those espoused by church leaders and academics. "Operant theology" will also be used rather than "ordinary theology," which assumes substantial differences between the theology of ordained church leaders and that of "ordinary" lay Christians due to differing levels of theological education.[50] As subsequent chapters will explain, some American church planting movements require little or no formal theological training for church leaders, and the denominations that have been most active in planting new churches typically have less demanding requirements for pastoral training.[51] In addition, a growing wealth of resources is now available to "ordinary" church members through online media and widened access to theological education.[52] Furthermore, ordained leaders can and often do influence the theological convictions of church members, making the distinction between leaders' theology and that of lay church members fuzzier.[53] It is also important to recall that ordained church leaders are rarely the only voices shaping operant beliefs.[54] This book will therefore use the term "operant missional ecclesiology" in order to avoid unwarranted clericalism, to account for important practical dynamics within planted American congregations, and to include clergy and lay members in a shared body of corporately discerned, negotiated, and enacted beliefs.

Methodology: Richard Osmer's Four Tasks of Practical Theological Reflection

Richard Osmer's description of the pastoral cycle will guide theological reflection in this book. Osmer proposes that theological reflection occurs in four tasks: the descriptive-empirical task, the interpretive task, the normative task, and the pragmatic task.[55] According to Osmer, each of these tasks participates in some aspect of Christ's threefold office.[56] The descriptive-empirical task participates in Christ's priestly office by practicing "a form of priestly listening, grounded in a spirituality of presence."[57] The aim of the descriptive-empirical task is thus not objective reporting, but "gathering information that helps us discern patterns and dynamics" at work in a given setting.[58] Osmer's second task, the interpretive task, participates in Christ's kingly office by drawing together relevant insights from different academic fields in order to practice "a form of wise judgment, grounded in a spirituality of sagely wisdom."[59] The normative task participates in Christ's prophetic office, identifying relevant resources within Christian theological tradition with the aim of "helping others hear and heed God's word in the particular circumstances of their lives and world."[60] The pragmatic task draws together insights from the first three tasks in order to effect practical changes.[61] As Osmer describes it, the pragmatic task is "grounded in a spirituality of servant leadership," marked by "taking risks on behalf of the congregation to help it better embody its mission as a sign and witness of God's self-giving love."[62] This four-step process offers a Christ-centered, comprehensive approach to theological reflection. Osmer's method encourages churches to weigh their situation and context carefully in light of Christian doctrines in order to identify constructive ways forward.

Several features of Osmer's approach suit it especially well to this inquiry. Osmer frames theological reflection in the context of actual church ministry and praxis, giving helpful focus to this examination of operant missional ecclesiology. The four tasks that comprise Osmer's approach also include questions about social and contextual factors at play within churches. As Osmer puts it, "congregations are embedded in a web of natural and social systems beyond the church."[63] As we will see, this statement is particularly true of planted American congregations, which frequently borrow forms and patterns from their surrounding culture in the hopes of offering more relevant, contextualized proclamation. Osmer's method particularly encourages both academic researchers and church planting practitioners to learn from problems and challenges, a move that echoes current academic and popular interest in troubled planted churches.[64] Drawing on the work of Heidegger, Gerkin, and Ricoeur, Osmer argues that human interpretive processes often go unnoticed until we are "brought up short," and it becomes clear that current paradigms no longer fully explain present realities.[65] Particularly in light of recent scandals, the Covid-19 pandemic and its aftermath, and shifting cultural norms and demographic patterns, many planted churches have indeed been "brought up short" in recent years. Osmer's theological reflection offers a constructive way forward that is balanced and redemptive, appropriately sensitive to troubling experiences and well suited to analyze cultural complexities.

Osmer's method also has limitations which bear equally careful consideration. Some critics worry that Osmer's method is too prescriptive and unidirectional in approach to explain complex situations fully.[66] This critique is well placed, particularly in the context of a written text, which necessarily presents ideas as a single unidirectional argument. By contrast, Osmer himself described the practice of developing theological reflection as both recursive and integrated.[67] Findings under one task naturally lead to reassessment of a different task.[68] Such a process occurred frequently in the research behind this book, though it might not be fully evident within the final written form. More seriously, others express concern that Osmer's approach describes the process in four discrete tasks, only one of which is explicitly theological, and so confines genuinely theological thinking to one section of the project.[69] Astley's account of ordinary theology offers a solution to this problem, even though Astley does not directly address Osmer; Astley writes, "The descriptive task of the study of ordinary theology requires us to engage in 'theological listening': listening out for it and attempting to portray it."[70] Following Astley, this book will approach the descriptive-empirical and interpretive tasks by "listening out" carefully for theological patterns at work and articulating theological nuances embodied within patterns of praxis. Similarly, the aim of the fourth task will be to identify strategies for bringing praxis into closer alignment with espoused theology. There will thus be genuinely theological reflection evident within all four tasks.

Overview of Chapters

The chapters that follow will develop sustained theological reflection on important patterns within the operant missional ecclesiology at work within contemporary American planted churches. Chapters 1 and 2 address Osmer's descriptive task by describing the development of existing patterns of operant missional ecclesiology within American church planting movements. Chapter 1 examines missiological discussions which preceded and broadly influenced twentieth-century American church planting efforts, even though these discussions were generally focused on missions in non-Western contexts. Chapter 2 examines the rise of church planting movements in the United States from the 1960s to the present day and describes ways that they gradually developed distinct patterns of operant missional ecclesiology. The focus shifts to Osmer's analytic task in chapter 3, which analyzes how the operant missional ecclesiology of planted churches interacted with broader historical, cultural, and sociopolitical developments in late twentieth-century America. Osmer's normative task is the focus of chapter 4, which revisits important threads in Christian theological tradition to articulate ways that churches can rightly participate in the *missio Dei*. Chapter 4 includes reflection on the doctrine of the Word as it appears in biblical texts, Reformation teachings that describe church as a creature of the Word, and threads of twentieth-century theologies of proclamation and ecclesial witness. Chapter 5 engages in Osmer's pragmatic task and considers how planted churches can draw their operant theology into closer alignment with their espoused callings and beliefs. As part of the pragmatic task, chapter 5 includes a practical example of church planting from the United Kingdom that complements the work of American church planters and is well suited to American cultural realities. Chapter 5 also outlines a framework for using the four Nicene marks of church to help planted congregations and scholars of church planting movements assess congregational ministries in a comprehensive, theologically grounded, and actionable way. The conclusion sums up the research by reflecting on an example of corporate ecclesial witness from Lesslie Newbigin's own missional experiences and suggesting new directions for further research.

Reflective Considerations: Locating My Own Perspective

Every theologian is shaped by his or her time and place, making it appropriate to locate my own perspectives relative to the field of church planting. A kind friend once described me as "a theological mosaic" because my faith includes fragments drawn together from a variety of Protestant Christian traditions. I spent my childhood in United Methodist congregations as a pastor's daughter and have been a member of SBC churches since my teenage years. I began formal theological study within an evangelical nondenominational seminary with Reformed leanings, where I currently serve on staff. I am also an American who spent three years in further theological study within an evangelical Anglican Bible college in the United Kingdom among a diverse international student body. During my years in the United Kingdom, I primarily attended charismatic Anglican churches and served with one on short-term cross-cultural mission teams. I enjoyed learning from the breadth of Anglican traditions. For example, I have fond memories of an informal theological "supper club" with committed Anglo-Catholic friends whose perspectives deeply enriched and challenged my own. My doctoral research was conducted at an ancient Scottish university but completed remotely from the United States during the Covid-19 pandemic, when video chats suddenly united us all. My understandings of church and mission are therefore eclectic, with a broad appreciation of the strengths and limitations of a wide range of Protestant confessional traditions and ecclesial structures.

My experiences with church planting and missional ecclesiology have been similarly rich and varied. My formal membership has long been with a planted church affiliated with the SBC, which I watched grow from a small fellowship into the large multisite megachurch it became. My church has always been committed to church planting and has sponsored more than thirty other planted congregations to date. These church planting partners are located primarily, but not exclusively, in North America. Several years ago, I participated in an official church visit to one of our church planting partners in Quebec, where I met and heard stories from about a dozen active church planters ministering in very diverse contexts throughout the province. As part of my postgraduate theological studies in the United Kingdom, I conducted research into Fresh Expressions' ecclesiology under Michael Moynagh's generous and gracious supervision. While completing that research, I participated in university missions in the United Kingdom and in Belgium, where I met still other church planters and saw ministries serving very different cultures. These experiences have left me all too aware that books and popular media accounts of American church planting have had a wider influence than some might realize. They also helped me to see that a variety of different approaches to mission, church, and missional church planting can be fruitful.

The collective weight of these experiences has left me, as Stefan Paas put it, a "skeptical advocate" of church planting.[71] I am skeptical because I am all too aware of the theological and logistical complexities facing missional churches and have seen unaddressed problems damage planted congregations. Nonetheless, I remain an advocate of church planting, having been repeatedly moved by the sincere commitment, compassion, and creativity that I observe in many planted congregations. The energy and enthusiasm of church planters, along with their genuine eagerness to share ideas with other Christians, encourage me to this day. May this book allow me to serve as "an interpretive guide,"[72] equipping scholars to explain the complex terrain that many planted churches have already traveled and empowering congregations to identify fruitful, well-trodden paths that will guide their ministries forward.

1

A Prehistory of Modern Church Planting

New Missional Directions

In 1974, when contemporary church planting movements were only beginning to appear in some parts of the American landscape, a major missional conference convened in Lausanne, Switzerland. Throughout the twentieth century, Christians had been wrestling with profound questions about the way missions had been conducted in earlier generations. Post-colonial concerns began before the official collapse of empires, as missionaries wrestled with long-standing problems and unanswered questions. When do overseas "missions" become "churches," and why does that distinction matter? What is the place of churches in the broader project of Christian mission? What kinds of missional outreach should Christians prioritize, and which remain ethical in twentieth-century contexts?

The 1974 Lausanne Congress was hardly the first group to examine twentieth-century missiology, but the debates and voices that emerged from Lausanne would directly inspire church planting pioneers like Rick Warren. For fifty years prior to Lausanne, concerned missionaries had proposed "church planting" as a reform measure to remedy growing concerns about overseas missions. At the time Lausanne met, there were real questions about whether cross-cultural Christian mission remained tenable in light of growing awareness of some historical abuses of power. The Lausanne delegates had to articulate what responsible mission looked like in the late twentieth century. Within their arguments, though, we can see the early threads of an emerging missional ecclesiology that would find concrete expression over the next fifty years in America's planted churches. Consequently, if we are to understand the development of

American church planting movements, we must first examine contemporaneous debates about mission, church, and the agency of churches in modern missions.

Church Planting: A Proposed Corrective in Cross-Cultural Missions

Twentieth-century discussions about church planting initially arose in the context of cross-cultural missions. Two former missionaries, Roland Allen and Donald McGavran, became foundational voices within these conversations. Allen and McGavran each redefined mission as planting churches in order to remedy problems they had observed while serving in cross-cultural missions during the first half of the twentieth century. Allen's and McGavran's works continue to shape discussions of church planting and remain widely cited.[1] For all these reasons, we will begin our look at contemporary church planting by exploring Allen and McGavran's advocacy of the practice as a primary missional strategy.

Roland Allen initially proposed "planting churches" as a corrective reform measure for overseas missions during the 1910s and 1920s. Allen was particularly concerned that Western mission agencies had persistently deemed overseas congregations "missions," rarely calling them "churches."[2] His concern was not merely rhetorical. Allen had also observed many overseas congregations remaining under Western leadership for long periods of time without ever being recognized as autonomous, locally led churches.[3] Allen therefore urged cross-cultural missionaries to reimagine their task as "church planting" in order to demonstrate an appropriate respect for local congregations, church leaders, and the Spirit's ministry among all Christians.[4]

The theology that emerged within Allen's work would have a lasting influence on the operant theology of American church planting movements in several key ways. Allen's discussion of "church planting" placed a heavy emphasis on evangelism, primarily the personal evangelism of Spirit-empowered believers.[5] According to Allen, missional churches can expect Spirit-led personal evangelism to produce a "spontaneous expansion" in membership.[6] As this emphasis suggests, Allen's missional ecclesiology rested on a strong pneumatology, foreshadowing both the rise of missional church planting among charismatic American congregations and the work of charismatic American church planting scholar C. Peter Wagner.[7] In addition, Allen's arguments consistently prioritized the local church, often describing sponsoring agencies beyond the local church as overly controlling entities that could arguably limit effective ministries.[8] This emphasis made Allen an early postcolonialist voice, but it also reframed the goal of missions as producing new, autonomous, local churches. Allen's work thus defined "church planting" as an evangelistic mission led by the Spirit which produces new, autonomous, and rapidly growing local congregations. As the next chapter will examine, Allen's vision of church planting remains readily discernible in many of America's planted congregations today.

Allen's theological justifications for church planting have also been widely influential. The title question of *Missionary Methods: St. Paul's or Ours?*[9] signaled a common approach to church planting: restorationism. According to this approach, the act of planting churches should be understood as an attempt to restore a lost form of missional ecclesiology that was once common in "the early church." The structure of Allen's question framed contemporary missional praxis and biblical methods as mutually exclusive alternatives. Allen's phrasing admitted the possibility that Paul might have employed multiple "missionary methods," but left little doubt that contemporary Christians should imitate Paul's praxis. For Christians who took the Bible seriously, the underlying logic behind Allen's title represented a major critique of contemporary missions. A similar pattern remains common in twenty-first-century theological arguments for planting churches: establishing a dichotomy between common current praxis and biblical praxis, then advocating a return to biblical praxis, as the author understands it.[10]

The exegetical work underlying Allen's arguments, though, bears further reflection, as it reveals important limitations of this approach to church planting. Contemporary missional praxis was Allen's primary interest, not biblical exegesis.[11] Robert Gallagher rightly observed that Allen was highly selective in citing New Testament texts, resulting in an incomplete picture of missions in the New Testament.[12] Allen's focus on Paul led him to primarily discuss Acts and the Epistles, particularly passages which describe evangelistic proclamation and the founding of new churches.[13] Allen's choice of Paul as the paradigmatic Christian missionary was not an entirely obvious one, either. Newbigin, Guder, Gibbs, and Bolger all focused instead on Christ's ministry as the paradigm of sound missional practice.[14] Focusing on Christ led them to fuller exegesis of gospel narratives and stronger accounts of "incarnational" missions, a term used to advocate Christians living as witnesses in communities and offering practical, loving service to others.[15] It seems, then, that Allen's preference for Pauline passages aligned well with his preferred missional strategies, but overlooked other potentially significant biblical texts. Preferred praxis seemed to be driving exegesis, not the other way around.

Even if we agreed to focus on Pauline texts, Allen's framing of those texts failed to capture the full picture of Paul's missionary efforts. As James Thompson pointed out, in Paul's own discussions of mission he "never mentions the numerical growth of his congregations."[16] Thompson added, "While Paul undoubtedly wanted the churches to grow, he gives primary attention in his letters to the transformation of communities into the image of Christ (Rom 8:29)."[17] Paul's missional writings arguably frame the most natural form of "growth" in churches as the spiritual and ethical development of church members, not the "spontaneous" membership increase that Allen's work envisions. Eddie Gibbs highlighted yet another dimension of Pauline missions that Allen overlooked: the "spontaneous expansion of the church" described in Acts and the Epistles provides important examples of contextualized ministry.[18] As Gibbs explained, even Paul had to "translate the message of Jesus and his discipling methods—originally developed within a Jewish and largely rural context—into the urban Greco-Roman world."[19] Gibbs therefore concluded that it was actually Paul's willingness to contextualize the gospel that made him a model for twenty-first-century church planting.[20] Allen's question, "Missionary Methods: St. Paul's or Ours?" overlooked the very real possibility that missionary methods in contemporary churches might rightly differ from Paul's in order to contextualize the gospel as faithfully as Paul did. Allen read Pauline texts through the lens of his own missional understandings, as is understandable. It is significant, though, that Christians interested in mission could read the same Pauline texts and identify very different models of praxis within them. Missional church engagement with a wider culture has always been a complex calling, and it remains so today.

Like Allen, Donald McGavran similarly advocated the practice of planting missional churches, but with slightly different emphases. McGavran's work primarily appeared during the 1950s through the 1970s and echoed both Allen's sincere commitment to cross-cultural missions and Allen's frustrations with ineffective missional praxis. Unlike Allen, McGavran was primarily concerned that definitions of "mission" had become so broad and varied that missionaries and sponsoring organizations lacked clarity about their calling.[21] McGavran noticed that some overseas missional hospitals, schools, and relief agencies could carry on for years without offering clear gospel proclamation.[22] He even lamented, "Where great populations have not turned to Christ, there are great hospitals; and where great populations have turned to Christ, there are few great hospitals."[23] As a result, McGavran argued, too many missionaries had become distracted by "secondary aims" like health care or education and forgotten their first calling: gospel proclamation.[24] He worried that this state of affairs might even lead some people to conflate the gospel with more tangible benefits, like health care, education, or community resourcing.[25] Citing Allen's work approvingly, McGavran wrote that he preferred "the Pauline Approach" to mission, which prioritized evangelism and planting new churches over all other missional strategies.[26] Church planting, McGavran argued, would help missionaries maintain a proper focus by drawing more attention to new believers and numerically growing churches.

McGavran's account of missional church planting as a means of fostering evangelism provoked varied responses. Some were concerned by how easily McGavran collapsed church planting into evangelism, arguably instrumentalizing churches for the sake of gospel proclamation.[27] Even more powerfully, J. C. Hoekendijk argued that McGavran's missional vision overemphasized the growth of churches themselves and overlooked the cosmic, broadly redemptive dimensions of the *missio Dei*.[28] Hoekendijk's critique provoked a direct response from McGavran and broadly influenced missiologists, many of whom eventually concurred with Hoekendijk that mission must include both evangelistic proclamation and community relief ministries.[29] The lasting influence of McGavran's arguments explains why missiologists who advocate holistic missions sometimes avoid references to "church planting," even when discussing missional church praxis.[30] McGavran's advocacy of planting churches linked the practice to evangelistic proclamation; whether this was helpful or problematic was a matter of perspective.

Nonetheless, it is important to emphasize that neither Allen's nor McGavran's work envisioned planting churches in the United States. America's long history of Christianity and its wide variety of Christian churches make twenty-first-century American contexts very different from those that Allen and McGavran envisioned. Allen, for example, primarily described planting churches in contexts where Christianity had little or no visible expression.[31] McGavran described planting churches in contexts where new converts to Christianity risked significant isolation, hostility, and even persecution from family and friends.[32] By contrast, in post-Christendom America, a "Constantinian captivity" of the gospel to cultural and power structures seems a far greater risk to churches than the persecution that McGavran described.[33] Hoekendijk even worried that "the call to evangelism is often little else than a call to restore 'Christendom,' . . . a solid, well-integrated cultural complex, directed and dominated by the Church."[34] According to Hoekendijk, missional activities in a post-Christendom context like today's America can easily become "a flurried activity to save the remnants of a time now irrevocably past."[35] Hoekendijk added that the impulse to grow churches can even obviate genuine missional engagement with a culture by increasing the "protective shell of the Church," which serves as "a shock-breaker," insulating Christians from encounters with other belief systems.[36] Thompson similarly saw a desire to restore Christendom behind some Western missional church efforts, writing, "The Pauline model does not guarantee that the church will regain its prominent place in our culture or appear relevant to the majority population."[37] Mission looks very different in contemporary America than it did in the contexts where Allen and McGavran ministered. Allen and McGavran had thus begun a helpful conversation about contemporary church planting, but American church planting movements would need to wrestle with the particularities of American culture to apply their ideas faithfully.

The 1974 Lausanne Congress: Context, Concerns, and the Lausanne Covenant

Allen's and McGavran's proposed reforms were not the only concerns facing the Lausanne Congress in 1974. The Lausanne Congress met in the wake of troubling developments that had occurred in cross-cultural missions from the 1950s through the early 1970s. Opportunities for cross-cultural missional engagement were increasingly limited, forcing missionaries and mission agencies to make significant adjustments. Mao Zedong's government had expelled Western missionaries from China, a move that sent shock waves throughout Christian missionary agencies.[38] The end of colonial rule in India and various parts of Africa and Asia raised the specter of more missionary expulsions to come.[39] Historic connections between a wide range of Christian missions and colonial authorities raised serious concerns about the ethics of earlier missionary engagement.[40] In the wake of Vatican II and *Lumen Gentium*, Catholic missiologists acknowledged some terrible abuses in Catholic missionary history.[41] Some missiologists even questioned whether Christian missions remained morally defensible.[42] Furthermore, by the late twentieth century, churches in some formerly "receiving" countries were thriving and no longer needed the same support from Western missions agencies that they once did.[43] Protestant and Catholic missiologists affirmed that cross-cultural Christian missions were still needed, but considerable uncertainty lingered about how to conduct them.[44] At the same time, declining church attendance led missiologists to increasingly concur that both Western Europe and the United States were becoming mission fields.[45] As early as 1962, American theologians were arguing for fresh missional engagement within American cities.[46] The Lausanne delegates therefore had serious questions to answer about the nature and practice of modern Christian missions.

In addition, the Lausanne delegates faced long-standing theological disagreements about the agency of churches in Christian missions.[47] In the 1930s, Karl Hartenstein, a key voice of *missio Dei* missiology, had described a central place for churches within God's mission, insisting, "Whoever says church says mission. And vice versa: whoever says mission says church."[48] By contrast, in the 1950s and 1960s, Hoekendijk had criticized ecclesiocentric missiologies by underscoring the cosmic dimensions of God's redemption.[49] Hoekendijk thus reminded Christians that mission is not primarily designed to increase church attendance nor to satisfy internal concerns about the local church's survival; instead, a missional church is called to be "a dynamic entity serving salvific ends that reach beyond itself."[50] As a result, Hoekendijk's missiology assigned churches a peripheral place within God's mission.[51] This move risked missional complacency within churches, who might come to see mission as entirely God's work, not theirs.[52] Hoekendijk's broad vision of mission also arguably opened the door for any seemingly "redemptive" activity to be classified as mission, obscuring the distinctive calling of Christian witness.[53] In view of these conflicting ideas, the 1974 Lausanne Congress also needed to articulate the place of churches within Christian mission.

The 1974 Lausanne delegates hoped to find a middle way, addressing Hoekendijk's critiques while still affirming churches' unique calling within the *missio Dei*. The final Lausanne Covenant echoed some of Hoekendijk's arguments; as Tennent observed, it indicated that "mission is not primarily a subset of the doctrine of the church which is seeking to grow and extend its reach and influence around the world."[54] The Lausanne delegates went even further, as Tennent noted, by insisting that

> mission is first and foremost about God and his redemptive purpose and initiative in the world, quite apart from any actions or tasks or strategies or initiatives which the church undertakes. To put it

> plainly, mission is more about God and who He is, than about us and what we do.[55]

The delegates to Lausanne thus accepted the central premise of *missio Dei*: mission is primarily a function of God's nature, for God's own redemptive purposes. At the same time, the sixth article of the Lausanne Covenant refuted Hoekendijk's effacement of church from mission, stating plainly: "the church is at the very center of God's cosmic purpose and is his appointed means of spreading the gospel."[56] Delegates to Lausanne overwhelmingly rejected any missiology that advocated "the separation of God's work from the life and witness of the church."[57] Indeed, the Lausanne Covenant insisted that churches remain at the center of God's mission, affirming that "missional ecclesiology" remained both a valid and an essential concept. The inherent contradictions between Hoekendijk's arguments and those he was critiquing remained unresolved.

The Lausanne Covenant never defined exactly how churches should participate in the *missio Dei*.[58] Two main opposing viewpoints dominated the discussions at Lausanne. The first was a common evangelical perspective, best articulated by McGavran, who argued forcefully that Christian missions must prioritize evangelism and planting churches, much as he had always said.[59] McGavran's views reflected a wider concern among evangelical missiologists that some reforms designed to address postcolonial abuses might ultimately undermine evangelistic ministries.[60] By contrast, Latin American missiologist and missionary Samuel Escobar insisted at Lausanne that Christian missions must be holistic, encompassing social justice and relief ministries alongside evangelistic proclamation.[61] Indeed, Escobar objected to "a missionary strategy that in its concern for numerical growth reduced evangelism to the transmission of verbal summaries of the Gospel from the distance of non-involvement."[62] This statement was particularly important, as it underscored both the extent of McGavran's influence and serious potential problems within his approach to missions. Escobar's statement rightly highlighted the reality that McGavran's vision of "evangelism" largely meant verbal proclamation, to the exclusion of other more practical ministries.[63] As Escobar characterized it, McGavran's approach risked projecting some "distance" from local communities by striking a posture of "non-involvement" in local concerns. Two conflicting missional visions were indeed present at Lausanne, representing fundamentally different responses to the challenges facing Christian missions in mid- to late twentieth-century contexts. McGavran's influence was clear, but his was not the only voice.

The final Lausanne Covenant did not resolve the conflict between these two missional visions, either, but again sought a middle way, combining McGavran's emphasis on evangelism and planting churches with Escobar's call for social justice and community involvement.[64] This compromise reflected the Lausanne Covenant's function as a conciliatory document, presenting a broad and unified statement on evangelical missiology. Unfortunately, this irenic approach opened the Lausanne Movement to critiques that it lacked "good theological and missiological reflection" and focused on practical concerns instead.[65] Such critiques were unfair to the delegates, who indeed wrestled with significant missiological questions, but they reflected the reality that the final Lausanne Covenant occasionally included conflicting views of mission without addressing their inherent contradictions. Consequently, the 1974 Lausanne Covenant gave missional churches a clear sense of their importance within the *missio Dei*, but could not necessarily offer clarity on what "mission" actually meant for churches.

On a more practical level, the Lausanne Movement, which began at the 1974 Congress, created a supportive, transnational network that would nurture and be nurtured by key church planting leaders within the United States. Rick Warren, who attended the 1974 Lausanne Congress and went on to found Saddleback Church in 1980, cited Ralph Winter's presentation on unreached people as life-changing, saying, "Ralph Winter engineered a revolution and it changed all of us."[66] Warren added, "No one would ever look at the world again the same after that. It influenced an entire generation."[67] Warren later served on the advisory council for the 2010 Lausanne Congress in Cape Town.[68] C. Peter Wagner participated in the 1989 Lausanne Congress in Manila.[69] Tim Keller, founder of the City to City church planting movement, presented keynote addresses on urban missions at the 2010 Lausanne Congress.[70] Influential leaders of contemporary American church planting movements thus engaged deeply with the Lausanne Movement, both in 1974 and in the years that followed. Even beyond this, the Lausanne Covenant has been "widely regarded as one of the most important theological documents in the evangelical movement."[71] The Acts 29 Network, for example, adopted the Lausanne Covenant as part of its statement of faith.[72] It was therefore wholly unsurprising that in the years following the 1974 Lausanne Congress, American church planting movements would encourage new congregations to understand themselves as missional. It was also unsurprising that these congregations might struggle to define what being a "missional church" really meant.

Church Growth Theory and Its Critics

Of the various voices at Lausanne, perhaps none would have a wider influence on American church planting efforts than McGavran's. McGavran would most directly influence American church planting movements through his foundational work in Church Growth Theory. This thread of highly pragmatic missional ecclesiology emerged out of McGavran's research during the mid-twentieth century at Fuller Theological Seminary in Pasadena.[73] Because definitions of mission varied, McGavran grew increasingly concerned that sponsoring churches and mission agencies were directing precious resources toward ineffective missions, while others seeing massive revivals lacked adequate support.[74] Consequently, McGavran's 1970 book *Understanding Church Growth* advocated further statistical research in order to identify and study growth in missional churches.[75] McGavran still defined mission narrowly as evangelism and planting churches, but now argued more directly that effective missional praxis would generally produce increased membership in local churches.[76] This point is worth repeating, because it is the central assumption behind Church Growth Theory: effective missional praxis yields church membership growth.

Church Growth Theory has been a common implicit or explicit thread in much church planting literature. Before McGavran formally articulated it, Allen had similarly argued that churches under the Spirit's leadership will "spontaneously expand," unless there are "causes that hinder" growth, like ineffective leadership.[77] Like McGavran, Allen implicitly defined "growth" as numerical membership increase and framed it as a normative experience for effectively functioning churches. McGavran's work expounded on this vision, which has remained dominant in discussions of church planting in America in the years following the 1974 Lausanne Congress. In 1995, Warren approvingly cited both Allen's and McGavran's work when describing the missional vision behind Saddleback Church.[78] In 2006, SBC church planting researcher Ed Stetzer noted that some planted American churches still treat attendance growth as an indicator of effective missional ecclesial praxis.[79] There is enduring power in the core assumption of Church Growth Theory: effective missional praxis yields growth, where growth is defined as numerically increasing church membership. As Charles Van Engen memorably put it, missional

Christians eventually came to see membership growth as "a mark of the true church," a sign of effective leadership, proper theological focus, and even divine favor.[80] Such understandings overlook spiritual growth, community transformation, or other ways that church or its missional influence might demonstrably "grow." There is no doubt that sincere missional commitment lay behind Church Growth Theory, and the desire to see people come to faith was genuine. Nonetheless, the emphasis Church Growth Theory placed on numerical membership increase became its most visible contribution to American church planting efforts.

One controversial element of Church Growth Theory is its advocacy of the Homogeneous Unit Principle, or HUP. McGavran defined a "homogeneous unit" as "a section of society in which all the members have some characteristic in common," such as a language group, tribe, or caste.[81] McGavran conceded that demographic diversity in worship is desirable, but insisted that the church's priority is "not to assist detribalization" nor "to fuse the various populations of the metropolis into one people," but rather to "disciple all who can be persuaded to believe on Jesus Christ."[82] Consequently, McGavran argued that as far as possible, missional worship should be offered for a single homogeneous unit, for example, local speakers of a specific language.[83] If the aim is numerical membership growth, the HUP is likely to succeed; sociological studies have since confirmed that homogeneous churches are indeed likelier than others to grow.[84] Far from being a tangential point, church planting advocates and practitioners have broadly endorsed the HUP as a viable strategy to foster membership growth.[85] Some in the United Kingdom have even cited McGavran's work on the HUP to justify the common missional practice of planting churches within homogeneous "affinity groups," which share a hobby or interest.[86] Within the United States, some planted congregations began as targeted attempts to reach youth or young adults by offering separate youth worship services; these services eventually developed into new churches comprised primarily of younger adults.[87] Warren advocated a strategically "targeted" approach to church planting, drawing on the HUP to encourage planted churches to concentrate outreach efforts on people similar to those already in their congregation.[88] Interest in the HUP thus enacted McGavran's overriding interest in numerical membership growth and made demographically targeted outreach a common strategy within planted churches.

Predictably, Church Growth Theory sparked further statistical studies of church membership growth and decline, most notably Roger Finke and Rodney Stark's "Rational Choice Model."[89] Rational Choice Model attempted to explain why some churches grew while others declined, much as McGavran had done. Unlike McGavran, Finke and Stark focused much of their research on American churches, though they similarly assumed that effective praxis produces membership growth.[90] According to the Rational Choice Model, individual Americans, faced with a range of church options, will weigh the benefits and the costs of membership and choose their church accordingly.[91] Tellingly, Finke and Stark offered only positive explanations for growth and negative explanations for decline, echoing McGavran's and Allen's confidence that effective churches will grow.[92] Their work thus espouses a form of ecclesial Darwinism, in which the most effective churches survive while ineffective churches eventually fade away. Finke and Stark drew their methodological lenses not from missiology, but from marketing and economic models, which study human choices without reference to theology.[93] To a large extent, Finke and Stark applied core ideas of Church Growth Theory to American churches in order to further explain historical patterns in membership statistics.

Unlike McGavran, though, Finke and Stark postulated little, if any, conversion growth.[94] Their project thus directly contradicted a central operant assumption of McGavran and many other church planting advocates: planting churches is a means of fostering evangelistic conversions.[95] Indeed, their work drew attention to important historical evidence which contradicted this key assumption underpinning Church Growth Theory. For example, Finke and Stark's assumption that planting churches does not necessarily foster evangelistic growth has been borne out by statistical evidence.[96] Subsequent studies have found that churches in Western contexts can indeed grow without winning any new converts, particularly if they are located in a rapidly growing community.[97] For example, Warren planted Saddleback Church in a rapidly growing community, making it at least possible that some of Saddleback's growth resulted from a large population of dislocated Christians seeking a new church home.[98] Stefan Paas even argued that it was a "wrong assumption" of many planted congregations in the 1980s and 1990s "that the expansion of [church] supply would automatically lead to an increase of demand."[99] As Paas explained, recent data implies that "church planting is a response to a growing religious demand, rather than a cause of it."[100] Finke and Stark have been proven correct in assuming that a variety of different explanations for church membership growth is possible, especially in countries like the United States, where Christian churches already abound.

By emphasizing statistical studies of church membership, Church Growth Theory and Rational Choice Models both became subject to further methodological critique. Comparing membership statistics between churches is notoriously problematic since subtly differing operant theologies can yield wildly differing definitions of "church member."[101] For example, if infants and children are counted as "members," the overall membership count will be higher, while churches that only count as members people who have espoused a personal faith in Jesus Christ will have lower membership counts, even if the same number of people attend on any given Sunday. McGavran, Finke, and Stark all acknowledged this difficulty and focused on attendance statistics instead of membership, but all three remained confident that effective ecclesial praxis means more people in churches.[102] Steve Bruce carried such methodological critiques further, highlighting flawed assumptions behind some accounts of church growth and decline.[103] Finke and Starke's work, for example, implied that if some churches grew while others declined, the growing churches likely drew members away from the declining churches.[104] By contrast, Bruce found it highly unlikely that members of theologically liberal churches in decline had decamped to rapidly growing conservative churches, as Finke and Stark's analysis suggested.[105] According to Bruce, a more likely explanation is that some people leaving theologically liberal churches had left Christianity altogether.[106] In order to demonstrate that membership had actually shifted from one church to another, or that such a shift was tied to theological preferences, one would need surveys and other qualitative research, which Finke and Stark's analysis did not include.[107] Bruce also pointed out that church attendance does not neatly correlate to Christian faith; church attendance in medieval Britain was routinely low, even though espoused Christian faith was nearly universal.[108] Bruce's compelling logic raises serious questions about the common assumption that membership growth indicates an increase of faith, particularly without further evidence. In the contexts McGavran envisioned, where Christianity had never had much visible expression, this assumption was more reasonable. In Christianized countries like the United States, church membership growth is not so easily explained. As Bruce rightly argued, assuming that effective praxis yields membership growth can obscure clear analysis of what is actually happening with people's faith. Numbers alone prove little.

Theological critiques of Church Growth Theory have been far more trenchant. One of the most thorough came in 1981 from Charles Van Engen.[109] Van Engen argued that while sincere desire for evangelistic growth is a valid expression of the *missio Dei*, actual conversions are God's work and cannot be interpreted as a "mark of the true church."[110] Newbigin also critiqued Church Growth Theory extensively.[111] He was particularly concerned that McGavran's reading of the Great Commission separated "making disciples," McGavran's term for evangelism, from teaching Christian faithfulness.[112] According to Newbigin, this distinction might encourage missional churches to accommodate sins in order to win converts.[113] McGavran's advocacy of the HUP indeed seemed to do this at times. McGavran argued that churches should be offering demographically homogeneous worship rather than "putting barriers" between the gospel and those who harbor racial, class, or linguistic prejudices.[114] Missiologist David Bosch objected to such practices, insisting that churches are called to speak prophetically against cultural sins like racism even as they proclaim the gospel.[115] Catholic theologian Jordan Bishop added that historical examples of abuse within some early missions in Latin America suggest that when numerical growth is the primary goal of missions, moral compromise and human tragedy can easily result.[116] Churches risk serious theological confusion and even ethical compromise when membership growth becomes their mission, metric, and identity.

Critiques of Church Growth Theory have done little to quell its influence. This is in part because some critics framed their objections as narrow critiques of McGavran's work or a particular aspect of it, like the HUP. Newbigin even coupled his critique of McGavran's work with sympathy for Allen's, which similarly assumed membership growth as normative for well-run churches.[117] Consequently, it has been too easy for advocates of church planting to dismiss important critiques of Church Growth Theory. Indeed, American church planters have broadly accepted Church Growth Theory, in spite of its inherent problems. For example, Wagner, who succeeded McGavran at Fuller, penned a statement which has been widely quoted: "The single most effective evangelistic method under heaven is planting new churches."[118] Tim Keller similarly tied the act of planting churches to measurable evangelistic growth, writing in 2009, "The only way to be truly sure you are increasing the number of Christians in a town is to increase the number of churches."[119] Church Growth Theory thus exerted a prominent influence on the operant missional ecclesiology that would become common in America's planted congregations, as we will see in subsequent chapters.

Fresh Opportunities and Unanswered Questions

In retrospect, the emergence of missional church planting movements in the United States in the late twentieth century seemed natural. As the Lausanne Congress of 1974 demonstrated, Christians had been actively rethinking the nature and practice of contemporary missions throughout the twentieth century. Allen and McGavran, among others, raised valid concerns about the conduct of cross-cultural missions in the early twentieth century. Church planting, as they described it, seemed a better way forward than other missional strategies because it encouraged autonomy and due respect to local congregations. McGavran also provided a clear definition of "mission": evangelistic proclamation and planting churches. Church Growth Theory offered a tantalizingly precise set of metrics by which sending agencies and missional churches could evaluate their praxis, though it also created methodological inconsistencies and theological challenges. McGavran's work had coupled the practice of planting churches with evangelistic proclamation, something that seemed more important than ever in formerly sending countries like the United States. Escobar, Newbigin, Bruce, and others offered helpful critiques of McGavran's missiology, but they did little to quell its influence among missional church leaders, who were often eager to foster quantifiable growth in local congregations out of sincere evangelistic faith.

Sincere missional commitment abounded at the First Lausanne Congress of 1974, but so did unresolved questions about what mission actually looked like. The importance of churches to Christian mission was clear, but considerable uncertainty remained about exactly how churches might honor their missional callings faithfully. American church planting movements would find fertile ground for theological reflection in the half century of missional ecclesiology that preceded Lausanne, and in the important debates that occurred at and in the years following Lausanne. Nonetheless, considerable work remained. As church planters began to enact missional ecclesiologies that were debated at Lausanne, they would have to negotiate the inherent contradictions and challenges that were already evident within them.

2
Developing Operant Theology Within American Church Planting Movements

High-profile pastors in some planted American churches have become household names. As a result, it can be tempting to think of their churches as isolated examples, the product of a uniquely charismatic and innovative leader's personal ministry. Popular and scholarly accounts of church planting have only reinforced this perception by offering local histories of individual congregations and focused, qualitative studies of a small subset of churches.[1] When a church like Mars Hill tragically collapses, a vision of planted churches as isolated, autonomous local ministries can even be comforting, reassuring those outside the immediate fold that problems were the result of a uniquely "bad apple." In reality, the picture is more complicated, and planted churches are not as isolated as they might appear. Many shared patterns of praxis and operant theology developed during the late twentieth century. These have remained visible in churches planted well into the twenty-first century, for good and at times for ill.

Contemporary American church planting movements began to appear shortly before the Lausanne Congress of 1974, but in the years following Lausanne they would explode in visibility and numbers. New practices like informal dress and contemporary worship music began as a part of a missional reform movement within Southern California's charismatic churches and gradually became standard praxis in many planted churches from varied confessional traditions across the United States. More subtle, but equally consistent, were other features of a shared operant missional ecclesiology: an emphasis on autonomous local congregations, a gradual narrowing of the pastoral office to "preacher," and a focus on reaching the "unchurched."

A genuine subculture in American Christianity formed, with shared practices that reflected recognizable beliefs about church and mission.

It is therefore particularly important to address Osmer's first task of theological reflection and ask of American church planting movements, "What is happening?" Osmer describes the first task of theological reflection as "the descriptive-empirical task," which requires discerning "patterns and dynamics" at work in a particular situation.[2] This chapter will prefer the term "descriptive," since "empirical" suggests scientific objectivity, a construct which practical theologians acknowledge is unrealistic.[3] By contrast, the term "descriptive" ties theological reflection more closely to a skill Osmer calls "priestly listening": attending carefully to the particularity of events and locating them within a broader narrative or situation.[4] Christians do not practice faith in isolated congregations, but engage with one another and with shared traditions.[5] Therefore, this chapter will identify important patterns within many descriptions of planted congregations in order to locate each specific episode within a broader narrative of American church planting efforts. Local operant missional ecclesiologies varied somewhat, but they also exhibited clear patterns, reflecting the reality that many planted American churches enacted understandings of both mission and church in demonstrably similar ways.

One important critique of Osmer's descriptive-empirical task is that it does not offer completely theological reflection because its focus is on observable human behavior, not theology.[6] As one researcher explains, describing churches solely in terms of observable human behavior is like describing "a soccer match in which only half the players are visible."[7] For this reason, Pritchard even identified a form of "empirical atheism" within some practical theological research.[8] In light of these critiques, Christians must acknowledge that God is at work in churches, though God's hand might not be readily apparent, particularly when examining churches with sociological or anthropological lenses. On the other hand, Christians must also avoid the assumption that all observable Christian practices are divinely inspired. Imperfect human beings develop and enact church practices, and so observable behavior in churches will not always reflect God's perfect intentions.[9] Practices do not always follow theology, and theology does not always inform practices. For this reason, practical theology necessarily attends to both practices and espoused theology, which are deeply intertwined, though not perfectly equivalent.[10] What people actually believe about church and mission sometimes becomes clearer when examining behavioral patterns, which both reflect and "complexify" espoused theology.[11] Following Astley, this chapter will therefore engage in "theological listening": attending to observable human behavior in order to identify the theological nuances and responses that are embodied within patterns of praxis.[12]

As the twentieth century unfolded, American Christians began to enact a growing consensus that "mission" was now a category that applied to churches in formerly sending countries, including the United States. Declining church attendance and growing social unrest during the 1960s made missional strategies like planting churches seem freshly relevant to Americans. The same sincere missional commitment that abounded at Lausanne became commonplace in planted American churches, where Christians began to rethink their own congregations' missional engagement within local communities. Embodied understandings of mission in the United States also began to resemble key elements of McGavran's and Allen's visions for planting churches overseas: an emphasis on evangelistic proclamation, church planting as a vehicle for evangelism, and an abiding faith that effective missional ecclesiology would produce numerical membership increase. At the same time, operant understandings of "church" became hazier. New missional ecclesiologies brought missional concerns to the fore, but subtly obscured understandings of congregational identity and spiritual formation, limiting important reflection on how either of these might function within the *missio Dei.*

1960s to 1970s: New Paradigm Churches

The mid-1960s through the late 1970s saw not only thoughtful discussions about the nature of Christian mission, but also networks of charismatic churches planting innovative new congregations throughout Southern California and the American Southwest.[13] These churches have rightly been called "New Paradigm churches" because they enacted a new paradigm of missional ecclesiology, features of which would continue to influence planted churches well into the twenty-first century.[14] The first New Paradigm church was Calvary Chapel, planted in 1965 as a ministry to surfers and people involved in countercultural movements.[15] Hope Chapel was planted in 1971, and the first Vineyard Church was planted by people with previous ties to Calvary Chapel in 1974.[16] Many New Paradigm churches initially defined themselves as charismatic renewal churches, but their strongly missional vision and rapid growth soon led them to plant additional new churches.[17] Like the missiological discussions at Lausanne, the pioneering practical reforms of New Paradigm churches would have a lasting impact on the operant missional ecclesiology of American church planting movements.

New Paradigm churches operated out of a highly missional ecclesiology. In the wake of unrest following Vietnam War protests and the Civil Rights Movement, both Calvary Chapel and the Jesus People movement began offering missional outreach to Southern California's largely unchurched countercultural communities.[18] Calvary Chapel's missional vision, though, was much more ecclesial; where the Jesus People went to hippies, Calvary Chapel designed its worship services to be welcoming to unchurched visitors, including hippies. Like the Jesus People movement, New Paradigm churches encouraged informal dress and developed new, contemporary styles of sung worship.[19] The Christian community in New Paradigm churches was therapeutic, individualistic, and localized, prominently espousing contemporary values like openness, honesty, tolerance, and authenticity.[20] These practices and values were designed to make church more appealing to disaffected young baby boomers in the late 1960s. Other than sandals and guitar music, New Paradigm churches remained relatively traditional charismatic congregations. They retained many common charismatic practices, including "bodily participation" in worship, "Bible-centered" sermons, and conservative family values.[21] There is no evidence that they engaged much in any of the political or social justice causes that were deeply important to California's countercultural communities. New Paradigm churches thus broadly rejected Escobar's vision of holistic missions, which included political and ethical engagement within local communities.[22] Instead, their missional vision was highly attractional and evangelistic, which aligned well with McGavran's call for gospel proclamation, church growth, and planting churches.[23] Informal worship, culturally relevant emphases, and eagerness to plant new congregations were the most significant innovations within New Paradigm churches.

The rapid growth of New Paradigm churches made them a particularly attractive model for other American church leaders who would become interested in church planting. By 1974, only nine years after its launch, Calvary Chapel had built and quickly filled a new worship space with seating for twenty-three hundred people.[24] By 1982, Vineyard had grown from a small in-home fellowship to a church of fifteen hundred people.[25] This growth likely happened in part because the population of Southern California itself was growing rapidly in the 1960s and 1970s.[26] Furthermore, the wave of new arrivals to Southern California at this time included many conservative American Christians from the Bible Belt as well as Latin American immigrants from charismatic backgrounds.[27] Nonetheless, conversion growth was clearly a significant factor. In the summer of 1968, just three years after its launch, Calvary Chapel baptized more than five hundred people.[28] One survey conducted in the early 1990s found that 25 to 30 percent of New Paradigm members reported no prior church affiliation, suggesting that conversion growth remained a central feature of New Paradigm church culture many years later.[29] These statistics were tracked and reported because they mattered to New Paradigm churches, which embodied many of McGavran's missional emphases, particularly his interest in fostering churches with rapidly growing membership.

As New Paradigm churches began planting additional congregations, they also began to embody some anti-institutional tendencies.[30] Calvary Chapel quickly standardized worship practices across its congregations, but its congregations collectively identified as an informal "network," not a formal denomination.[31] Under John Wimber's leadership, Vineyard Churches eventually became a denomination, but the process was hardly straightforward.[32] Many Vineyard members argued that the very concept of "denomination" "conjured up images of control, structure, and bureaucracy," which they feared could too easily stifle local innovation.[33] In the last twenty years, some charismatic church planting networks have formalized their organizational structures, while others have preferred to remain an "informal network of influential leaders."[34] This resistance to organizational structures partly reflected countercultural tendencies in the late 1960s, when some younger Americans justifiably questioned long-standing American institutions in the wake of the Vietnam War and the Civil Rights Movement. In that context, avoiding institutionalization was a potentially important missional strategy. It was also an intriguing echo of Allen's concern that entities beyond the local church can too easily become controlling, limiting Spirit-led ministries in missional churches.[35] Whatever the motivations, local church autonomy has remained an enduring feature of New Paradigm churches.

Emphasizing local congregations caused the operant missional ecclesiology of New Paradigm churches to shift in other ways, perhaps most notably in understandings of the pastoral office. Instead of deriving authority from denominational structures like "deacon boards, boards of trustees, presbyteries, general assemblies" or even shared doctrinal statements, New Paradigm pastors derived their authority from the "trust" of their congregations and other leaders within the movement.[36] Consequently,

New Paradigm churches made theological education optional for church leaders.[37] As Christerson and Flory explained, their leaders

> gain their legitimacy and influence from their perceived ability to access supernatural power to produce "signs and wonders" rather than through speaking ability, educational credentials, or position in a hierarchy.[38]

Institutional structures thus played little role in identifying or validating local church leaders. Over time, these changes gradually meant that the office of local pastor was both narrowed and elevated. Pastoral responsibility narrowed considerably in scope as small group ministries effectively shifted much of the burden of pastoral care from the lead pastor to volunteer lay leaders and/or other church staff.[39] In large, rapidly growing congregations, where pastors could not build relationships with every church member, it was necessary to delegate some pastoral responsibilities to others. In practice, delegating pastoral care indeed freed time and allowed pastors to focus more closely on preaching and developing the Sunday services, but it also removed pastors from involvement in the everyday cares and concerns of their congregation. At the same time, with no ecclesial authority above the local pastor, the pastoral office was also effectively elevated, granting pastors more authority over the theology and practical functioning of their congregations. As Wagner explained, "the pastor now functions as the leader of the church instead of as an employee of the church."[40] Pastors in New Paradigm churches thus became "leaders" of the congregation, positioned in authority over them, not an "employee," one who serves a wider church and is accountable to other ecclesial authorities. Perceived charismatic gifts further elevated some pastors; Christerson and Flory noted that some church leaders made decisions via "direct 'words from the Lord' . . . rather than relying on a consensus-based process with other believers."[41] The pastoral office in New Paradigm churches was thus narrowed into a focus on preaching and elevated into something arguably closer to a Catholic priesthood, where church leaders exercise considerable spiritual and practical authority, particularly in discerning God's voice.

Founding pastors of New Paradigm church planting networks occupied an even more elevated position, shaping the theology and identity of many local congregations. Calvary Chapel initially had no formal statement of faith; instead of crafting one, they offered recordings of founding pastor Chuck Smith's sermons to prospective church planting pastors.[42]

This practice was likely intended to give local pastors greater freedom to innovate, attend to the Spirit, and respond to local communities, but it created the impression that Smith's preaching was the only guidance that local pastors would need. Without a clear confessional statement, it would be difficult to determine if any pastor or congregation had drifted or erred theologically, particularly if other leaders had little or no theological education either. Within some New Paradigm networks, prominent pastors were said to "exert their influence . . . through media, conferences, and their relationships with other individual leaders in religious and secular professions."[43] Founding pastors of new movements thus became more like public media personalities or social media "influencers" than traditional bishops, who are held accountable to doctrinal standards and other ecclesial leaders. As a result, there was a real risk that New Paradigm networks might become cults of personality around founding pastors and other high-profile leaders.

The ideas debated at Lausanne would not have seemed abstract or theoretical to all American churchgoers; indeed, by 1974, many of the missiological discussions at Lausanne had already found tangible expression in the praxis of New Paradigm churches. Their missional vision aligned particularly well with McGavran's calls for evangelistic proclamation and planting churches, and these churches embodied key elements of Church Growth Theory. New missionally focused congregations grew rapidly and emphasized outreach to unchurched Americans. They also pioneered new informal styles of Christian worship that would be more accessible to younger generations. New Paradigm churches thus included many "Seeker Sensitive" features long before the term came into popular usage. This is an important contribution which sparked ongoing creative innovations among churches that hoped to minister well in a rapidly changing culture. At the same time, New Paradigm churches also eschewed denominational structures and formal theological statements, locating spiritual authority instead within informal charismatic leadership networks and local congregations. Subsequent church planters would have to negotiate the challenges these moves created; otherwise, a founding pastor's spiritual authority and personal charisma might too easily transform a sincere missional Christian congregation into a cult of personality.

1970s to 1990s: Seeker Sensitive Churches

From the mid-1970s through the 1990s, Seeker Sensitive church planting movements became more common and more visible. Like New Paradigm churches, Seeker Sensitive churches operated from a highly missional ecclesiology. In fact, Seeker Sensitive churches were even more direct in stating their missional intentions. Their leaders drew heavily from Church Growth Theory to develop attractional evangelistic missional strategies. They designed gathered services "specifically to appeal to 'unchurched' people."[44] There are numerous examples of Seeker Sensitive churches,[45] but Saddleback Community Church in Southern California and Willow Creek Community Church outside Chicago offer particularly helpful case studies. These churches each became known as pioneering and influential models of Seeker Sensitive church planting, sparking thoughtful research into their praxis.[46] Although their ministries developed some new patterns of praxis and theology, Seeker Sensitive churches also shared much of their operant missional ecclesiology with New Paradigm churches.

Saddleback Community Church placed mission at the heart of its ecclesial identity. Its founding pastor, Rick Warren, had felt a calling to overseas missions and attended the 1974 Lausanne Congress, but ultimately decided that God was instead leading him to plant a "missionary-sending church" within the United States.[47] Warren planted Saddleback in 1980 and came to see its ministry as inherently missional. He hoped the church would grow primarily by conversions and wrote in 1995 that he "openly discourages" Christians from transferring their membership from another church to Saddleback.[48] Warren's aim in church planting was thus demonstrably similar to that seen in New Paradigm churches: attractional evangelistic ministry to unchurched people. Warren's interest in missional church planting also reflected that of his denomination. Warren and Saddleback were both affiliated with the Southern Baptist Convention (SBC), a denomination which has long been one of the most active in church planting, with "more missionaries and church planters in both North America and abroad than any other evangelical church group."[49] This commitment has been enduring; a 2021 report from the SBC's annual meeting indicated that the denomination hoped to add five thousand new congregations in North America by 2025.[50] Saddleback was thus one highly visible expression of a much wider interest in planting churches within the SBC.

Willow Creek Community Church similarly placed mission at the heart of its ecclesial identity. Willow Creek's founding pastor, Bill Hybels, had been serving as a youth minister in another church, where he worked to make meetings feel accessible to students' unbelieving friends.[51] In 1975, Hybels and his team planted Willow Creek, hoping it would be a church where young adults might feel similarly comfortable inviting their unchurched friends.[52] The founding missional vision of Willow Creek, like that of Saddleback and New Paradigm churches, was thus highly attractional, with a particular eye to young baby boomers. Hybels's founding vision proved enduring; in 1995, Lynne Hybels described Willow Creek as "a church for the unchurched."[53] This concise catchphrase indicated that Willow Creek members did not describe their church as existing for Christians or even for God's glory, but for the sake of missional outreach to the "unchurched." One qualitative researcher wrote about Willow Creek:

> In response to many of my questions on why the church did or did not do something, staff members and volunteers would repeat to me the church's motto: "Lost People matter to God." In practice, Willow Creek's commitment to reach the unchurched is the axis of its ministry.[54]

Evangelistic mission to the unchurched was thus more than a motto; it became the "axis" of the church's entire ministry and culture. Willow Creek unapologetically instrumentalized church for the sake of evangelistic mission.

Some of the most visible, practical features of Seeker Sensitive churches echoed patterns set by New Paradigm churches.[55] For example, like New Paradigm church pastors, Warren dressed informally and encouraged Saddleback members to do likewise.[56] As in New Paradigm churches, Hybels made sung worship selections, church language, and the worship space itself more contemporary in style.[57] Warren and Hybels both projected an informal, friendly persona, much as New Paradigm pastors had done.[58] Many of these moves were designed to make church appealing to baby boomers, without the specific focus on countercultural groups that marked the founding vision of some New Paradigm churches. Wilford's recent qualitative study of Seeker Sensitive churches even included Calvary Chapel alongside Willow Creek and Saddleback,[59] underscoring the many practical similarities between New Paradigm churches and Seeker Sensitive churches. Saddleback and Willow Creek did not hail from the same charismatic tradition as New Paradigm churches, but they largely followed New Paradigm churches' pattern of offering informal, contemporary styles of worship.

Like New Paradigm churches, both Willow Creek and Saddleback soon experienced rapid membership growth. By 1995 Willow Creek saw over 15,000 people attending each weekend, and by 2011, that number had swelled to 23,500.[60] Saddleback similarly saw 10,000 people attending weekly by 1995, a number that more than doubled by 2011, when over 50,000 people attended Saddleback's Easter services.[61] Echoing core tenets of Church Growth Theory, each church's founding narrative suggested that much of this was conversion growth. Willow Creek, while not offering specific numbers, reported that at times they "didn't have many Christians" in attendance, which created challenges when seeking volunteers to disciple new believers.[62] Saddleback tracked baptisms, reporting that in 1995 four out of five members had been baptized into the church.[63] In early 2011, Saddleback baptized more than 1000 people during a single service.[64] When seeing such numbers, it is important to remember that as an SBC church Saddleback only recognized believer's baptism by immersion.[65] Consequently, it is not clear how many of the people baptized at Saddleback might have been Christians who were previously baptized as infants. Nonetheless, both churches ultimately became models for later churches in part due to their rapid growth, as had New Paradigm churches before them.

The emphasis on growth in both Saddleback and Willow Creek's founding narratives reflected their interest in Church Growth Theory, which became central to the operant missional ecclesiology of Seeker Sensitive churches. Warren recalled reading about McGavran in 1974 and described his reaction by saying, "I felt God directing me to invest the rest of my life discovering the principles . . . that produce healthy, growing churches."[66] Warren thus framed the act of planting Saddleback Church as a practical expression of McGavran's missiology. Citing both McGavran and Allen, Warren wrote, "It's the natural thing for living organisms to [grow] if they are healthy. . . . [S]ince the church is a living organism, it is natural for it to grow if it is healthy."[67] Like Allen and McGavran, Warren used the term "growth" primarily to describe increasing in numerical membership, and he saw growth as both natural and normative for effectively functioning churches. Warren therefore reasoned that instead of asking how to make a church grow, leaders should be asking questions like, "'What is keeping our church from growing?' What barriers are blocking the waves God wants to send our way? What obstacles and hindrances are preventing growth from happening?"[68] Warren's emphasis on eliminating "obstacles" or "hindrances" to growth echoes Allen's work, which similarly argued that when churches do not grow, an unhelpful "barrier" is likely in the way.[69] Both Saddleback and Willow Creek therefore sought to identify and eliminate "barriers" to church attendance. Warren recalled unbelieving friends accompanying him to another church and finding the services confusing and unclear.[70] Warren also worried about logistical barriers like insufficient parking, inconvenient service times, and inadequate childcare.[71] Willow Creek's early leaders conducted an informal survey of their community to learn why people did not attend church.[72] Few details or data from this survey survive outside Hybels's impressionistic memories. Hybels did not mention any theological objections to Christianity or conflicting religious beliefs. Instead, Hybels recalled that the most common "barriers" people cited were ineffective, unclear, irrelevant, and/or insensitive elements within church services.[73] Both Willow Creek and Saddleback Churches, like other Seeker Sensitive churches, saw "barriers" to church growth as primarily logistical or stylistic, not theological.

Rapid growth created very real constraints on space, which required creative solutions lest space itself become a barrier. Saddleback opted to become a multisite church.[74] Like some multisite churches, Saddleback appointed separate pastoral and worship teams for each campus.[75] Each Saddleback campus thus became a small church to some extent, but all Saddleback campuses remained a single legal and financial entity, sharing administrative and financial resources, collegial relationships, and some programming.[76] Saddleback thus more or less reinvented some traditional denominational structures, albeit on a far more limited scale. Saddleback leaders explained their approach by saying that they were "one church in many locations."[77] This is an interesting reformulation of an older theological distinction between the one Church universal and local churches, though at Saddleback, "one church in many locations" referred only to Saddleback congregations, not to a global body of Christian faith. By contrast, Willow Creek initially adapted to its swelling congregation by expanding its facilities and programming, becoming a model "megachurch."[78] This move risked making its gathered services seem "impersonal" or even "corporate," but according Hybels, large services allowed new visitors to maintain "the anonymity they desire."[79] Eventually, though, Willow Creek grew too large for any single space to accommodate and switched to a multisite model.[80] Spatial reconfigurations thus allowed Seeker Sensitive churches to accommodate membership growth.

In addition, Seeker Sensitive churches offered highly contextualized forms of Christian worship, something that contemporary missiologists also advocated.[81] Saddleback, Willow Creek, and other Seeker Sensitive churches sought to leverage connections between Christian teachings and popular culture, using a "conspicuous amalgamation of widely shared secular narratives, symbols, and places with narrower, explicitly evangelical Christian narratives, symbols, and places."[82] Sermons in Willow Creek's "Seeker Services," for example, frequently referenced contemporary art and pop culture to explain the gospel.[83] Similarly, Warren opted for topical rather than expositional sermons and chose sermon titles that would seem relevant to people with no church background.[84] Both Warren and Hybels prioritized the "felt needs" of individuals within the local community, particularly in their sermons.[85] These practices aimed to make Christianity seem more relevant and accessible to contemporary Americans, key hallmarks of contextualized worship.

Missiologists, though, had also warned that ineffective contextualization poses serious risks, foreshadowing important limitations of Seeker Sensitive approaches to church planting. Newbigin criticized churches which, for the sake of relevance, absolutized local cultures over and against the gospel, something he called "false contextualization."[86] Newbigin described "false contextualization" as something like a thinly disguised version of Hoekendijk's missional ecclesiology, which had placed the world's felt needs, not the gospel, at the center of Christian mission.[87] According to Newbigin, when the gospel is falsely contextualized, "the world is not challenged at its depth but rather absorbs and domesticates the gospel and uses it to sacralize its own purposes."[88] Newbigin's critique was not directed specifically to Seeker Sensitive churches, but laid alongside descriptions of Saddleback and Willow Creek's praxis, the problem becomes clear: some of their sincere attempts to eliminate "barriers" to church attendance could inadvertently domesticate the gospel, prioritizing cultural relevance over the gospel's more challenging, culturally problematic demands. Sermons and ministries that focused too intently on "felt needs" risked subtly reframing the gospel in utilitarian terms, as a text to be consulted primarily to solve one's own perceived problems. One researcher aptly observed that the strength of Seeker Sensitive preaching was that it "starts where people are. Its weakness is that it leaves them there."[89] Neither Warren's nor Hybels's sermons presumed biblical literacy, but they seemed unlikely to increase it much, either.[90] Instead, the primary responsibility for discipleship and biblical literacy shifted from pastors to small group ministries. Nonetheless, the best estimates have consistently indicated that approximately 40 percent of people in Seeker Sensitive churches did not attend small groups.[91] Seeker Sensitive churches thus risked becoming a very comfortable environment for people who were not particularly interested in Christian discipleship or spiritual formation. Willow Creek's three-year internal Reveal study in 2007 famously discovered that just such a pattern had become widespread, with many Willow Creek members reporting low satisfaction with their church's discipleship and spiritual growth offerings.[92] Seeker Sensitive churches certainly grew numerically, but not everyone in them understood how to grow in their faith.

Willow Creek carried the push for "seeker sensitivity" so far that they fundamentally redefined gathered weekend services. One qualitative researcher reported that at Willow Creek, "church staff recognizes that the weekend service is not a worship service."[93] This was a significant departure from the operant ecclesiology of almost all other Christian churches. "Believers' services" happened, but only on Wednesday or Thursday nights, not on weekends.[94] Willow Creek saw weekend services as something like Jesus's hillside teachings, Paul's Areopagus sermon, or John Wesley's open-air revivals: a "public forum" where unbelievers might encounter the gospel.[95] A "public forum" is not a sacred space, and so Willow Creek's worship space was designed to resemble a shopping mall, food court, or other public commercial venue. One visiting researcher even observed, "There is nothing in the lobby that appears overly religious, except for the occasional bookcase of Bibles. I suspect some people could walk through the space and never realize it was a church."[96] Willow Creek so fully prioritized evangelistic mission that sacred space became difficult to identify, and long-standing beliefs about Christian Sunday worship were arguably sacrificed.

Willow Creek's approach was not universal, even among Seeker Sensitive churches. Indeed, Saddleback maintained a traditional understanding of weekend church services as gathered Christian worship, and Warren insisted that services must be "Seeker Sensitive" but not "seeker driven."[97] He also maintained that worshiping God is a central purpose of church.[98] Warren argued that only Christians can truly engage in Christian worship, but quickly added that non-Christians can experience God's presence by witnessing Christian worship.[99] Saddleback thus maintained a clearer ecclesial identity and encouraged its members to see a variety of spaces within and outside Saddleback as sanctified by God's presence.[100] Unlike Hybels, Warren insisted that discipleship, Christian fellowship, worship, and practical ministries are also core purposes of the church alongside evangelism.[101] Many congregations that admired Hybels's ministry but were understandably reluctant to abandon traditional understandings of Christian worship therefore adopted the Saddleback model instead.[102] Warren's approach to Seeker Sensitivity thus preserved a more traditional understanding of ecclesial identity, particularly that of church as a Christian worshiping community.

Both Willow Creek and Saddleback have significantly influenced many other planted American congregations. In 1995, each church published an account of its founding narrative which included recommendations for others hoping to plant similar churches.[103] Furthermore, Willow Creek and Saddleback each operated a leadership training network for church planters.[104] In 1995 one researcher identified approximately 650–700 member churches within the Willow Creek Association, interviewed two dozen church pastors operating Willow Creek–style church plants, and conducted site visits to ten Seeker Sensitive churches in four different US states.[105] Striking as this is, Willow Creek and Saddleback had an even wider influence than their training networks. Pritchard identified four levels of Willow Creek's influence: people within their massive flagship church, "hundreds of churches" that were planted according to Willow Creek's model, still other churches that included some Seeker Sensitive elements, and "thousands of churches and individuals around the world who have been influenced by the Willow Creek programs, principles, books, and tools."[106] By the late 1990s, Willow Creek and Saddleback had shaped popular understandings of church planting in the United States and beyond, influencing many pastors and congregations.

One could qualify this picture somewhat by arguing that Willow Creek and Saddleback's influence on planted churches was primarily practical, not theological. For example, one researcher noticed that people attending Willow Creek and Saddleback training events seemed "interested primarily in methodology, not theology. They are looking for practical marketing suggestions, not theological justifications."[107] Such observations, though, belie the subtle but significant effects that Seeker Sensitive practices had on operant missional ecclesiology. Seeker Sensitive practices were built around specific assumptions about mission and church, such as Church Growth Theory, and their ministries were practical expressions of that operant theology. Churches would therefore find it difficult to adopt too many elements of Seeker Sensitive praxis while enacting a fundamentally different understanding of missional church. Furthermore, many Seeker Sensitive churches remained structurally independent, like Willow Creek, or affiliated with loosely organized, congregationalist denominations, like SBC-affiliated Saddleback.[108] Consequently, many Seeker Sensitive churches lacked the denominational structures that traditionally provided theological training, doctrinal standards, and practical oversight to local congregations, leaving little to counter the operant theology that Seeker Sensitive praxis embodied. For this reason, it is hardly surprising that Wilford's research comparing Saddleback and Willow Creek to other Seeker Sensitive churches concluded, "The most important differences are in aesthetic and organizational style. By contrast, theological differences are minimal."[109] Without careful theological reflection, congregations that adopted Seeker Sensitive practices might find that these practices carried more theological influence than was initially obvious.

In numbers and in visibility, Seeker Sensitive churches carried the praxis and operant theology of New Paradigm churches forward, encouraging wider swaths of the American population to understand church as fundamentally missional. Their approach enacted core assumptions of Church Growth Theory, making its missional vision familiar to many Christians who had never heard of Donald McGavran or Roland Allen. Seeker Sensitive churches popularized the growing missiological consensus: churches have a vital role to play in mission, and mission is relevant to congregations throughout the world, including those in seemingly "Christianized" countries like the United States. Rapid membership growth and relevant evangelistic proclamation were hallmarks of these congregations. Seeker Sensitive churches embraced a calling to missional engagement and sparked widespread interest in finding effective ways to minister well in rapidly changing cultures. These were important developments, which Seeker Sensitive churches achieved on an impressive scale. Some of these churches, though, also adopted approaches to contextualized worship that risked eroding long-standing theological understandings of church itself. Willow Creek's sacrifice of Christian worship to create a "public forum" where people might encounter the gospel belied substantive challenges that remained, as did more widespread limitations in fostering Christian discipleship. Missional outreach was clear; ecclesial identity and Christian spiritual growth had become hazier.

1990s to 2010s: Emerging Church Movements and Other Proposed Reforms

By the 1990s and early 2000s, concerns about Church Growth Theory and some common features of church planting praxis grew louder.[110] Emerging church movements (ECMs) proposed a series of practical responses which they hoped would address many of these concerns.[111]

This new stream of church planting began in the mid-1990s as a loosely connected network of missional congregations seeking to offer alternatives to Seeker Sensitive churches. Their responses accurately identified some of the most important unanswered questions and potentially problematic developments within contemporary American church planting efforts. Some of the reforms they adopted still offer tantalizing pictures of what missional church planting might become. Nonetheless, many congregations that identified with ECMs did not go far enough in reexamining the operant theology that had developed within contemporary church planting movements. Indeed, as we will see, their reforms addressed some stylistic features of church, but Emerging churches could still embody demonstrably similar assumptions as their predecessors about the nature of church and mission.

The term "Emerging church" bears definition. In this book, "Emerging church" denotes planted missional churches that self-identified with ECMs, began between the 1990s and the mid-2010s, and targeted Gen X and younger Americans.[112] It is particularly important to clarify that "Emerging churches" are distinct from the "Emergent Village," an informal network of politically progressive Christians which also arose in the 1990s.[113] These two groups are often confused, for understandable reasons. Like the Emergent Village, Emerging churches positioned themselves as a "protest" against conservative American evangelicalism and some of its common expressions within Seeker Sensitive churches.[114] To maintain a clear distinction between them, the term "Emerging church" will be preferred over "Emergent church," which some writers have used to describe the same congregations and church planting networks.[115] The now defunct Mars Hill Church in Seattle, which founded the Acts 29 Network, offers the best documented case study of an Emerging church,[116] though it is important to underscore that Mars Hill was both more theologically conservative and more troubled than many other Emerging churches.[117]

The espoused missional ecclesiology of Emerging churches differed from that of Seeker Sensitive churches, in part because its leaders cited different missiological sources. Where Seeker Sensitive church leaders like Warren cited McGavran and Church Growth Theory, Emerging church leaders typically cited Lesslie Newbigin.[118] Some of Newbigin's most influential books, including *The Gospel in a Pluralist Society* and *Foolishness to the Greeks*, appeared in the United States in the late 1980s, making his a fresh, formative voice speaking to American Christians around the time Emerging churches began.[119] Newbigin's works particularly encouraged

Western Christians to learn from overseas missions and to prioritize the relationships between a congregation and its surrounding community.[120] Newbigin argued that congregations can only contextualize the gospel properly "when the word is not a disembodied word, but comes from a community which embodies the true story, God's story, in a style of life which communicates both the grace and the judgment."[121] This is why Newbigin called local congregations "the hermeneutic of the gospel," the living illustration of God's grace that makes Christ's redemption visible and understandable within local communities.[122] Advocates of ECMs agreed, citing a partially realized "kingdom" eschatology to argue that missional churches can and must become authentic worshiping communities with a strong ethos of local social engagement.[123] The espoused theology of ECMs thus differed demonstrably from that of Seeker Sensitive churches, which had focused on evangelistic proclamation, broadly following McGavran and Church Growth Theory; ECMs, by contrast, articulated something much closer to the holistic missional vision that Escobar had advocated at Lausanne in 1974.[124]

Some of the distinctive elements of ECM praxis reflected their espoused theology. Newbigin's influence is especially clear in Bielo's description of ECMs' operant missiology:

> Being missional means seriously cultivating relationships—not before or after conversion attempts, but in place of them. To accomplish this goal, they advocate mimicking the acculturating foreign missionary: settling into a locale and becoming intimately familiar with a place and its people.[125]

The comparison between Emerging church members and "acculturating foreign missionaries" is a bit strained, since most of them were Americans living within their home culture. Nonetheless, it underscored the sense of estrangement that many Emerging church members felt from evangelical church culture. People within Emerging churches commonly crafted narrative accounts describing their personal experiences of "deconstruction" or "deconversion" from evangelical Seeker Sensitive churches.[126] These narratives frequently expressed frustration with a church culture that "prioritizes megachurch growth over spiritual growth," "is overly invested in being Seeker Sensitive," "allows for complacency and a lack of commitment to faith," "follows 'culture' blindly but constantly fails to create it," and "has a skewed sense of what 'worship' means."[127] For this reason, common Emerging church praxis included participatory multisensory worship, emphasis on "authentic" local community, and active social and political engagement.[128] Some churches used the arts to create richer worship spaces and a more thoughtful, thorough engagement with contemporary cultures.[129] All of these practices have proven to be enduring, even in newer congregations that might not self-identify as Emerging churches.[130]

Bielo's description also highlighted ECMs' missional focus on relationships, an intentional contrast from Seeker Sensitive churches' perceived focus on "conversion attempts."[131] Emerging churches consequently sought to foster a more "intimate familiarity," as Bielo put it, between congregations and their surrounding community. Seattle-area churches that another researcher identified as recognizably Emerging distinguished themselves by "the regularity and intentionality with which they share more substantial meals."[132] This is a notable difference from the approach fostered by Hybels, who spoke favorably of large, impersonal services that allowed seekers some "anonymity."[133] Unlike Seeker Sensitive churches, which emphasized the relevance of sermons, Emerging churches emphasized the importance of authentic lived witness; as Newbigin wrote, mission "is not only declaratory; it is performatory. It can be the first because it is the second."[134] For this reason, it was hardly surprising to see Emerging churches practice "radical hospitality" by welcoming marginalized groups into their fellowship, to hear Emerging worshipers "pray corporately for justice and liberation and for specific political and social issues," and to experience Emerging congregations actively prioritizing practical service within local communities.[135] ECMs' operant missional ecclesiology echoed threads of Newbigin's missiology and heeded the calls for ethical living and social justice that were voiced at Lausanne,[136] but less obvious in New Paradigm and Seeker Sensitive congregations.

It is important to acknowledge that ECMs' efforts to articulate and embody a different missional ecclesiology did not fully obviate the risks of instrumentalizing church for the sake of mission. Newbigin himself had worried that an overly realized view of "kingdom" could create "a corpus of ethical demands" that would "sacralize whatever is the contemporary program for justice and peace."[137] There was indeed a genuine risk that ECMs might simply baptize the Democratic political leanings of some younger American Christians. Indeed, many people in the politically progressive Emergent Village were sympathetic to ECMs, and one qualitative researcher observed that "self-identified Emerging churches are predominantly theologically progressive."[138] In churches where a progressive political ethos became too strident, ECMs risked creating the impression that social transformation rather than the gospel lay at the center of God's mission, much as Hoekendijk arguably had done.[139] As Van Engen explained, under the lens of this kind of missional ecclesiology, the gospel can easily get "lost in the jungle of sociopolitical and economic agendas."[140] Such a situation, he worried, "essentially amounted to the euthanasia of the church."[141] Bosch expressed similar concerns, adding that Hoekendijk's missiology made it "hard to define exactly how mission differed from the ethos and activity of the Peace Corps."[142] Such a missional approach could easily become ineffective contextualization of the gospel, bowing to the felt needs of a new generation rather than creating a prophetic encounter between the gospel and contemporary culture. ECMs would need more than an ethos of "protest" and an understandable passion for tangible social engagement. They needed a clear understanding of what it meant to be a missional church.

ECM congregations were very concerned about maintaining a distinctly Christian identity, and so many adopted ancient-future practices, which they hoped might restore a more tangible experience of "church" to gathered services.[143] Examples of ancient-future practices include:

> closer attention to the annual church calendar than conservative Evangelicals have required; designing multisensory worship experiences; performing monastic disciplines; integrating pre-Reformation theologians into public and private reading rituals; and rethinking the role of materiality in worship events.[144]

The rise of these practices represented a clear rejection of Seeker Sensitive styles of worship, which used contemporary music and pop culture references to bring church praxis, style, and sermon content into closer alignment with contemporary culture.[145] By contrast, ECMs went backwards in time, seeking much older forms and practices that Christians had experienced for many centuries. Indeed, some ECM churches saw Seeker Sensitive worship as a form of "unwelcome modern influence" over churches.[146] ECMs had rightly diagnosed that churches like Willow Creek arguably veered into ineffective contextualization, potentially compromising their identity as "church" in order to offer culturally relevant services for the "unchurched." It was therefore unsurprising to see ECMs turn instead to more traditional worship practices, like candles and liturgical calendars. Some Emerging Christians created complex, interactive, multisensory spaces for prayer analogous to the Stations of the Cross, while others shortened their sermons, incorporated Taizé worship, and offered the Eucharist or Communion weekly.[147] ECMs' attention to materiality in worship and thoughtful recovery of earlier practices created space for quiet, prayerful contemplation that could too easily be lost in noisy, busy, media-driven modern American life.[148] In place of the media spectacles that one might observe in a large Seeker Sensitive church, ECMs created more intimate, tangible experiences that many people in their communities might associate with historic expressions of Christian faith.

Ancient-future practices, though, also carried theological and cultural baggage that required careful consideration. Some ancient-future practices were drawn from neo-liturgical traditions, which subtly and effectively reinforced a local church's connection to other congregations and to historic Christian traditions.[149] Others, like "multisensory" worship and "monastic disciplines," hailed from contemplative Christian traditions, which were less likely to create a sense of worshiping community and more likely to heighten individual spiritual experiences.[150] As a result, some ancient-future practices unintentionally reinforced the highly individualistic engagement with Christian spirituality which ECM leaders rightly associated with Seeker Sensitive services.[151] For example, Bielo observed that after a guided meditation on art led by one Emerging Christian leader, the leader had real trouble fostering meaningful discussion within the group about their individual spiritual reflections.[152] More problematically, most ancient-future practices reflected an imagined medieval Christian past that was very European and very white. Ancient-future practices reflected neither the richness of global Christian traditions nor the ethnic diversity within many twenty-first-century American communities. They thus subtly contradicted ECMs' espoused desire to be more "inclusive."[153] Churches that adopted ancient-future practices intended to restore a sense of ecclesial identity, which was important. On their own, though, these practices were not a perfect solution to the gaps in operant theology that ECMs rightly identified within many Seeker Sensitive churches.

Despite helpful attempts to offer constructive alternatives, the operant missional ecclesiology of some Emerging churches ultimately echoed many of the patterns seen in earlier American church planting movements. Some researchers saw the operant theology of Emerging churches as recognizably evangelical, much as it had been in many Seeker Sensitive churches.[154] According to one study, some Seattle-area Christians even described Mars Hill as another Seeker Sensitive megachurch, admittedly with an edgier pastor.[155] Other observations supported this characterization; Gibbs and Bolger wrote that early Emerging churches

> were characterized by loud, passionate worship music directed toward God and the believer (not the seeker); David Letterman-style, irreverent banter; raw narrative preaching; *Friends* (the popular TV series) type relationships; and later, candles and the arts.[156]

Emerging churches' initial preference for "loud, passionate worship music directed toward God and the believer (not the seeker)" might seem like a clear reaction against Willow Creek's style of Seeker Sensitive services, which were not configured as Christian worship.[157] Their insistence on authentic Christian worship music, though, as well as their later embrace of contemplative ancient-future practices, aligned well with Warren's more balanced missional ecclesiology, which similarly prioritized authentic worship.[158] More strikingly, some features that Gibbs and Bolger described, like "irreverent banter" and "raw narrative preaching," might seem like a reaction against Warren's easygoing, crowd-pleasing, Seeker-Sensitive style.[159] Using *Friends* or "the arts," though, actually followed the underlying Seeker Sensitive pattern: leveraging references to contemporary popular culture to explain the gospel. ECMs simply updated their cultural references and overall style to recontextualize the gospel for a younger generation, exactly as Seeker Sensitive and New Paradigm churches had previously done. The primary difference was the targeted demographic. Even the "raw narrative preaching" and "irreverent banter" echoed an interest in informality and authenticity which went all the way back to New Paradigm churches and continued in Seeker Sensitive churches. Bielo observed a preference for irony within ECMs as a humorous and serious means of critiquing contemporary cultures.[160] The style is different, but the interest remains engaging with contemporary culture, particularly among cynical Gen X Christians. Gibbs and Bolger therefore concluded that within Emerging churches, the "bulk of church practice . . . remained the same as their conservative Baptist, seeker, new paradigm, purpose-driven predecessors; only the surface techniques changed."[161] This pattern is hardly surprising given their history; one of the first Emerging churches was founded near Saddleback Church in 1986, by a pastor who admired New Paradigm churches, attended a Baptist seminary, and worked at Willow Creek under Hybels.[162] People in Emerging churches had already internalized much of the operant theology that had been visible in earlier approaches to American church planting. They updated the look and feel of services but retained many shared assumptions and values. Their espoused theology was different; their operant theology was at times demonstrably similar.

In particular, Emerging churches did not fully address the real risks of allowing a cult of personality to emerge around a founding pastor, risks which had first appeared in New Paradigm churches. Indeed, at Mars Hill Church, such risks were arguably amplified. At its peak, Mars Hill boasted thirteen thousand people attending weekly.[163] When it became a multisite church, Mars Hill began to simulcast Mark Driscoll's preaching across all campuses rather than appointing local preachers, as Saddleback Church had done.[164] Driscoll defended this move by comparing simulcast sermons to Paul's pattern of writing long kerygmatic letters to be read aloud in remote first-century congregations.[165] Driscoll's comparison, though, overlooked the infrequency of Paul's letters; no first-century congregation received weekly letters from Paul, but all Mars Hill congregations received teaching from Driscoll nearly every week. It also ignored the important fact that the first-century congregations that received Paul's letters also had local leadership.[166] Driscoll also argued that simulcasting was analogous to using amplifiers and projection screens, a common practice in many larger worship spaces.[167] This analogy, though, only holds if all pastoral communication were one-way preaching. By contrast, most pastors see and hear congregants while preaching and have opportunities to converse with them before or after services. Mars Hill's approach thus heightened the pattern that began to develop in some New Paradigm churches, where a gap arose between pastor and congregation. At Mars Hill, it became difficult to imagine the office of pastor as anything beyond a distant preacher.

The Mars Hill pattern of remote preaching exaggerated still other problematic patterns seen in earlier planted congregations. Once Mars Hill began streaming services, it was relatively easy to record them and post them to the internet. According to Mars Hill's own literature, the internet was framed as something like "the Greek Marketplace of Acts 17," "the place in which people gather to dialogue thoughts, philosophies, opinions."[168] Mars Hill's very name attested to its desire to create a public forum like Mars Hill in Athens, also known as the Areopagus, the site where Acts 17:16–34 records people outside the faith encountering the gospel message through Paul's innovative, contextualized preaching. Mars Hill's approach to missional church thus was a clear echo of Willow

Creek's operant understanding of Seeker Sensitive services as public space for gospel preaching.[169] Mars Hill never addressed the inherent risks of this approach. Over time, one staffer even noticed that Driscoll had begun preaching to the cameras, not the congregation.[170] Mars Hill's services did not require physical attendance and prioritized engagement with those who might never enter their fellowship, echoing Willow Creek's commitment to the unchurched. This impersonal approach marked a significant distinction between Mars Hill and many other Emerging churches, which stressed embodied local experiences, but it is significant that such an approach was possible even when a congregation aligned itself with key tenets of ECMs. Earlier models of church planting still held considerable influence, in spite of Emerging churches' critiques of them.

It is important to clarify that Emerging churches were not the only voices in the 1990s and early 2000s that identified limitations in the operant missional ecclesiology of planted churches. In response to widespread concerns that planted American congregations had adopted an ecclesiocentric missional theology, some Christians within and outside ECMs began advocating for "Disciple-Making Movements" (DMMs).[171] As the name suggests, DMMs focus on empowering lay Christians to disciple others.[172] This approach deemphasized preaching and prioritized relationships between individual Christians and individual seekers. DMMs also reflected a common critique of Seeker Sensitive churches: they focused so much attention on evangelistic conversions that they risked neglecting discipleship.[173] As Jeff Vanderstelt put it, "If we fail to connect decision-making moments to disciple-making processes, we unnecessarily create immature deciders instead of mature disciples."[174] For Vanderstelt, this was hardly a theoretical concern; when he began ministering to what was left of the congregation in Mars Hill Seattle after Mark Driscoll's fall, he found that while people in his congregation "knew about" common Christian "spiritual practices like solitude, silence, sabbath, prayer, Bible reading, and such," many of them "had not been well equipped" in practicing such disciplines and "lacked the motivation and empowerment that comes from abiding in Christ."[175] As Vanderstelt's observations note, shifting the language from "church planting" to "disciple-making" also addressed missiological concerns that Church Growth Theory had drawn artificial distinctions between evangelism and discipleship, which needlessly encouraged churches to see the two as competing, not complementary priorities.[176] DMMs therefore combined discipleship and evangelism into a single continuous process of faith development, creating time and space for seekers to explore the gospel before and after conversion.[177] The rise of DMMs thus demonstrably highlighted the lack of emphasis discipleship had received in many Seeker Sensitive churches and addressed some of the theological problems that created this gap.

DMMs, though, did not respond fully to the operant missional ecclesiology behind the patterns that they justifiably saw as problematic. Like ECMs, some advocates of DMMs unwittingly embodied much of the thinking behind the praxis that they rightly critiqued. For example, early advocates of DMMs broadly echoed Church Growth Theory's emphasis on numerical growth by framing "disciple-making" as generating rapidly multiplying networks of believers.[178] Fostering the "rapid multiplication" of disciples was not all that different from fostering rapidly growing churches; it similarly privileged numerical growth. Win Arn even stressed the importance of identifying "responsive populations" in order to fuel the rapid numerical increase of disciples.[179] This strategy was not materially different from McGavran's work identifying "receptive populations" in order to fuel rapid church attendance growth.[180] More critically, some DMM advocates risked moving church from the center of mission to its periphery, at best, by labeling churches as merely a "support" or "partner" to the actual disciple-makers.[181] Some DMM advocates also argued for planting house churches, but connections between DMMs and house church planting were not immediately obvious.[182] Like Willow Creek's Seeker Sensitive services, DMMs lacked any obvious function for gathered Christian worship, replacing the spiritually formative elements of worshiping communities with highly individualistic discipling patterns. Vanderstelt, for example, rightly critiques an overemphasis on worship attendance, saying, "Public gatherings are important, but they are not sufficient," and adds, "Jesus certainly engaged in this space but didn't expect much from it" because "his time with the crowds had little lasting impact."[183] As Vanderstelt rightly notes, swelling attendance at gathered services does not automatically create spiritual maturity, and public engagement does not automatically generate widespread public faith, but corporate Christian worship still matters. DMMs thus rightly pointed to important limitations of existing American church planting praxis, but they ultimately failed to offer a fully viable alternative to the operant missional ecclesiology common to planted churches.

The 1990s and early 2000s saw a series of proposed alternatives to earlier models of church planting. Each of these proposals reflected growing discontent with Seeker Sensitive churches, and some espoused a more holistic missional vision. Their critiques were valid, and the alternatives they proposed rightly reminded churches of the significance of long-standing Christian traditions, holistic mission, and spiritual formation. In the end, though, Emerging churches never fully articulated an alternative missional ecclesiology that could move planted churches forward. Individualism loomed large in many proposed alternatives, and "church" in some seemed little more than a platform for a preacher or a tangential support to individual disciple-making efforts. The operant missional ecclesiology of American church planting movements had unfortunately grown hazier, and operant understandings of "church" seemed particularly strained.

2000s to Present: Problems Exposed

By the mid-2000s, some planted American churches began making the headlines for the worst reasons. In 2006 Ted Haggard, a prominent evangelical pastor tied to charismatic church planting networks, was fired over allegations that included sexual impropriety and drug use.[184] In 2014 Mark Driscoll resigned from the leadership of Mars Hill Church following allegations of bullying, misogyny, dishonesty, plagiarism, controlling behavior, abusive leadership, and misappropriation of funds.[185] Soon thereafter, Mars Hill announced that it was closing its doors and selling its properties.[186] The Acts 29 Network had appointed new leadership before Driscoll's fall and thus survived its founding church's demise.[187] Charges of spiritual abuse, though, were lodged against Steve Timmis in 2020, ending his seven-year leadership of Acts 29.[188] In 2017–18, credible allegations of sexual misconduct against Bill Hybels came to light,[189] ending his long-time leadership of Willow Creek Church and the Willow Creek Association.[190] Hybels's longtime mentor, Gilbert Bilezikian, was also accused of inappropriate conduct, but permitted to continue serving at Willow Creek after the allegations surfaced.[191] As a result, Willow Creek's entire elder board eventually resigned and the Willow Creek Association rebranded itself as the "Global Leadership Network."[192] Allegations of pastoral abuse and troubling responses to abuse survivors generated a wave of accusations within the SBC, a denomination that had long championed and supported planting churches.[193] By the summer of 2022, investigators found that the SBC Executive Committee had covered up allegations of abuse within their ranks.[194] The collective weight of these scandals, coupled with increasingly divisive American politics, led to the departure of some key

SBC leaders.[195] This list is only a selection of the recent scandals that garnered the most national media attention.

It is worth emphasizing that many—indeed, most—planted American congregations did not experience anything like these situations. Many planted churches have ministered faithfully, blessing their congregations and local communities. Discussing problems that have occurred is in no way intended to malign these faithful churches. Instead, the aim is to help them safeguard their ministries and their missional witness. Scandals have come to light in a wide range of Christian churches and ministries in recent years. It is both unrealistic and unhelpful to assume that problems can be managed quietly, outside the public eye. In this context, it is the responsibility of every church, including planted churches, to transparently acknowledge shortcomings, to lament the pain and brokenness that sin engenders, and to actively seek better ways forward. It is also our responsibility to address potentially damaging consequences of existing practices in the hopes of avoiding preventable problems and reducing planted churches' vulnerability to bad actors. As Paul wrote in 1 Corinthians 12:26, when any one part of the body of Christ suffers, "all suffer together"; indeed, scandals in any church affect the witness of every church. When people have been hurt in churches, and when many more now harbor suspicions of Christian ministries, responding well to problems is an important step toward rebuilding trust. Churches must always be a safe space where hurting souls can find a God who sees and heals.

One could describe recent scandals as solely the byproduct of a few individual leaders' moral failures. Planted churches have felt some pressure to do so. For reasons that the next chapter will explore more fully, many planted churches operated from a highly individualistic soteriology, and so the understandable instinct might be to explain scandals not as a systemic or structural problem, but a poor personal decision by a sinful individual.[196] Many church planting networks formed as loose associations of fully independent or congregationalist churches, making it even more natural to frame problems as isolated local issues.[197] To be sure, individual moral failings were a genuine concern, and the scandals described in the previous paragraph were not wholly equivalent. Still, the list of scandals in the previous paragraph was not confined to one any one phase of church planting; it included planted churches within independent charismatic networks, Seeker Sensitive churches, and Emerging churches. Nor have scandals been isolated to one local community; the planted churches represented in the above list were located across a wide geographic area that includes most of the United States. Sadly, the troubling pervasiveness of scandals raises important concerns that bear careful consideration. As this book has demonstrated, seemingly independent planted congregations were often more closely interrelated than they might appear. As this final section will explore, some of the very practices that became common among planted churches inadvertently left them more vulnerable to bad actors and less equipped to respond well when problems arose.

Some potential vulnerabilities came as unfortunate side effects of the widespread influence of Church Growth Theory. In many planted congregations, membership growth seemed to offer a tantalizingly clear metric for identifying faithful ministry. Membership statistics for planted congregations were not difficult to find; qualitative researchers generally included them in the opening pages of their studies, and they featured prominently in the founding narratives of many planted churches and church planting movements. Warren's writings popularized Church Growth Theory, linking McGavran's missional interest in increasing church attendance to the project of contemporary American church planting.[198] It was therefore not surprising that rapidly increasing membership eventually came to be seen as a mark of effective ecclesial praxis in planted American congregations.[199] For example, when concerned peers advised Mark Driscoll to seek mentoring from John Piper, Driscoll reportedly rejected this advice because Piper's church was smaller than his own.[200] If this account is true, it is only one example of widespread operant beliefs that subtly framed small or slowly growing churches as less effective than larger or more rapidly growing churches.[201] This ecclesial version of a prosperity gospel made it natural for large, growing churches assume that their swelling numbers were a sign of effective leadership that enjoyed God's favor. This perception could too easily tempt some congregations to overlook the shortcomings or struggles of a pastor who could draw a crowd.

Widespread interest in growth created another challenge: problems in planted churches became more difficult to identify as both popular and academic discussions of "megachurches" increasingly and unfairly stigmatized large churches on the basis of little but their size.[202] Some smaller planted churches and some Emerging churches even defined themselves as an attractive alternative to "megachurches," reflecting a growing perception that larger churches were inherently problematic.[203] Hybels felt the need to defend Willow Creek's size in a discussion of "frequently asked questions" about the church; he did so by arguing that there were "tremendous benefits" to the "wide-ranging inventory of ministries" that a large congregation can offer.[204] The form of his response suggests that size alone was a critique, not the church's operant theology, which prioritized growth. One recent academic study concluded that in many churches, "the push for increased size . . . fosters vulnerabilities unspoken by leaders and unseen by members and supporters."[205] As this phrasing suggests, what deserved attention was perhaps not size itself so much as "the push for increased size," which results from an operant missional ecclesiology drawn from Church Growth Theory. The same problematic patterns seen in large churches could just as easily occur in a small church that shared their interest in growth. The arbitrariness of critiques based on size alone made it all too easy to dismiss the critics of large churches and to overlook potential problems facing smaller ones. Focus on congregational size thus became a tantalizing distraction for both critics and practitioners of church planting.

Given the widespread interest in membership growth, it was hardly surprising that many planted churches came to see their missional calling as both attractional and ecclesiocentric. Personal evangelism existed, but its stated aim was often to invite unchurched friends to come to church.[206] Similarly, articulated plans for "discipleship" at times focused primarily on building up the church. For example, Willow Creek's seven-step discipleship paradigm explicitly envisioned "unchurched Harry and Mary" moving from "seekers" to committed church members, who in the final stage of their discipleship volunteered at Willow Creek and supported the church financially.[207] In this model, connections to God are assumed to develop alongside growing commitment to church. From New Paradigm churches to Emerging churches, many planted congregations poured most of their energy into gathered weekend services, where the largest numbers of people would assemble.[208] At the same time, reforms proposed by each new stream of church planting focused on the look, feel, and content of services, potentially neglecting other elements of ecclesial life, like discipleship. DMMs had attempted to address this problem by rightly refocusing attention on spiritual formation, placing emphasis on discipleship that went beyond church allegiance. Nonetheless, as we have seen, in many planted churches spiritual formation was at times secondary to membership growth, and even DMMs did not offer an entirely clear articulation of the relationship between "discipling" and the church. It was therefore sadly predictable that spiritual immaturity could persist for years, even among some church leaders.

The weight of these pressures gradually reduced popular understandings of "church" to a platform for a preacher. Oddly, the pastor seemed to exist apart from the congregation, differentiated not only by lighting and physical location but also by relationships. As pastors focused more on preaching, they and the congregation could easily drift apart, with neither really knowing the other well enough to offer the accountability, support, and encouragement that all Christians need. Saddleback's leaders envisioned church as a series of concentric circles of commitment; tellingly, "lay ministers" occupied the church's innermost circle.[209] Pastoral staff did not appear in this diagram, as if they somehow occupied another space, removed from the church's discipleship patterns but still overseeing the organization. Many independent planted churches espoused the importance of communal leadership and decision-making,[210] but in churches like Willow Creek and Mars Hill, the founding pastor eventually became the only authoritative voice.[211] It was therefore not wholly surprising to see some pastors exploit a congregation to advance their personal brand or relate to their congregations transactionally. Mars Hill was one tragic example; one researcher even described the church as "Mark Driscoll's evangelical empire."[212] One complaint brought against Driscoll involved the use of church funds to help advance one of his books up the bestseller lists.[213] If people believed that church were primarily a platform for the preacher, then increasing his or her platform through larger worship services, screens, amplifiers, online media, and/or best-selling books could seem a viable way to advance the *missio Dei*. Many "models" of church planting in fact became so closely tied to a particular pastor's personality that they became impossible to replicate or even continue after the founding pastor departed.[214] This reality could too easily tempt pastors to press on rather than seek help when difficulties mounted. Preaching had become far too lonely an office.

Pastors within this culture also felt immense pressure to perform, which created additional temptations. Plagiarism has long been a common temptation for pastors,[215] but when preaching became the primary attraction within an attractional missional strategy, temptations to "borrow" a more compelling sermon likely grew stronger. Indeed, charges of literary plagiarism were lodged against Driscoll, and charges of sermon plagiarism were lodged against church planter and SBC president Ed Litton.[216] With little theological training or denominational support, some pastors of planted churches found themselves with insufficient resources to draw on when pressure to deliver a good sermon mounted.

If problems arose within a planted congregation, there was not always enough outside help to summon. As we have seen, planted churches often rejected denominational affiliations and other formal ecclesial structures that have historically provided local congregations with leadership training, support, and accountability.[217] Many either resisted denominational affiliations or conspicuously omitted denominational labels from their name.[218] Loosening ecclesial oversight gave planted churches helpful freedom to engage in creative ecclesial experimentation and to develop freshly contextualized worship services,[219] which doubtless proved a blessing to many congregations and seeking souls. Loose oversight, though, could also leave pastors without help when challenges arose. Informal networks and leadership conferences created some opportunities for pastoral support and mentoring, but relationships between pastors and church planting networks could sometimes prove more transactional than supportive.[220] In addition, high-profile leaders of large planted churches have not always been held to shared denominational standards of faith and praxis.[221] For example, Warren ordained three women at Saddleback Church in 2021, something counter to the SBC's complementarian theology.[222] In response, some delegates to the SBC's 2021 Convention discussed removing Saddleback from the SBC, but no action was taken until February 2023, several months after Warren's retirement.[223] Whatever one's beliefs about women's ordination, it is concerning that any pastor's high profile might exempt him or her from denominational standards. In this context, planted churches could easily find themselves with little beyond local internal structures and pastoral integrity to safeguard their congregation.

Lacking support and facing immense pressure, burnout and struggle among pastors of planted churches became a massive risk. Tim Morey has explained the spiritual challenges facing church planters, writing, "I realize just how much of my vocation as a church planter is my trying to do what I cannot possibly do."[224] Citing research on the health of pastors, Morey explains,

> Pastors have higher rates of anxiety and depression than the general population. They have poorer lifestyle-related health markers, including higher rates of obesity, hypertension, diabetes, and metabolic syndrome. Research would indicate that at any given time, one-third of pastors are experiencing burnout and/or depression. Only one-fourth of pastors . . . finish well with vitality.[225]

As he adds, the specific pressures of church planting only compound the stresses and strains felt by other pastors; the pressures Morey cites include functioning as a "solo pastor, not part of a staff," less accountability from within or outside the congregation, "few (or zero) established leaders to share the work," and tension with other local pastors who might feel threatened by a new congregation.[226] All of these factors risk further isolating a struggling church planting pastor and exaggerating the strains that are common among Christian ministers. The results have at times been tragic. In 2019, a thirty-year-old church planting pastor named Jarrid Wilson died by suicide, sparking a national conversation on the very real mental health struggles facing many clergy.[227] The burden of mission in planted churches has too often rested primarily on the pastor's shoulders, making their ministries more stressful and less sustainable than they ever needed to be.

The tragedies documented in recent headlines were not inevitable. To find a way forward, planted congregations must avoid blaming problems solely on the flaws of individual pastors or even local congregations. To be sure, personal accountability is needed, but gaps in accountability and support coupled with unsustainable pressure must also be addressed. A way forward requires careful reflection on the operant missional ecclesiology that created accountability structures and informed ministry and missional decisions. Systemic vulnerabilities and unreasonable expectations are not solely the fault of a pastor but can be symptomatic of a wider culture around church planting that must be thoughtfully reexamined by all who share in it. The unintended consequences of Church Growth Theory on missional church praxis bespeak a profound need for better methods to assess the ministries of planted churches so that potential problems can be identified and addressed more effectively. Scandals, heartaches, and the lesser strains felt by too many people serving planted churches all underscore the need for clear missional ecclesiology. Churches are more than their pastors, and planted congregations must always seek healthy ways to participate together in the *missio Dei*.

Developments and Lingering Challenges

There has been much to celebrate and much to lament in the recent history of American church planting. It is important to recall that description is only the starting point of theological reflection. The aim of Osmer's first task is neither to laud nor to criticize churches, but to honestly examine present realities so that churches can find better ways forward. Upon reflection, the rise of church planting movements and their operant missional ecclesiology includes many commendable developments. Over the last sixty years, planted churches made Christian mission a consistent focus, allowing important missiological understandings to "come home."

Delegates to Lausanne had reminded all churches of their central place within the *missio Dei*, and American church planting movements took this calling to heart. Each phase of church planting generated creative, fresh ideas, which produced contextualized, contemporary worship services that could adapt alongside American culture. Charismatic renewal churches introduced casual, contemporary worship within networks of like-minded churches. Seeker Sensitive churches carried these practices further, making the "unchurched" a focus of ministry and emphasizing the importance of clear, evangelistic preaching. Emerging churches identified weaknesses in earlier church planting models, reintroducing older Christian practices and reemphasizing discipleship and relationship in order to further churches' missional engagement. Many ordinary Christians who had not read or even heard of leading missiologists like Allen, McGavran, and Newbigin were guided by planted church ministries to embody some of their most important insights. Church planting movements thus showed a commendable desire to be ever reforming Christian traditions so that they might proclaim the gospel clearly in ever-changing cultural contexts.

Unfortunately, proposed improvements to church planting praxis frequently fell short; while operant understandings of mission became clearer, operant understandings of church became strained. Charismatic renewal churches began subtly redefining the pastoral office, which over time was gradually reduced to the task of preaching in many planted churches. In addition, an emphasis on local church autonomy within key movements limited the theological grounding and accountability that denominational structures traditionally offered local ministries. Seeker Sensitive churches risked conflating "mission" with ever-increasing church attendance, at times diminishing a sense of church as sacred space. Emerging churches identified valid concerns within existing church planting praxis, but never fully addressed the operant missional ecclesiology behind that praxis. It was therefore tragically predictable that some planted congregations might struggle, and that some pastors might crumble under the weight of inappropriate expectations. The story of church planting as it developed in the United States over the last sixty years makes clear the need for careful theological reflection on operant missional ecclesiology. It is vitally important that American church planting movements articulate a missional ecclesiology that is appropriately contextualized, theologically grounded, and practically feasible.

3
Cultural Influences and American Church Planting Movements

Cross-cultural missionary Andrew Walls once reminded readers, "All churches are culture churches, including our own."[1] As we will see, shared operant beliefs about church planting indeed became genuinely American, reflecting key threads of late twentieth-century American culture, history, and values. The Americanization of church planting is somewhat surprising. After all, as we have seen, McGavran and Allen originally envisioned very different contexts when they proposed missional church planting with an emphasis on evangelism and local church autonomy. Nonetheless, by the late twentieth century, networks of evangelistic, autonomous local churches had proliferated throughout the United States, a nation with a long history of Christian witness. Why did this happen? Why did these specific forms of operant missional ecclesiology become so popular in a country that differed substantially from the cross-cultural contexts where they originated?

Planted American congregations focused much of their missional energy on accommodating contemporary cultures in order to offer a relevant, timely, evangelistic gospel witness. To do this, they adopted elements drawn from America's long-standing revivalist traditions and borrowed some practices from popular entertainment industries. Unfortunately, neither of these features of American culture offered sufficient resources to develop a clear operant missional ecclesiology. Billy Graham helpfully raised popular awareness of the importance of gospel preaching in contemporary American contexts. Graham's ministry, though, was not based in any local church and could not answer lingering questions about a church's place in the *missio Dei*. Planted churches also drew consumeristic, businesslike practices from entertainment industries. Eventually, though, some also bowed to consumeristic cultural preferences for homogeneous congregations, which ultimately limited their missional outreach. Advocates of contextualization have long argued that mission-minded Christians must weigh carefully how historical, cultural, and social realities might affect gospel proclamation.[2] As we will see, it is vitally important to consider how culture might affect the vision and practices of planted American churches, allowing their operant missional ecclesiology to subtly, gradually drift from their espoused beliefs and stated callings.

It is therefore appropriate to turn to Osmer's second task of theological reflection: the analytic task. This task aims to help churches understand and explain significant patterns, like those described in the last chapter, by setting local developments within a broader cultural context.[3] As Cahalan and Nieman explain, analytic work "is not so much a matter of translating something completely unfamiliar as it is making public something that would otherwise remain unnoticed and undeveloped."[4] This task will require "sagely wisdom," drawn from academic fields like history, economics, sociology, and politics, to highlight subtle cultural dynamics at play within American church planting movements.[5] These missional churches felt a strong calling to respond well to their culture in light of the gospel. Richard Niebuhr observed that the gospel has the potential to respond to a culture in a variety of ways; it might oppose, accommodate, transcend, paradoxically engage, or transform a culture.[6] As we will see, planted congregations focused much of their missional energy on accommodating American culture. This choice reflected sincere missional aims, but it also had unintended consequences. Over time, American cultural factors obscured planted churches' ecclesial identity, at times counteracting their stated missional aims and even compromising their witness. Understanding these cultural influences will equip planted congregations to discern more clearly how their gospel witness can engage well with local American cultures.

One potential concern is that Osmer's analytic task, like his descriptive task, arguably brackets out properly theological thinking and unduly privileges "objective" approaches drawn from social sciences and other purely human streams of wisdom.[7] Cahalan and Nieman, for example, complained that Osmer's method risks reinforcing "the stereotype that practical theology concerns only the application of Christian thought to actual situations that have first been understood by other means."[8] Indeed,

Osmer's second task does invite wisdom from nontheological disciplines, but it does so primarily to answer questions that arose out of theological concerns. In this chapter, the primary theological concerns in focus will be the missional witness and ecclesial identity of planted churches. The analytic task will therefore be conducted "with an eye for what is missing, forgotten, or distorted" in the operant missional ecclesiology shared by many planted American congregations.[9] Cultural analysis will also "complexify" understandings of American church planting,[10] revealing facets of operant theology that seem more cultural than theological. The aim, then, is that the analytic task will highlight aspects of espoused belief and current praxis that bear reexamination in the following chapters.

Historical Precedents: Billy Graham and Revivalist Ministries

Perhaps the most obvious cultural influence on the ministry of planted churches was America's rich history of revivalism. Revivalism has long been an enduring feature of American religious life. At least three "Great Awakenings" have occurred in American history, the first in the early eighteenth century.[11] During the eighteenth century, traveling evangelistic speakers like George Whitefield and John Wesley preached the gospel in large public revival meetings.[12] Under the influence of Charles Finney in the late nineteenth century, revival meetings became better planned and more organized.[13] Revivals remained common through the late nineteenth and early twentieth century, when Dwight L. Moody and Billy Sunday ministered.[14] By the mid- to late twentieth century America's most visible revivalist by far was Billy Graham, the only revivalist still in living memory when today's church planting movements began.[15] Graham's ministry drew fresh attention to the missional possibilities of professional, well-produced, well-organized, public evangelistic preaching events. Understanding Graham's influence will therefore shed important light on facets of American revivalist history that shaped its contemporary church planting movements.

It is almost impossible to overstate Graham's influence on late twentieth-century American evangelical thought and culture. Speaking for contemporary Americans, Scot McKnight rightly commented, "the only real revivalist most of us have known is Billy Graham."[16] Graham had access to a wider range of broadcast media than any previous revivalist and enjoyed a longer life and ministry than any of his predecessors.[17] Consequently, the scope of Graham's ministry is nothing short of staggering. According to one recent estimate, Billy Graham "evangelized over two billion people during his sixty-year long career."[18] Graham also created helpful space for theological reflection on evangelical missiology. The Billy Graham Evangelistic Association (BGEA) helped to organize and fund the Lausanne Congress of 1974, where Graham was a keynote speaker.[19] Furthermore, Graham engaged students and professors on many university campuses and oversaw the creation of Gordon-Conwell Theological Seminary, which offers academically rigorous evangelical theological training.[20] Graham's work thus influenced at least two key church planting leaders during their formative years: Rick Warren and Tim Keller.[21] On a more popular level, Graham helped to transform *Christianity Today* into a serious journal of contemporary evangelical thought.[22] Graham's influence was thus so wide-ranging that one must consider his ministry when examining late twentieth-century American church planting movements, which shared Graham's commitment to evangelistic mission.

On the most practical level, Graham's ministry enacted many well-established patterns of revivalist practice, bringing America's revivalist history to life for generations born after the Second World War. Like that of many of his predecessors, Graham's gospel preaching emphasized the need for individuals to personally repent from sin and receive Christ's salvation.[23] Some local pastors even described Graham's preaching as a "punitive, hellfire-and-brimstone presentation of sin and guilt."[24] These descriptions seemed arguably better suited to earlier revivalist preaching than to Graham's, especially as his ministry developed.[25] Instead of eliciting an overly emotional response, as had many of his predecessors, Graham offered listeners the decidedly calmer, more rational invitation to "make a decision for Christ."[26] Like Finney had done, Graham invited converts to walk down an aisle at the end of meetings to demonstrate their newfound faith.[27] McLoughlin underscored links between Graham and revivalist history, writing, "Graham, like Sunday and Moody, has reduced revivalism to such a science that there is never a night when scores of converts do not come forward."[28] Some mid-century observers even argued that "Graham's early crusades were the death rattle of the old revivalism."[29] Quite the contrary; Graham's ministry kept older revivalist traditions alive, demonstrating to late twentieth-century Americans the potential impact of evangelistic preaching in their own generation.

The form of Graham's crusade meetings did more than echo earlier revivalist ministries; it also prefigured many of the forms and practices that church planting movements would adopt. In *Rediscovering Church*, Bill Hybels even wrote that he was "surprised" by criticism of Seeker Sensitive services, since "our approach isn't very different from what Billy Graham has done with nearly universal blessing for the last several decades."[30] For example, Graham generally held meetings in sports arenas or other large "neutral" spaces, not churches.[31] This move allowed him to accommodate very large crowds and to avoid any obvious preference for one local congregation. It also leveraged the comfortable, nonthreatening atmosphere of a space where people could "buy a hot dog, and you don't have to wear a coat and tie."[32] Planted churches like Willow Creek similarly sought to hold services in an apparently "neutral" space in the hopes that people without a Christian background would find the environment comfortable and accessible.[33] Graham encouraged informal dress at his meetings as early as his 1949 Los Angeles revival, something that would become a hallmark of planted churches from the 1960s to the present.[34] Graham read local newspapers and adapted his messages to address concerns and crises of the moment, modeling features of "relevant preaching" that later church planting pastors would adopt.[35] Like church planting pastors, Graham eagerly leveraged popular culture to foster interest in his meetings, even inviting celebrity testimonies in order to attract their fans.[36] Over time, Graham's personal celebrity turned him into the main attraction in an attractional model of mission.[37] When Graham was in town, the primary missional responsibility of most local Christians was simply to invite friends "to come along with you to an attractive performance."[38] Largely the same missional model appeared in many planted churches: an evangelistic, "relevant" sermon did most of the missional work, and the rest of the service was designed to heighten responses to this message.[39] Graham's ministry thus served as a bridge that connected older revivalist ministries with contemporary forms and practices that would become common in many planted churches.

One subtle but important point on which Graham's ministry prefigured that of church planting ministries was the meticulous count that BGEA kept of decisions. When someone made a decision at a crusade, a volunteer or staffer would carefully record and categorize it, and BGEA would later publish the totals.[40] Graham was hardly the first to adopt this practice; Finney had similarly tracked "immediate visible results" like decisions, which he argued offered "a quicker and more public way of telling converts" and of demonstrating the validity of his praxis and theology.[41] BGEA's eagerness to document and publish such statistics partly reflected a similar desire to offer "concrete evidence" to financial sponsors and local church partners that investing in Graham's crusades was a valid decision that would "reap some fruits."[42] Finney's and Graham's practice resembled that recommended by McGavran and other disciples of Church Growth Theory, who similarly thought that increasing numbers of church members demonstrated the validity of a church's missional practice.[43] What was new to Graham's ministry was the scale and visibility of decisions made at events. Late twentieth-century audiences could watch Graham's televised events and see thousands of Americans streaming down an aisle at the conclusion of his preaching. These images created the distinct impression that evangelism done well would yield significant, measurable results, much as Finney and McGavran had argued. Graham crusades thus reinforced a key Church Growth paradigm and suggested that untold numbers of Americans might convert to Christianity after a well-delivered evangelistic event.

Images and statistics from Graham's ministry, though, belied somewhat more complex realities. As McLoughlin argued, "The fact that 50 per cent of those standing in front of the platform after the invitation are counsellors is sometimes lost on the reporters."[44] Unless television audiences were aware of this possibility, too, they might imagine a larger response than what actually occurred. According to BGEA's own statistics, among people who made decisions in crusades up to 1960, as many as 55 percent were already "born again" church members who were simply making a recommitment of faith, 65 to 75 percent were already church members, and almost 90 percent indicated ties to or interest in a specific local church.[45] Combining these statistics, one could argue that potentially no more than a quarter of the people seen walking down an aisle during Graham's early crusades were new converts, and very few were genuinely "unchurched." These statistics might indicate that Graham was preaching to the choir more than he realized, or that America was still broadly Christianized in the immediate postwar years. After all, the term "revival" implies, at least in part, a reigniting of an already existing faith. Still, these statistics at least suggest that existing American churches might have been effectively connecting with many curious and seeking souls at the very time when New Paradigm churches began to take form. The compelling images of thousands of converts streaming down an aisle at a Graham meeting need to be understood in light of the historical and spiritual context in which they arose.

In later years, Graham was called "America's pastor,"[46] a title that subtly reflected a significant redefinition of the pastoral office that many planted churches had also experienced. Like that of other revivalists, Graham's primary ministry was preaching. Graham faithfully answered letters from individuals and penned a syndicated advice column,[47] but he only provided personal pastoral care and counseling to a select few, including many American presidents and world leaders.[48] Graham had little direct contact with or pastoral responsibility for most of the people who heard him preach. This pattern was entirely understandable for an itinerant evangelistic speaker like Graham, particularly given the large crowds attending his events, but it was far more unusual for a congregational pastor. Nonetheless, many planted churches similarly assigned discipleship and pastoral care to other staff or to small group leaders so that the lead pastor could give more time and energy to preaching.[49] Graham's ministry thus subtly reflected, or perhaps unintentionally reinforced, a growing impression that evangelistic preaching was a missional pastor's primary calling, while pastoral care was a separate responsibility that others in a church could fulfill.

On an even more subtle level, the individualistic soteriology implicit in Graham's events offered important insights into the operant missiology behind contemporary church planting movements. Graham leveraged current national or global concerns to establish the relevance of the gospel, but in the end, "the personal was always paramount," and individual faith decisions were his main goal.[50] Consequently, Graham's sermons emphasized personal salvation and individual redemption from individual sins. Graham rarely mentioned structural or cultural sins like racism and said little about social inequalities, particularly in the early years of his ministry.[51] He believed firmly that lasting social change was only possible if and when enough individuals repented and became Christians.[52] Graham's individualistic emphasis was criticized,[53] but it became a hallmark of modern American evangelical thought and preaching.[54] N. T. Wright even argued that "the movement that has long called itself 'evangelical' is in fact better labelled 'soterian,'" because many evangelicals "have thought we were talking about 'the gospel' when in fact we were concentrating on 'salvation.'"[55] "Salvation," understood as an individual experience, is still a common emphasis of operant theology in many American evangelical churches.[56] As we will see, Graham's theology that framed saving faith as an individual choice would have significant consequences for planted churches.

Graham found further grounds for his individualistic approach to mission in premillennialist dispensationalist eschatology, a theology which he helped to popularize.[57] Indeed, this element of his theology remains a widespread feature of modern American evangelical thought.[58] Premillennialist dispensationalist eschatology teaches that "natural disasters and social chaos will accelerate as Christ's return draws near."[59] This highly pessimistic eschatology also implies that human efforts to battle injustice or improve society will ultimately prove futile.[60] Melvin Hodges described a very similar operant eschatology at work within contemporary Pentecostalism:

> Pentecostals do not expect all the world to become Christian through the efforts of evangelism. Rather, they see that the remedy of many of earth's ills must await the Second Advent of the King of Kings, for which they earnestly pray and wait. His coming will solve the problems of the social order. Until then, Christians must faithfully witness by life and word.[61]

Operant eschatology thus shaped operant missiology, much as missiologists had predicted,[62] and a laissez-faire approach to "problems of the social order" naturally followed an eschatology like Graham's. It was therefore unsurprising that premillennial, pretribulationist dispensationalism coincided with an increasingly separatist position in some American churches, which sought first to avoid being corrupted by the world and only second, if at all, to engage with it.[63] Some in attendance at the 1974 Lausanne Congress even worried that Christians might "bury their heads in the sand and wait for Christ's second coming,"[64] much as Hodges's description had suggested. The best evidence indicates that many of today's planted American churches also operate from a pretribulationist eschatology.[65] Understanding Graham's eschatology helps to explain why so many planted churches emphasized evangelistic proclamation and resisted the more holistic missional visions that Escobar advocated at Lausanne. Tellingly, churches that preached different eschatologies often adopted very different patterns of missional engagement.[66] For example, in Mosaic Church, which had some ties to ECMs, postmillennialist eschatology encouraged its leaders to embrace a hopeful sense that "purposeful human agency can affect history" and "actualize the mission of the church."[67] Similarly, Bielo's research identified a small number of Emerging church leaders whose preterist beliefs led them to "see themselves as 'partners with God' and 'active agents' in making the kingdom known to all."[68] These pastors "emphasized [an] ethic of responsibility for their surrounding social and environmental conditions" in light of their belief in "the absence of a future event promising to usher in perfection."[69] Eschatology shapes missiology. Planted American churches that shared Graham's eschatology tended to conclude that the redemption of the world was in God's hands alone.

A close study of Graham's ministry accounts for many features of contemporary American church planting ministries, but it does not explain their ecclesiocentric missional focus. Unlike church planting ministries, Graham's ministry was intentionally distinct from that of local churches. Graham generally held events in public spaces other than churches and carefully timed them to avoid conflicts with local church services.[70] This was a long-standing pattern among itinerant revivalists like Wesley, who wanted to avoid any perception of competition between their ministry and that of local pastors.[71] While there were noble intentions behind this pattern, it unintentionally created the distinct impression that evangelism and church ministries were two separate things. Eighteenth- and nineteenth-century revivals had occasionally even raised the specter that local churches were not doing enough to proclaim the gospel; if they were, after all, revival meetings might not be needed.[72] Furthermore, perhaps because Graham was so focused on individuals and their decisions, his preaching made little "explicit mention of the necessity of church or a more organic notion of believers as incorporated into a broader community."[73] Graham was even somewhat critical of America's postwar church attendance boom, which he found to include much that was "shallow and superficial."[74] Graham therefore concluded that "high levels of church attendance were not an indication of spiritual vitality."[75] Unlike many planted churches, Graham was openly skeptical of a core assumption of the Church Growth movement: he did not believe that high levels of church attendance necessarily indicated strong faith. As a result, Graham's ministry had the potential to serve as a helpful check on ecclesiocentric missions, since his desire to win new converts was clearly not a desire to build up any one local congregation.

Indeed, one can argue that Graham's ministry was so distinct from that of local churches that it had little impact on local church attendance. Some early studies suggested that few of the people who made decisions at Graham's crusades in New York, Toronto, or the United Kingdom in the 1950s became new church members, in part because many were already members of local churches.[76] For this reason, the impact of Graham's ministry on local churches sometimes seemed "superficial and ephemeral" to early observers.[77] One even notes that "pastors in crusade cities were generally less sure of Graham's prophetic importance to area churches," and some remained "ambivalent at best about the value of Graham's campaigns."[78] Graham's methods were developed in an era when most Americans claimed some Christian background, so perhaps this is not an entirely surprising outcome. In fairness, Graham's crusades typically involved considerable planning and coordination with local churches, who were expected to continue discipling people who made decisions long after the crusade ended.[79] There was thus a very real possibility that Graham's ministry had other, less tangible spiritual benefits for local churches, including helpful discipleship training. Nonetheless, in 1972 Wagner observed that even genuinely new converts to Christianity sometimes never found their way from revival events to local churches and wrote, "This is still a major problem for Billy Graham, Campus Crusade, and almost anyone who has been active in evangelism."[80] Revivalist ministries were a step removed from churches, and connections between revival meetings and local church ministries were not always obvious.

In theory, church planting movements represented an important correction to American revivalist traditions by reemphasizing the significance of churches to the *missio Dei*. The espoused theology of planted churches, particularly their emphasis on inviting people to services, assigned churches far more agency than was obvious in other evangelistic ministries. In practice, though, many planted congregations similarly struggled to connect new believers to an existing church fellowship. Recent studies of church planting in the United States, United Kingdom, and Europe have found that many planted congregations drew most of their membership growth from Christians seeking a new church, not from conversions.[81] There is also evidence that many American churches have struggled to retain members who make a conversion decision. Recent research found that while most children and teenagers raised in Protestant homes eventually made "a decision" to become a Christian, no more than 50 percent of them remained actively engaged in church as young adults or reported regular spiritual practices that reflect ongoing engagement with Christianity.[82] Researchers also found that a significant majority of Americans, potentially as many as 75 percent, have made "some kind of decision to accept Christ," but only about a quarter attended church regularly.[83] These findings suggest that many planted churches have shared Graham's challenge to communicate the significance of a faith community to those who espouse Christian faith.[84] Weak operant ecclesiology has had similar effects within planted congregations to those seen within Graham's early ministries.

Church planting ministries owe a significant debt to Graham's ministry and to American revivalist traditions more broadly. Planted congregations adopted many practices that resembled those seen in Billy Graham revival meetings. Like Graham, they transformed services to make the sermon central and the space comfortably neutral. An attractional, individualistic missional model like Graham's became prevalent. Graham's ministry offered further evidence that in the perception of many Americans, the office of "pastor" had narrowed to "preacher," preferably one who can draw a crowd. Graham's eschatology helps to explain why evangelistic preaching and a focus on "individual decisions" became prominent in planted churches while holistic missional strategies and engagement in social justice were comparatively rare. Graham's ministry, though, operated primarily outside of churches, as had most itinerant revivalist ministries. Consequently, American revivalist traditions offered planted congregations few models of pastoral ministry in a local missional church setting, and few resources that might strengthen their operant ecclesiology. Planted churches that sought to integrate Graham's revivalist strategies into the normal patterns of a local congregational ministry had little historical precedent.

Economic Models: The Business of Entertainment

Understanding features of the economic culture surrounding planted American congregations offers further insights into their shared operant missional ecclesiology. Church planting movements hoped to make gathered services more appealing and accessible to Americans, and so they borrowed forms and practices from America's popular entertainment industries. This move was entirely understandable, since American entertainment industries have long wielded enormous cultural appeal and influence. Unfortunately, the practices that planted churches borrowed were not as theologically neutral as they might have seemed; over time, they subtly reshaped operant understandings of missional church.

Connections between American churches and entertainment industries have historical roots that go as deep as revivalism.[85] Early American Protestant churches encouraged literacy, fueling a growing market for reading material.[86] In the nineteenth century, talks from visiting revivalists often resembled contemporary theatrical performances or popular lecture circuits.[87] The film industry, though, developed the most complex relationship with churches. Film initially offered churches a new medium for presenting biblical stories.[88] One Episcopalian priest with an interest in children's ministry even invented reel-to-reel film technology.[89] Before purpose-built cinemas existed, filmmakers frequently rented church buildings to screen films.[90] This arrangement offered churches both supplemental funding and missional opportunities, since they could invite those who came for a film to stay for a service.[91] Eventually, the development of "talkies" demanded better audio equipment than many congregations could afford, and so purpose-built cinemas became the normal site for screening films.[92] Church leaders also became more vocally critical of films' moral content over time, deepening the divide between churches and filmmakers.[93] Still, even today, traces of an older symbiotic relationship between the film industry and missional churches persist. Many planted congregations, including Willow Creek, have rented or converted space within cinemas to host worship services,[94] and Regal Entertainment Group now has a special marketing unit offering support to new churches looking to start in a cinema.[95] Some churches still rent space in cinemas to host private screenings of Christian-themed films as a form of evangelistic outreach.[96] Perhaps, then, it is no accident that pioneering congregations within every stream of church planting began in the greater Los Angeles area, just a stone's throw from Hollywood.[97] Los Angeles–area churches have long enjoyed an unusually high concentration of people who are blessed with creative talent and receptive to creative innovation.[98] This energy gave Southern California's congregations a unique freedom and capacity to experiment with praxis. It was therefore no wonder that church planting and entertainment industries might become inextricably connected in popular imagination.

The metaphor of artistry actually provides a helpful way to describe possible forms of missional engagement between a church and its surrounding culture. As Niebuhr wrote, the gospel has the capacity to oppose, accommodate, transcend, paradoxically engage, and transform culture,[99] and the same can be said of the arts. Artists do not simply reflect culture; they also interpret and respond to it, giving expression to inchoate fears and unresolved questions. Artists also prophetically confront injustice, drawing sympathy to marginalized people and awareness to overlooked problems. The arts encourage people to engage with one another, reflect on the present moment, remember their history, and imagine hopeful future possibilities. These features of artistic expression all have natural affinities with the aims of missional churches, which at their best also engage with culture in probing and thoughtful ways. Additionally, many forms of art like music, theatre, and film require creative collaboration among teams of artists with a wide range of talents and abilities. Churches are similarly designed to draw the varied talents, gifts, and voices of members into a unified corporate ministry, as chapters 4 and 5 will discuss more fully.[100] Practically speaking, artistic training has proven valuable for church leaders; George Whitefield, for example, credited theatrical training with improving his preaching style.[101] Paas proposed artistic experimentation and artists' havens as viable patterns for planted churches that hope to engage creatively and courageously with ever-changing cultures.[102] For all of these reasons, some planted congregations intentionally embraced artistic patterns of creative collaboration and cultural engagement.[103] Churches and the arts can coexist very fruitfully.

Combining churches and entertainment industries, though, generated far more challenging complexities. As qualitative researchers have observed, many missional churches tried to "copy successful entertainment formats from the secular sphere . . . in order to let individuals 'have a good time' during their rituals and religious services."[104] Rereading this observation, the conflict becomes evident: entertainment industries are designed to please and amuse people, helping them to "have a good time," while Christian worship is designed to direct human attention toward God. In practice, it can sometimes be hard to distinguish whether a congregation is using media as a creative means to contextualize the gospel or whether they have allowed "entertainment" to become the focus.[105] Early Emerging churches, for example,

> were characterized by loud, passionate worship music directed toward God and the believer (not the seeker); David Letterman-style, irreverent banter; raw narrative preaching; *Friends* (the popular TV series) type relationships; and later, candles and the arts.[106]

According to this account, Emerging churches were not simply leveraging pop culture references to explain the gospel; they actively patterned worship practices after popular entertainment. Willow Creek was similarly accused of being in the entertainment business.[107] Hybels and other leaders understandably found this charge deeply offensive,[108] but evidence suggests it was not as far-fetched as one might have hoped. Willow Creek highly valued "excellence" in gathered services and worked to offer a "professional production" that could "compete" with media outlets like *Sesame*

Street and Disney World.[109] Consequently, at Willow Creek "all participants in the service are highly skilled and thoroughly prepared. They are also generally attractive people who are well-dressed."[110] The appearance of people at the front matters deeply to a casting director or concert producer, but not to a Christian congregation. Christian worship is not traditionally understood as a celebration of the talents of the most skilled or attractive people, but a humble acknowledgment of God's own majesty. Hybels frequently stressed to "visiting church leaders" that Willow Creek had "several hundred thousand dollars' worth of sound and lights in this auditorium."[111] Both this massive investment and Hybels's characterization of the space as an "auditorium" indicate substantial conflation between Christian worship and popular entertainment. Willow Creek was hardly alone in this challenge; many planted churches similarly sought "to align their products with those typically found in the entertainment complex."[112] For example, most planted churches focused their missional energy on sermons, which drew attention to a human on a stage-like platform. Some included architectural features, lighting, or other design elements borrowed from cinemas and other entertainment venues.[113] Larger congregations frequently used cinematic or concert-like screens to project song lyrics and Scriptures, or live video that would help those in distant seats see the pastor more clearly.[114] The combination of these features with Seeker Sensitive churches' desire for high production values transformed worship into multisensory performance artistry.[115] One could thus be forgiven for conflating planted churches with popular entertainment.

Given the widespread borrowing of entertainment forms, it was only natural that a kind of celebrity culture grew around some pastors.[116] Billy Graham had enjoyed some aspects of his own celebrity but remained conscious of problems that media attention could create and worked to "adapt himself to television, and to an array of other media, without straying into show business."[117] Planted churches have much to learn from Graham's prescient insight. One observer noted that Graham was concerned that "show business" can create a "passive intimacy" between speaker and audience, allowing the audience to "feel connection to the figures on the small screen without risking anything themselves."[118] Pete Ward defined a celebrity as a "mediated individual" who is "consumed" by the public, not an individual with whom one has a genuine relationship.[119] As we have already seen, planted churches often reassigned pastoral care to others, making it more likely for congregants to see their pastor as a "mediated individual." Professional sound and lighting equipment only reinforced such a perception, as did arena-style seating that physically distanced congregants from their pastor. Using projection screens too liberally risked further transforming worship into cinema; one qualitative researcher noted that although she could clearly see the people at the front of a church service, she and her companions "found our eyes repeatedly drawn to the screens, rather than to the live people standing before us."[120] Being framed as an on-screen celebrity performer posed additional risks for pastors. If pastors imagined themselves as performers, temptations mounted to avoid engaging authentically with the congregation, since in many performance arts, the "audience" sees "only what you, the artist, show it."[121] Churches needed more than a distant celebrity pastor; they needed a community of authentic lived faith, which included the pastor.

Entertainment forms also subtly reduced the congregation from a living community of active worshipers into a passive, consumeristic "audience." At best, Christian worship services feature a carefully crafted "dramaturgy" which can "mobilize conventions of active and passive response."[122] By contrast, entertainment forms bypass such conventions, encouraging passive consumption from everyone except the people on stage. For example, loud music made worship services feel like a concert, which could create powerful, immersive spiritual experiences;[123] however, loud music did not facilitate quiet, reflective moments or silent prayer, which have long been important, spiritually formative elements of Christian worship. Concert-like volume also precluded conversation, encouraging attendees to sing collectively with the person on stage, but not to connect with one another. Even concert-style lighting made it difficult for the pastor or worship leader to see the congregation or engage with their responses to the service. Understanding worship as cinema, with all the "added layers of mediation" between pastor and congregation, predictably fostered a "sense of spectatorship rather than participation."[124] At Willow Creek, for example, visitors frequently came and went anonymously, listening to services without interacting with the congregation or pastors.[125] This is normal, indeed, polite and expected behavior when attending the cinema, but hardly the worshiping community or Christian fellowship that churches traditionally offered. Mars Hill's decision to live stream sermons across multiple campuses transformed church into little more than a cinema, a space where people gathered to watch an absent celebrity deliver an on-screen performance.[126] In such an environment, the congregation risked becoming, as one church planting pastor put it, reduced to "faceless numbers" whose primary function was to "fill churches."[127] One can understand the appeal of such a model for congregations, as little was required of them, and services actively accommodated their interests and preferences. Entertainment practices thus subtly eroded congregational participation, replacing traditional understandings of Christian worship with something far less personal and more passive.

As congregations became more passive, descriptions of church members as "consumers" became more frequent.[128] Church planting ministries subtly reframed their mission as identifying "current and potential customers" and creating new "firms seeking to serve that market."[129] Therefore, there was considerable interest in finding ways to "market" church in order to draw in new "customers,"[130] much like a film or concert producer might hope to promote a performance. Interest in church marketing was hardly new; in the early twentieth century, books had appeared with titles like *Principles of Successful Church Advertising.*[131] In the 1980s, planted churches' interest in growing their membership sparked fresh waves of church marketing research, which unapologetically borrowed "research tools and norms from secular advertising and commercial public relations rather than sociology, anthropology, or Church Growth experts."[132] Consequently, many church planting practitioners adopted marketing strategies in the hopes that they would identify a "target" audience and craft specific appeals to that audience.[133] Hybels's early survey to understand why people were not attending church differed little from research any marketer might conduct before opening a new business in a crowded market.[134] One researcher described a leading church planting consultant's video, which ironically and unfavorably compared churches' marketing strategies to those used by Starbucks.[135] The video was hardly a "broadside against Christianity for being too much like Starbucks."[136] Instead, it was an emphatic assertion "that Christian churches are *not enough* like Starbucks," which even suggested that marketing concerns "should shape a congregation's whole identity."[137] Many planted churches have agreed, and so devised "branding" strategies.[138] Such moves foster the appearance of "corporatization," an attempt to turn Christianity into "a religious 'product' that is uniform, stable, and predictable."[139] Paas, for example, lamented that a "main emphasis" of church planting movements in the 1980s and 1990s "was on the replication of existing models of being church, rather than innovating them."[140] In some cases, a church's "brand" became tied inextricably to the teaching pastor's personality, transforming the pastor into a spokesperson for the congregation and its brand.[141] In such situations, it is no wonder that pastors might be sorely tempted to aggressively manage their "image" in order to continue attracting consumers.[142] The pastor could easily become the "brand." Unreflective use of marketing and branding strategies might work in entertainment industries, but they further undermined ecclesial identity and threatened to undermine the calling of churches as worshiping communities.

As advertising and promotional practices became more common, churches began to be framed as competitors, much like businesses or cinemas that compete for customers. Finke and Starke even wrote,

> Some readers may shudder at the use of market terminology in discussions of religion, but we see nothing inappropriate in acknowledging that where religious affiliation is a matter of choice, religious organizations must compete for members and that the "invisible hand" of the marketplace is as unforgiving of ineffective religious firms as it is of their commercial counterparts.[143]

Finke and Stark's comments about competition between churches and the "invisible hand" of the marketplace were clear references to Adam Smith's foundational economic theory.[144] Economic and marketing theories have long postulated competition for customers.[145] Rational Choice Theory similarly presumed little or no conversion growth and therefore framed churches as competing for members.[146] Economic theorists have generally argued that such competition is healthy; Smith, for example, even wrote that competition between churches prevented clerical complacency.[147] Finke and Stark concurred, adding that competition between churches gives "consumers a wider range of religious rewards" and "forc[es] suppliers to be more responsive and efficient."[148] These arguments, though understandable, failed to account for many important beliefs and practices of planted churches, reflecting fundamental and important differences between missional churches and businesses. Those who stress the value of competition seemingly assumed that churches had little or no intrinsic motivation "to be more responsive" to members of a community, or to avoid complacency. By contrast, planted churches' espoused missional calling created a strong motivation to present the gospel effectively and to respond to local communities. Furthermore, most planted churches actively sought conversion growth, not competition with other churches. Warren, for example, openly discouraged Christians from transferring their membership from another church to Saddleback.[149] By valorizing competition between churches, business models never fully aligned with planted churches' commitment to evangelism.

Business and marketing models also prioritized growth, which reinforced some elements of Church Growth Theory while also revealing its limitations in explaining the operant theology behind church planting. The aims of an entertainment industry, like those of any business, are to profitably satisfy consumers' demands. As Stark and Finke argued, "the religious subsystem of any society is entirely parallel to the subsystem involved with the secular (or commercial) economy: both involve the interplay of supply and demand for valued products."[150] Finke and Stark, like others, erred in assuming that churches are "entirely parallel" with businesses. Churches have a very different calling. Newbigin, for example, argued against any sense that "the world-wide Church has to be built up with the same sort of prudent calculation of resources and costs as is expected of any business enterprise."[151] In business, growth increases profits, and can be "for the sake of growth" rather than for "any overarching purpose."[152] In church, the aim is not solely numerical growth, but the glorification of God and the transformation of hearts and lives. Newbigin therefore lamented the "kind of missionary zeal which is forever seeking to win more proselytes but which does not spring from and lead back into a quality of life which seems intrinsically worth having in itself."[153] Newbigin was rightly critical of Church Growth Theory for overlooking that "quality of life" that can be one of Christianity's main missional attractions.[154] Finke and Stark even conceded, "Economic principles will serve as tools for understanding religious change, but they imply nothing about the merits of such change."[155] This is an important clarification; churches are called to live ethically and cannot ignore the merits of or problems with their practices.

To some degree, planted churches actively resisted practices that are common to businesses, reflecting their different priorities. Strictly following business models might have encouraged churches to leverage an economy of scale, combining administrative functions and other resources, much as multisite churches did. By contrast, rather than fostering large congregations "by adding to their current building or looking to add a service to accommodate all the people," some Emerging churches "deliberately chose to scale back."[156] One might cynically argue that their push for smaller churches was just an alternative marketing pitch, like a small family-owned business, a farmer's market, or a microbrewery might use.[157] Even many multisite churches created the appearance of smaller congregations, belying the reality that these smaller congregations remained embedded within a larger church structure. Furthermore, many planted churches actively resisted the standardization that denominational structures and branding strategies might encourage. For example, there was early interest in standardizing worship across Calvary Chapel congregations, when leaders unapologetically turned to business models and said: "Look, when you go to a McDonald's, you know you can order a Big Mac. If someone walks into a Calvary Chapel, they should be able to know what's there. They shouldn't get any doctrinal surprises."[158] Not long after this discussion, John Wimber left Calvary Chapel and joined the growing Vineyard movement.[159] This incident illustrates a common tendency within planted churches to split and form new streams of church planting, effectively voting with their feet for local innovation over large-scale standardization. Emerging churches particularly avoided corporate models and actively questioned "the constructed nature of labels and identity."[160] Like many postmodernist thinkers, Emerging church leaders expressed deep concern that marketing strategies manipulate desires to create "a manufactured dissatisfaction."[161] Consequently, within Emerging churches, there was "an emphasis on things that cannot, by their very nature, be packaged and recreated time and time again."[162] On the whole, then, planted churches have consistently and thoughtfully resisted business models that encourage standardization and sometimes economy of scale, even when they embraced marketing strategies and other business practices.

Practices borrowed from entertainment industries were potentially helpful at times, but they were not theologically neutral. Popular entertainment industries offered a bank of cultural references to leverage when explaining the gospel, but their forms also exacerbated a growing celebrity culture around pastors, eroding authentic pastoral relationships and subtly pressuring pastors to "perform." Entertainment forms and practices also encouraged both churches and researchers to frame the congregation as "audience" or even "consumer," whose tastes and interests must be pleased. The economic culture surrounding planted churches thus explains their shared focus on the look and feel of gathered services. It also explains why Church Growth Theory was so persistently appealing: it resembled the interest that entertainment industries had in measurably, steadily increasing their audience. As Americans engaged with planted churches, they found many familiar forms which were accessible to believers and seekers alike and discovered fresh possibilities for creative innovation. What they risked losing was a clear understanding of their unique identity as "church." Consequently, planted churches needed a way to express espoused beliefs that diverged from the goals of consumer-driven entertainment. Otherwise, some of their sacred callings could too easily go unanswered.

Sociopolitical Factors: Race, Politics, and Homogeneous Congregations

Like entertainment culture and revivalist history, broader questions about race and politics in America have loomed large over the ministries of its Christian churches, including planted churches. Indeed, church planters were not blind to these long-standing tensions in American culture, which could hardly be ignored. Many planted churches that followed McGavran's missiology even came to see homogeneous congregations as a compelling growth strategy. This practice was consistent with American cultural history and with Church Growth Theory, but the churches that adopted it experienced a variety of unintended consequences. It is not the aim of this study to draw conclusions about the underlying attitudes that people within planted churches hold about race. Instead, the aim is to explore the subtle, unintended consequences of some church growth strategies, particularly the Homogeneous Unit Principle (HUP), against the backdrop of long-standing racial and political divisions within many American communities. As we will see, there is good reason to conclude that any damaging consequences of the HUP for American planted churches were wholly unintentional, since the HUP ultimately worked to undermine some of these churches' most frequently espoused missional aims.

One of the most striking features of American congregational life is its racial and political homogeneity. According to two recent studies, in at least 80 percent of American congregations and 86 percent of Protestant congregations, at least 80 percent of church members belong to a single racial or ethnic group.[163] Startling as these numbers might seem, they are a slight improvement from 1999, when a similar survey found that in 90 percent of American churches 90 percent of the members belonged to a single racial or ethnic group.[164] There is reason to suspect that this picture might be changing slightly; one 2020 study of megachurches reported that the number of multiracial megachurches have increased over the last twenty years, with 58 percent of megachurches reporting being multiracial as of 2020.[165] Another 2021 study found that among all American congregations, multiracial churches were more numerous and more rapidly growing than in previous decades.[166] Noteworthy as these trends are, we must temper their conclusions slightly, since their definition of "multiracial" was "having 20% or more minority presence in their congregation,"[167] which might not look that different than a congregation where 80 percent of the membership belongs to a single racial group. It is important to add that a demographically homogeneous church is not necessarily problematic. Some homogeneous churches may simply reflect the demographics of their surrounding community. Others, like immigrant churches and historically Black congregations, offer important, theologically rich ministries. Still, the best evidence has consistently indicated that few of America's congregations have enjoyed much racial diversity, and there is no clear evidence yet that planted churches are an exception.

In light of this context, one must carefully reconsider McGavran's Church Growth Theory, which advocated homogeneous congregations as a growth strategy. While working in cross-cultural missions, McGavran observed, "Men like to become Christians without crossing racial, linguistic, or class barriers."[168] McGavran left the basis of homogeneity open-ended, but made clear that congregational diversity in a wide range of categories, including language, class, or race, might be a "barrier" to unbelievers.[169] McGavran therefore concluded that churches hoping to win unbelievers to faith should honor the HUP rather than requiring seekers to eschew all their cultural prejudices before coming to church and hearing the gospel.[170] McGavran particularly hoped to avoid imposing any set of "legalistic requirements which must be met *before* men can become Christians."[171] McGavran's articulation of the HUP reflects a growing postcolonial awareness that cross-cultural missionaries have not always been adequately sensitive to important cultural nuances.[172] Sometimes this meant that needless cultural barriers indeed made it harder for people to hear the gospel.[173] Nonetheless, the open-endedness with which McGavran described the HUP left it unclear how far churches should go to accommodate local culture. This unanswered question would have significant consequences for America's planted churches.

There is also considerable historical precedent for planting racially homogeneous churches within the United States. The HUP even offered a clear explanation for the historical development of many American churches, as Damian Emetuche noted:

> [W]hether it is in reference to the evangelization of Native Americans or other immigrant groups that followed the Euro-Americans, the church from the beginning of the modern United States of America as a nation has adopted the homogeneous principle of church planting even when the concept was not known or used because it

> was rooted in the nature, tradition, culture, and constituency of the American history and migration pattern.[174]

Emetuche's observation accurately summarized much of American religious history. Arriving immigrant groups commonly formed churches comprised primarily of people from similar cultural backgrounds.[175] As a result, Christian confessions that were common within each immigrant group became most visible in regions where many of their compatriots settled.[176] Immigrant churches have been and continue to be an important feature of American Christianity. For example, many immigrants from Latin American countries settled in the American Southwest; those from charismatic Protestant backgrounds helped to spark the growth of New Paradigm churches.[177] Similarly, recent African immigrants have planted a variety of missional churches throughout the United States, though these churches have sometimes struggled to incorporate people who are not recent African immigrants into their congregations.[178] In the early twentieth century, Dietrich Bonhoeffer even observed that Americans generally select congregations for social or demographic reasons, not confessional ones.[179] As a result, Bonhoeffer concluded that the primary distinctions between many of America's churches were more likely to be demographic or cultural than theological.[180] The HUP was thus consistent with historical patterns of church planting throughout American history.

Furthermore, subsequent sociological research has broadly confirmed that McGavran's observations were accurate: people generally do prefer to join groups that are homogeneous, full of people like themselves.[181] According to various studies, people widely perceive homogeneous groups as less prone to conflict, better able to articulate shared goals and group identities, and thus more stable and satisfying to members.[182] This pattern might be starting to change; compellingly, one 2021 survey found that multiracial American congregations were actually growing faster than others, while another from 2020 reported that many megachurches were actively striving to be more diverse.[183] If so, this marks a very recent change; as late as 2015, 71 percent of evangelicals surveyed reported that their church was "diverse enough."[184] That same 2015 survey also found that only 37 percent of white Christians and roughly half of Black and Hispanic Christians wanted their congregations to become more diverse.[185] Given the racial homogeneity of many American congregations, these 2015 responses might seem surprising, but they actually confirmed McGavran's assumption that fallen human beings prefer homogeneous churches. Emetuche put it well when he wrote that the HUP "appeals to our fallen cultural sensitivity. We love to congregate with people of the same affinity; we resist integration across racial, ethnic, and class barriers because we cherish personal freedom and individualism."[186] Emetuche rightly connected the HUP to "fallen cultural sensitivity." In a highly consumeristic culture like the United States, where "personal freedom and individualism" are often emphasized, the HUP predictably appealed to many. Subsequent sociological research thus broadly confirmed that homogeneous worship has often seemed attractive to many of the people that planted American churches hoped to reach.

As a result, many planted American churches understandably expressed interest in the HUP. As one researcher concluded, "The strategy . . . was and is a popular one."[187] Planted churches typically grew by encouraging members to invite their friends to church,[188] and sociologists have confirmed that friendship networks are often relatively homogeneous.[189] Consequently, demographically homogeneous growth was the most natural outcome in planted congregations, unless they actively worked to foster diversity. Seeker Sensitive churches were particularly eager to remove cultural "barriers" to the gospel and so took McGavran's arguments for the HUP to heart. Sometimes their application of the HUP was subtle. Warren, for example, paraphrased key elements of the HUP and encouraged American church planters to "target" the focus of their outreach to specific "receptive" demographic groups, generally those most similar to the majority of existing church members.[190] By applying this strategy, whichever group was already a demographic majority would likely increase the most, resulting in a more homogeneous congregation. Some planted churches, like Saddleback, even used a multisite structure to offer different styles of worship in different locations, each of which was designed to appeal to different demographic groups.[191] Other churches did not apply the HUP in gathered worship but actively fostered "affinity groups" and/or other small group ministries tailored to a narrowly defined subgroup.[192] Interest in the HUP was not unique to majority-white congregations, either. One Black church planting advocate summarized the HUP, affirmed that people generally prefer worshiping with "their own kind," and concluded, "The homogeneous principle has promise as a tool for evangelism."[193] The HUP therefore needs careful analysis, as it has found widespread application within planted American churches.

The HUP might be borne out by sociological and historical evidence, but its application in the United States was hardly without controversy.

Even some advocates of church planting questioned whether it was justified to apply the HUP within American communities.[194] Most strikingly, McGavran personally opposed applying the HUP to American churches, adding that he attended a predominantly Black congregation while in the United States.[195] McGavran clearly identified racism as sinful, though he maintained that any renunciation of sins "should be regarded as the fruit of the Spirit" and could not be expected of people who had not yet come to faith.[196] It is indeed important to avoid legalism and give due deference to the work of the Spirit. As a missional ecclesial practice, though, applying the HUP proved theologically problematic by encouraging churches to maintain an appearance of complicity with cultural prejudices. Newbigin therefore justifiably complained that McGavran unduly accommodated sin in order to grow churches.[197] Bosch concurred, expressing particular concern that the HUP both justified and protected anyone who might have been tempted to plant racially homogeneous congregations for more sinful reasons.[198] Emetuche called the HUP "the cultural gospel of personal preference and individuality," rightly adding, "In the New Testament, individual preferences never dictated mission practices and church planting."[199] As Emetuche rightly pointed out, the HUP unduly allowed consumeristic personal preferences to shape churches. Emetuche even wrote, "By adopting the homogeneous unit principle, the American evangelical churches accepted a sociocultural reality in place of biblical principle."[200] Churches adopting the HUP did not attempt to transform "sociocultural realities," but only to minister to fallen individuals within those realities. At best, the HUP ignored sinful cultural prejudices; at worst, it risked baptizing them under the auspices of missional ecclesiology. These theological problems bear significant reflection, particularly for churches serving increasingly diverse American communities.

The HUP was not the only aspect of Church Growth Theory that created potentially problematic, unintended consequences for American church planters hoping to serve diverse communities. The research on church planting is currently far too underdeveloped to offer more than preliminary notes of caution. Far more study is needed to determine how popular rhetoric around church planting might be received in America's many monoracial and multiethnic congregations. Most of the current literature on church planting stems from white-majority congregations, and researchers often overlook similar practices at play in others. Part of the reason is that the term "church planting" is not as widely adopted outside white-majority congregations, even when demonstrably similar practices are at work. Richard N. Pitt's 2021 book *Church Planters: Inside the World of Religion Entrepreneurs* uses the terms "founder" and "founder-led church" interchangeably with the terms "church planter" and "church plant," and so identifies a huge range of minority-led congregations that broadly fit this book's definition of "planted church." For example, Pitt discusses many churches affiliated with the predominantly Black Church of God in Christ (COGIC), "a denomination where 60% of the churches are led by founding pastors" that features in few other studies of church planting.[201] Because they adopt terms other than "church planting," the omission of COGIC churches from existing studies of church planting is perhaps explainable, but it leaves a significant gap in our understanding. Far less information is available about church planting in congregations where other ethnicities than white or Black are in the majority. Still, enough information is available about missional theory and praxis in Black churches to offer some preliminary insight into reasons why non-white congregations might be reluctant to use the term "church planting." In order to minister well in many American communities, we must begin to explore reasons why church planting movements might struggle to connect beyond white-majority congregations, in the hopes of sparking further research to clarify and complexify the picture offered here.

Broadly speaking, Church Growth Theory likely seemed more compelling to white churches than to Black churches in part due to differing concerns around maintaining church attendance numbers. As of 2014, only about 66 percent of white Americans reported attending church at least a few times a year, and only 34 percent reported weekly attendance.[202] By comparison, in the same 2014 study, 83 percent of Black Americans reported attending church at least a few times a year, with about 47 percent attending weekly.[203] Reported church attendance by Black Americans was slightly higher than in 1990, when a comparable study found that 78 percent of Black Americans reported attending at least once in the last six months, with 44 percent reporting weekly attendance.[204] To the extent that church planting arose in response to declining church attendance, Black churches had fewer such concerns. In fact, in 1990, the very moment when Seeker Sensitive churches were proliferating, Lincoln and Mamiya observed, "The seven major black denominations have not suffered the kind of severe decline in membership experienced by some mainstream white denominations."[205] In fact, an unusually high 37 percent of Black Americans reported being "superchurched" in 1990, meaning they attended church more than one day a week.[206] Black churches were consequently less inclined to worry about bolstering membership rosters and more apt to worry about staffing needs.[207] Black denominations and congregations were also less likely to support church planters financially. As recently as 2021, Pitt found that Black church planters rarely reported receiving "even a one-time gift from their home church or denomination" to support their new ministry, while "more than half of the White founders" reported receiving either a large one-time gift or extended monthly support from their sending church.[208] One 2013 study found that only 52 percent of Black church planters were paid at all, only 38 percent were paid enough to meet their basic needs, and a staggering 69 percent were bi-vocational during their church's first two years, even though they performed at least forty hours of work for their church every week.[209] Given the weight of logistical differences, church planting likely seemed less urgent and less feasible to many Black-majority congregations than it did to white-majority congregations.

There are also important theological reasons why Black churches might have been reluctant to engage with church planting movements. Pastor Tony Evans recalled Billy Graham asking him why partnerships between Black and white pastors had ended abruptly after one joint evangelistic event; Evans wrote:

> I told him that this happened because the event was only tied to evangelism and not to community transformation as well. . . . The heart of African-American Christianity hinged on a broader perspective of the scope of the gospel rather than solely on the gospel's content.[210]

Evans's observation explains why church planting ministries might have seemed less appealing to Black congregations: church planting advocates historically tied their ministries to evangelism, not to social justice or "community transformation" ministries.[211] Civil rights leader John Perkins voiced similar concerns more strongly, writing:

> Something is wrong at the root of American evangelicalism. I believe we have lost the gospel—God's reconciling power, which is unique to Christianity—and have substituted church growth. We have learned how to reproduce the church without the message.[212]

For Perkins and Evans, the "message" or "scope" of the gospel involved much more than fostering membership growth; it involved the "reconciling power" of transformed lives within local communities. James Cone, for example, wrote that the "sole purpose" of a church's existence was "to be a visible manifestation of God's work in the affairs of men."[213] Many Black churches therefore defined mission as holistic ministry within a community, "including political, economic, educational, and social concerns."[214] These churches also prioritized social justice, much as Escobar encouraged the Lausanne delegates to do.[215] Differences in operant missiology explain why Black pastors like Rev. Dr. Martin Luther King Jr. marched on Washington demanding structural reforms while white pastors like Graham organized evangelistic preaching events. These differences in operant missiology made it less likely that church planting would become as high a priority for Black congregations as it became for white congregations.

The end result was that Black churches were less apt to self-identify as "planted," even if they largely meet this book's working definition of planted church: they began as entirely new congregations with missional intentions recently enough that their founding vision remains within living memory. Oak Cliff Bible Fellowship in Dallas offers a helpful case study. Oak Cliff began as a Bible study in 1976 in Tony Evans's living room.[216] Today it is a megachurch with seating for ten thousand, a wide array of ministries, a training network, and national and international media partnerships.[217] Furthermore, Evans mentored other Black church planters.[218] Evans's ministry thus closely paralleled the church planting ministries of Rick Warren and Bill Hybels. Unlike Hybels or Warren, though, Evans's stated missional aims focused primarily on racial reconciliation and ministries to at-risk youth and struggling communities.[219] The Urban Alternative, Oak Cliff's training network, makes no mention of church planting on its website; its stated priorities instead include "Church Health and Leadership Development," "Society and Community Impact," and "Community and Cultural Influence," and its most prominent missional program involves partnerships between churches and public schools.[220] Oak Cliff Bible Fellowship thus reflects very different missional priorities than those found in many predominantly white planted congregations. Church planting has certainly occurred within Black congregations, as Evans's ministry demonstrates, but even in large planted congregations like Oak Cliff Bible Fellowship, Church Growth Theory was not the major missional emphasis; holistic missional strategies were.

Given the striking differences in operant missional ecclesiology separating white and Black American congregations, multiracial church planting efforts have understandably proven challenging. Far more research on multiracial churches is needed,[221] but existing research has indicated that it is easier to begin a new multiracial church than it is for an existing congregation to become multiracial.[222] For this reason, church planting seems to offer a compelling way forward, an opportunity to start congregations with a more inclusive culture. Such churches offer a potential haven for multiracial families, second- and third-generation immigrants, and many others in an increasingly diverse America. In practice, though, this strategy has enjoyed only limited success. In California, for example, congregations have attempted multiracial church planting with some frequency and success,[223] but multiracial churches remain a small, if growing, percentage of American congregations.[224] One qualitative study of Mosaic Church reveals possible reasons why. Mosaic is a renewed, multiracial SBC congregation in Los Angeles with ties to New Paradigm churches and the ECM.[225] Mosaic became a haven to Christians whose racial identity was fluid or complex but struggled to attract Black members.[226] As Martí explained, "Music was the site of a specific culture clash,"[227] but the conflict ran much deeper. Martí's research found that Black Christians "equate Mosaic with assimilated 'white' culture" because Mosaic's approach to mission was deemed too individualistic.[228] Mosaic was actually more involved in holistic missions than many planted congregations, in part because its pastor's posttribulationist, amillennialist eschatology differed from that espoused by Graham and other evangelical church planting leaders.[229] Consequently, many planted American churches might easily face even greater struggles attracting Black members than Mosaic did. To foster diversity, planted churches must do more than invite Black Christians and people from other ethnic identities into a culturally white space. They must foster a clear ecclesial identity that can transcend differences and allow a truly inclusive operant missiology to find tangible expression.

As American politics became more racialized, political differences between white and Black populations began to create additional patterns of political homogeneity in American churches in recent years. One July 2020 survey found that 82 percent of white evangelicals intended to vote for Trump, a slight increase over 2016, while 88 percent of Black Protestants intended to vote for Biden.[230] Another survey conducted in 2020 found that among Americans who regularly attended worship of any kind, 70 percent of white respondents voted for Trump, while 90 percent of Black respondents voted for Biden.[231] One can therefore assume that many racially homogeneous American congregations are also likely to be politically homogeneous. Studies that focus on planted churches are rare, but one 2003 study found that 95.7 percent of Willow Creek Association churches had a white pastor, and 83 percent of Willow Creek Association pastors voted for Bush in 2000.[232] Established patterns of racial and political preferences thus seemingly held firm, at least among Willow Creek Association church leaders. Far more research is needed to clarify the picture among planted churches, but there is little evidence that it differs much from other American congregations.

This dimension of homogeneity in churches has affected their operant theology in ways that risk further alienating some people of color. Emerson and Smith wrote twenty years ago that "it appears that conservative religion intensified the different values and experiences of each racial group, sharpening and increasing the divide between black and white Americans."[233] Emerson and Smith's research found white evangelicals to be more individualistic and less sympathetic to structural explanations for social problems than other Americans were.[234] For example, in surveys, white evangelicals commonly reported that fostering evangelism, discipleship, and healthy relationships between individuals would prove a far more effective solution to racism than government interventions or structural changes.[235] This belief rightly reflected an understanding that racism is sinful, but it also aligned well with common Republican policies, not the Democratic policies favored by most Black Protestants. Emerson and Smith even described an operant theology common in many white evangelical churches called "accountable freewill individualism."[236] This set of beliefs postulates that individuals have free will, which must be respected, but individuals must also be held personally accountable for their choices.[237] By emphasizing a "freedom to choose," accountable freewill individualism harkens back to Enlightenment constructs which Republican politics typically embrace.[238] Emerson and Smith also found that white Christians, unlike Black Christians, typically defined freedom as being "free to pursue one's destiny without political or bureaucratic interference or restraint."[239] This understanding of freedom echoed late twentieth-century Republican political rhetoric, which similarly emphasized limited government and maximal individual freedom. Emerson and Smith's research thus traced a growing alignment between racialized perspectives, operant theologies, and political ideology in America's churches.

The origins of church planting as a missional strategy reflect similar political concerns and begin to explain why "church planting" might carry some conservative political baggage. In the early twentieth century, church planting arose in part as an alternative to the Social Gospel. The Social

Gospel was a common missional emphasis at a time when cross-cultural missional projects typically involved building schools and hospitals in the Global South.[240] McGavran complained that some of these missional efforts allowed theologically liberal Christians to "forego evangelism for the sake of social outreach."[241] Reinhold Niebuhr harbored similar concerns about the Social Gospel, which he worried rested on problematic connections with liberal worldviews.[242] Niebuhr rightly observed that the Social Gospel espoused an overly optimistic faith in human perfectibility that contradicted traditional Christian doctrines of sin.[243] It seemed, then, that much as church planting became aligned with conservative politics, so more holistic missions had previously become aligned with liberal theology and politics, at least in popular perception. Niebuhr therefore worried that in an attempt to counterbalance the theological flaws of the Social Gospel, evangelical Christians might lose sight of "the breadth and complexity of our social obligations."[244] Niebuhr's concern was well placed; as early as 1947, Carl F. H. Henry lamented, "against Protestant fundamentalism the liberals level the charge that it has no social program calling for a practical attack on acknowledged world evils."[245] According to Henry, this criticism was entirely justified, since too many Christians who rejected the Social Gospel behaved like "the modern priest and Levite, by-passing suffering humanity."[246] At the 1966 World Congress on Evangelism in Berlin, Wagner "spoke for many evangelicals in claiming, 'Too often we have rushed by the hungry ones to get to the lost ones.'"[247] Wagner's reference to "the lost ones" tracked uncomfortably well with Willow Creek's oft-repeated motto, "Lost people matter to God."[248] As David King put it, "Within the post-war American evangelicalism . . . the relationship between evangelism and social action served as a clear boundary marker for the movement."[249] In other words, modern evangelical identity in America seemingly required resistance to holistic missions, particularly if holistic missions drew resources or attention away from evangelism. As dear as holistic missions were in many Black churches, their absence would make it more challenging to connect Black Christians with majority-white planted churches.

Compounding these challenges, sociological research has found that churches are likely to grow more homogeneous over time unless they actively encourage diversity.[250] According to researchers, this happens because once a "niche" identity is established in a voluntary social group, members who fall outside or on the "edge" of that identity are far more likely to leave.[251] Over time, this sociological phenomenon, called the "niche edge effect," predicts growing homogeneity in congregations, particularly if a variety of nearby churches exists.[252] Homogeneity is self-reinforcing. Following this logic, if planted congregations become aligned with a specific racial identity, political worldview, or missional vision, people with different perspectives will soon feel out of place and leave, resulting in more homogeneous congregations. Perhaps in part for this reason, a recent study of megachurches found that many reported avoiding divisive political conversations and rarely engaging in overt politics.[253] Tellingly, though, the respondents for this study were primarily "the senior pastor or key leader," and most of these same churches relied primarily on small groups to build fellowship and conduct spiritual formation,[254] a pattern many planted churches have also followed. Consequently, much of the conversation and relationship in a church happens in small groups, where the lead pastor might not be involved. Even when the lead pastor is judicious about avoiding politics in the pulpit, small group members who perceive their fellowship as politically homogeneous can at times engage in unguarded discussions about politics that alienate people who hold different views. Apart from the pastor's notice, then, the niche edge effect can still develop, an unfortunate byproduct of insensitive conversations during Bible studies or unhelpful comments made when discussing prayer requests. Once this happens, genuine innovation and varied perspectives will become harder to nurture, and groupthink will become a greater risk.

The best evidence suggests that this is already happening. One 2013 study confirmed that Emerson and Smith's findings remained consistent with prevalent attitudes and preferences.[255] In 2021 Emerson summarized his current research by saying, "The divisions and conflicts we found [in the last three years] are intense, easily more intense than I have seen in my 25 years of studying the topic."[256] George Marsden concurred, writing in 2021, "Tribal instincts seem to have become overwhelming."[257] In the wake of increasingly divisive elections, many planted American churches have experienced deep and growing political tensions, sometimes fueling leadership conflicts or even church splits.[258] One researcher had found a healthy variety of political perspectives in Vineyard congregations in Southern California, but noted that several years later, "there was almost a split in the church where I had spent most of my time."[259] As one ethnographer recently concluded, there is a widespread perception of a "consistent connection with right-wing Republican political policy" and the evangelical expressions common in planted churches.[260] For example, one 2017 study documented a variety of expressions of Christian nationalism within Calvary Chapel churches.[261] In such churches, "Republicanism, nationalism, patriotism and evangelicalism are at times so closely tied as to appear indistinguishable."[262] Political nuances are even evident in Christians' responses to problems within planted churches. According to Tim Keller, "conservative listeners" were concerned about *Christianity Today*'s 2021 podcast series *The Rise and Fall of Mars Hill* because they saw its critique of Mars Hill as "too 'liberal'" due to its failure to emphasize that "the flaws that led to the blow-up were largely failures of leadership."[263] In other words, identifying problems as partly structural rather than wholly individual was seen as a mark of inappropriate "liberalism." The critique itself seems unfair, since the podcast documented in some detail both Driscoll's reported personal flaws and mistakes made by other church leaders. This response, though, speaks to the reality that in some planted churches conservative political perspectives have become so entrenched that people are not open to alternatives. In such an environment, it would be understandably difficult for a Democratic-leaning Black Christian to feel wholly at home in some evangelical planted churches.

The struggles of the ECM illustrate the profound challenges that this politicized church culture poses for planted congregations, even beyond racial considerations. Emerging church practices have had ongoing resonance,[264] but the ECM itself waned during the 2010s.[265] The reasons were complex. Emerging churches were especially resistant to organizational structures beyond the local congregation, with some leaders avoiding the title "movement" or even "church."[266] This made it difficult to sustain a broader church planting movement. Many people within Emerging churches were suspicious of megachurches and determined to "stay small,"[267] positions that limited their potential missional outreach. Theological controversy surrounding Rob Bell and other ECM leaders as well as scandal surrounding Mark Driscoll heightened concerns about the movement.[268] Politics, though, were clearly a factor. Emerging churches framed themselves as a reaction against politically conservative American evangelical culture.[269] This positioning, combined with the espoused Democratic politics of many ECM leaders, generated profound resistance to Emerging churches among conservative American evangelicals,[270] the group most likely to support church planting as a missional strategy. To put it differently, by the late 1990s, when ECMs began to appear, political alignments were already such that American Christians committed to church planting were less likely to engage with a politically liberal congregation, and politically liberal American

Christians were less likely to adopt church planting as a primary missional strategy. With the decline of the ECM, politically liberal church planting became almost a contradiction in terms.

The challenges facing multiracial planted churches and the ECM begin to explain why many planted churches might struggle to attract various demographic groups within American communities. Keller argued that a primary reason for the decline of evangelicalism in the United States is that the country "is slowly running out of traditionally-minded Americans to be converted, and conservative Protestants on the whole are unwilling or unable to reach the highly secular and culturally different."[271] Keller added that this problem is compounded by a "conservative politicization" of evangelical churches that has "turned off half the country" along with an unaddressed "race problem."[272] As we have seen, the problems that Keller cites are related. In 2006, SBC-affiliated church planting advocate Ed Stetzer argued that in his home county surrounding Atlanta, GA, 70 percent of the population had "little to no connection or interest in Christianity," and most of the remaining 30 percent who might be receptive to an attractional missional church were already connected to one.[273] It is no wonder, then, that some scholars and practitioners were drawn to business models, which envisioned churches competing for a limited, fixed body of potential members. The racial and political polarization felt by too many planted churches has confined their potential appeal to a small subgroup of Americans who are already well served by many churches. Planted congregations intended to offer attractive, "relevant" worship to the unchurched, but unintentionally allowed themselves to become unattractive and irrelevant to many unchurched Americans.

Planted American churches have struggled to look anything like the multinational, multiracial, and multilingual congregations seen at Pentecost or in Revelation 7:9. In small monoracial communities this is understandable, but in larger, more diverse communities it points to significant theological and practical shortcomings within common church planting strategies like the HUP. By failing to address America's racial and political divides, planted churches have missed important opportunities to speak and act prophetically as ministers of reconciliation in an increasingly divided culture.[274] Sociological research, contemporary surveys, and American religious history all confirmed McGavran's instinct: imperfect people often prefer homogeneous churches. Common church planting practices, especially the HUP, gradually, unintentionally reinforced tribal loyalties, at times accommodating potentially divisive behavior for the sake of missional outreach. Over time, racial homogeneity in planted congregations even reinforced an operant missional ecclesiology that carried strong perceived alignments to Republican politics, and this perception became self-reinforcing. As a result, today's planted American congregations must address their own culture, or they will unintentionally see their potential outreach become ever more limited than they intended. Serious theological reflection can help churches discern ways to practice courageous, compassionate, prophetic engagement within their local community in light of their shared history.

The Americanization of Church Planting

Church planting movements developed in harmony with important patterns in America's history and culture, becoming an authentically American phenomenon. This is remarkable, since modern church planting strategies arose amid discussions of mission in very different contexts. Understanding American culture helps to explain why American Christians widely embodied specific strategies developed within church planting movements. Revivalist traditions embodied by Billy Graham, consumerist ideology implicit in entertainment industry practices, and growing perceptions of political and racial alignments in America collectively explain why many planted churches have broadly prioritized individualistic, evangelistic missiology over holistic missions and social justice engagement. Under the influence of Graham's ministry, many planted churches focused their missional energy on crafting services with high production values and accessible, appealing evangelistic speaking, borrowing some forms and practices from the entertainment industry. Cultural patterns and historical precedents have inspired planted American churches to offer services that were compelling and creative. Contextualized worship was no longer a concept reserved for discussions of overseas missions; it became a living reality for many American Christians in planted churches.

Missiologists have long noted, though, that cultural forms and practices are rarely theologically neutral; they can carry subtle ideological baggage that needs careful evaluation, particularly when it conflicts with the gospel. The same creative energy that sparked new waves of church planting also unintentionally encouraged congregational passivity and consumerism, while allowing a celebrity culture to grow around leading pastors. A strong missional desire to increase attendance led many planted churches to foster homogeneous congregations, leaving some ill equipped to confront America's history of racial inequality or to respond effectively to an increasingly divisive political culture. As a result, the shared operant missional ecclesiology common to many planted churches at times conflicted with their stated goals, and their sincere missional calling to serve the unchurched has become more challenging than it ever needed to be. Christ does not always accommodate culture,[275] and planted churches cannot, either. America's planted congregations need a theologically grounded missional ecclesiology that will empower them to respond well to their culture in light of the gospel.

4
Theological Interpretation of Church and the Revelation of the Word

> In the beginning was the Word, and the Word was with God and the Word was God.
>
> John 1:1

"It felt like it had turned from a church into a business, and I was just done." A woman was explaining to me why she had left a planted church that was now mired in scandal. As the church grew, management concerns seemed ever more pressing, and her own spiritual growth took a back seat to programs, strategies, and other initiatives designed to draw new people into the congregation. This was not what church was meant to be, she felt, but she struggled to articulate exactly what she wanted it to be. Hers is hardly an isolated example. Planted churches minister earnestly and creatively, but many still wrestle with unanswered questions about what exactly "church" and "mission" mean, or how the two relate to each other. What is a missional church? How does a missional church offer ministries that are relevant to contemporary American cultures while also nurturing distinctly Christian fellowship? Turning from operant to espoused theology reveals numerous helpful resources that can answer these questions, grounding the practice of contemporary American church planting in the rich soil of Christian doctrine.

Planted churches take their call to proclaim the Word seriously, and rightly so. A long history of Protestant teachings provides important insight into the nature of the Word that Christian churches are called to proclaim, the nature of proclamation itself, and the significance of gospel witness in the life of churches. Churches are a creature of the Word,[1] the Reformers insisted; most modern church planters agree. Consequently, doctrines of the Word offer important insights into ecclesial identity. Close examination of John's Gospel reflects that Jesus's own ministry involves much more than one-way communication to be passively received; as the Word made flesh, Jesus embodies a relational God who speaks, hears, and actively responds to humanity. Churches therefore reflect God's own character by hearing and responding to their community by the power of the Spirit, who draws them together as the body of Christ. Churches proclaim the Word, and churchly proclamation encompasses far more than preaching. Indeed, gospel proclamation requires the corporate discernment and witness of the full body of Christ. The practical ministries, worship, and prayers of a congregation actively point the world to a receptive and responsive God. A doctrine of God's relational Word further clarifies that church is much more than an abstract concept or a philosophical tradition to be explained verbally. Church is a real community of flesh and blood which by its humanity and lived faith points to the historical reality of the Word made flesh. Church exists as a visible sign of Christ's incarnation that corporately makes the gospel audible and tangible to local communities.[2] Churches therefore have an indispensable place within the *missio Dei*, and their ecclesial life and practices matter deeply.

Having established what the operant missional theology of American church planting movements became and having analyzed reasons why it developed certain features, this chapter will address Osmer's third task of theological reflection: the normative task.[3] Theological interpretation, one of three approaches that Osmer offers for the normative task, will be the main focus. Theological interpretation identifies key patterns in Christian tradition that inform practices in a specific context.[4] The aim of this chapter will be to draw together threads from Christian tradition that develop helpful understandings of church and mission. The resources developed here will identify Protestant doctrines of the Word that most planted churches would naturally espouse and will honor their espoused callings to be a church on Christian mission, witnessing to the gospel.

A potential weakness inherent within theological interpretation echoes broader critiques of Osmer's overall method: theological interpretation risks treating theology and praxis as if they were separate.[5] A gradual decoupling of theology from praxis has created real problems in planted churches. As we have seen, some features of their operant missiology and ecclesial praxis developed for reasons other than clear, robust theological reflection. In some instances, a sincere missional desire to accommodate cultural preferences subtly undermined the espoused aims of planted churches. In other cases, pragmatic concerns like attendance growth created unhelpful blind spots, allowing gaps to emerge between espoused and operant beliefs about what mission really meant. This problem is not unique to planted churches; as Christoph Schwöbel once wrote, "often the institutional structures of the Church which were once established on the basis of the Reformers' ecclesiology seem to function quite apart from reflection on their foundation."[6] The same could be said of some practices and structures that became common within planted American congregations. This chapter will therefore examine foundational threads in Protestant theological tradition with a particular eye to the operant missional ecclesiology of contemporary American church planting movements. Theological interpretation of missional ecclesial identity will equip planted churches to identify gaps between theology and praxis and to reexamine praxis in light of their holy calling to participate in the *missio Dei*. Where appropriate, some brief preliminary comments about practical implications will appear, which the next chapter will develop more fully.

The primary theological conversation partners within this chapter will be Robert Jenson, Karl Barth, and Dietrich Bonhoeffer. Jenson's theology offers helpful insights for reflection on the Gospel of John, which describes Jesus as the embodied Word.[7] Jenson offers a contemporary reflection on Trinitarian theology from a Lutheran perspective which foregrounds theological understandings of relational speech for key elements of Protestant thought, including the nature of Christian worship. Barth's theology examines both the nature and theological significance of churchly proclamation in light of the Word, making his work a helpful conversation partner for planted churches that take preaching seriously.[8] Unlike other theologians who focus solely on the technique of preaching or on the theology of the Word, Barth considers how the two are connected, developing a rich theology of the preached Word and its implications for wider doctrines of revelation and ecclesiology in twentieth-century contexts. Bonhoeffer's ecclesiological reflections trace key implications of Christ's incarnation for ecclesial identity and praxis, taking seriously biblical imagery of church as the body of Christ.[9] Bonhoeffer's work is distinct among contemporary ecclesiological texts due to his focus on churches that operate within the complexities of a "religionless age."[10] This focus locates the concrete reality of church within contexts that closely resemble those in which contemporary American church planters hope to minister. Together, these theologians carefully interweave discussions of gospel witness with helpful clarity about a church's identity and callings, offering detailed Protestant understandings of how churches proclaim the redemptive Word as the body of Christ within a complex, modern world.

Church as a Creature of the Word: The Nature of the Word

The early Reformers grounded their ecclesiology in a shared understanding that church is a creature of the Word.[11] For example, the first of the Ten Theses at Berne insisted, "The holy Christian Church, whose only head is Christ, is born from the word of God, abides in the word, and hears not the voice of strangers."[12] This foundational Protestant ecclesiological statement invites examination of two closely related doctrines: the Word and the church. The Word shapes the church, not the other way around, making it vitally important to begin with careful consideration of the Word before examining church as a creature of the Word. Throughout John's Gospel, Jesus acts as the embodied Word who actively speaks, listens, and responds to humanity. John's Gospel therefore offers an important starting point for theological reflection on the Word made flesh in Christ Jesus.

Unlike the Gospel of Matthew, which features several lengthy sermons by Jesus, or the Gospels of Mark and Luke, which emphasize Jesus's miraculous deeds, the Gospel of John describes Jesus engaged in frequent, interactive conversations. In the Fourth Gospel, Jesus's first recorded words are not a sermon or even a wise saying, but a simple question, "What are you seeking?" (1:37).[13] By its very form, a question anticipates and invites a response. After the disciples respond to Jesus's question, he then offers them an invitation, "Come and you will see" (1:39). Throughout the Fourth Gospel, this pattern recurs frequently as Jesus asks questions and invites others to respond to him by word and deed. Later in John 1, Jesus invites Philip to follow him and then responds to Nathanael's questions, in part by asking another question, "Because I said to you 'I saw you under the fig tree,' do you believe?" (1:43–51). When urged by his mother, Mary, to address the lack of wine at a wedding, Jesus responds with a question, "Woman, what does this have to do with me?" (2:4). Similarly, Jesus's post-resurrection appearances in John include a series of questions that invite others to respond and engage. In John 20:15, the risen Christ's first recorded words are two questions to Mary Magdalene, "Woman, why are you weeping? Whom are you seeking?" (20:15). In John 20:24–29, Jesus responds to Thomas's unspoken questions, inviting Thomas to feel his hands and side, and then asking, "Have you believed because you have seen me?" Jesus later approaches the disciples on the beach and asks, "Children, do you have any fish?" before inviting them to cast their net on the right side of the boat (21:5–6). In the wake of their catch, Jesus engages Simon Peter with a series of three questions: "Simon, son of John, do you love me [ἀγαπᾷς με] more than these?" (21:15); "Simon, son of John, do you love me [ἀγαπᾷς με]?" (21:16); "Simon, son of John, do you love me [φιλεῖς με]?" (21:17). After briefly discussing Peter's responses with him, Jesus offers Peter a familiar invitation, "Follow me" (21:19). Shortly thereafter, Peter asks Jesus about the beloved disciple, to which Jesus responds with the last words the Fourth Gospel records him as saying, "If it is my will that he remain until I come, what is that to you? You, follow me!" (21:22). Jesus's last recorded words in the Fourth Gospel, like his first, are a question followed by an invitation. Jesus's interactions at key moments throughout the Fourth Gospel depict his deeply relational nature, calling humanity to respond to and engage with him.

Jesus's conversations are also a primary means by which the Fourth Gospel presents important, revelatory theological teaching. John 3:1–21 recounts Jesus's nighttime conversation with Nicodemus, which Nicodemus initiates (3:2). This theologically rich discussion includes key revelations about being born again (3:1–8) and the purposes of Jesus's ministry (3:9–21). It is important to note that this conversation unfolds as Jesus hears and responds to specific questions that Nicodemus raises (3:4, 9). Not long after this interaction, Jesus converses with a Samaritan woman in John 4:1–26. Jesus begins the conversation by saying to the unnamed woman, "Give me a drink" (4:7). Jesus thus invites her to respond to his presence in a tangible way. A conversation develops when the woman responds with a question of her own, "How is it that you, a Jew, ask for a drink from me, a woman of Samaria?" (4:9). As their discussion continues, Jesus listens to the woman closely enough to echo some of her wording, repeating her phrases: "I have no husband" and "on this mountain" (4:17, 20–21). Jesus only reveals that he is the Messiah following the woman's own description of the Messiah (4:25–26). Jesus thus continues the pattern of revealing important teaching by listening and responding to questions. John 13–16 similarly describes Jesus in extensive discussions with his disciples on the night before his crucifixion. Jesus responds to their questions about his immediate actions washing their feet (13:6–20), which of them will betray him (13:21–30), where he is going (13:36–14:4), how they can know the way to follow him (14:8–11), why he reveals himself to them (14:22–31), and what his words mean (16:16–33). This most rich and extensive theological revelation thus unfolds not as a lecture, but as a relational interaction between Jesus and his disciples, where Jesus listens and responds to them. Some of the most significant theological revelations that the Fourth Gospel offers about Jesus's identity, purpose, and ways thus come not in sermons, but in genuine, interactive conversations.

This pattern matters significantly because the prologue to the Fourth Gospel (1:1–18) explicitly frames Jesus as the Word (*logos*) made flesh (1:14). Jesus is no ordinary human teacher adopting a Socratic method, but the incarnate presence of the Triune God dwelling among humanity. Jenson's theology highlights the importance of conversational dynamics for revealing something about the Trinity, writing "the one God is a *conversation*."[14] Jenson later clarifies that Jesus is a "counterpart speaker of the triune conversation."[15] As Jenson explains, "'the Word' stands for God's identifying communication of himself, and is at once the content of God's self-conception . . . and the act of sharing that conception."[16] Jenson's theology thus sits particularly well with striking passages in the Fourth Gospel that describe Jesus revealing God's nature to humanity by allowing people to overhear snatches of his own prayerful conversations with the Father. For example, in John 11:41–42, Jesus prays aloud at Lazarus's tomb and says, "Father, I thank you that you have heard me. I knew that you always hear me, but I said this on account of the people standing around, that they may believe that you sent me." In this instance, Jesus engages in direct conversation with the Father, which others are explicitly invited to overhear. Jesus's status within the triune conversation is both the means and the content of revelation in John 11:41–42, which reveals the Father as the hearer of prayer and the Son as "the resurrection and the life" (John 11:25–26, 43–44), sent by the Father in response to human need. Similar moments occur in Jesus's priestly prayer to the Father in John 17 which reveal Jesus as the God-sent intercessor for humanity, the Father as the hearer of prayer, and the Father and Son as one. As Jenson rightly argues, framing the Word as conversation underscores both Jesus's divine identity in relationship with the Trinity and an important method by which Jesus reveals that identity throughout the Fourth Gospel.

By writing that "the Word became flesh" in the historical person of Jesus (John 1:14), the author of John makes a distinctive claim that "differentiates him from every other extant non-Christian source of Mediterranean antiquity."[17] The references to the Word in John 1 allow Jesus to appear as the fulfillment of Old Testament typology connecting divine revelation to God's relational engagement with humanity. The Hebrew formula "the word of the Lord" (דבר־יהוה) often describes a word that is not only spoken, but relational, as seen in its first usage in Genesis 15:1. The context is a conversation between Abraham and an almost personified "word of the Lord," which listens and responds to Abraham's concerns. In this exchange, Abraham asks about his childlessness and receives a specific response that expands into a revelatory promise of innumerable heirs (15:1–6). Abraham then asks for confirmation of his inheritance (15:8), and the Lord responds with more promises (15:12–16) and confirming signs (15:5, 17) that mark a sacred covenant (15:9–11, 17–20). As this conversation develops, the author switches from describing it as a conversation between Abraham and "the word of the Lord" (15:1) to describing it as a conversation with "the Lord" directly (Gen 15:6–8, 13). Conversing with the word of the Lord thus seems functionally equivalent to conversing with the Lord, prefiguring John 1:1, which says "the Word was with God and the Word was God." The Word in Genesis, as it is in John, is revelatory, and revelation occurs as humans engage in honest conversation with God. As Jenson rightly notes, "Where this Word has come, genuine conversation, even argument occurs."[18] Revelation can indeed occur through surprising conversational twists. This dynamic is perhaps most obvious in Genesis 18 when the Lord discusses Sarah's impending pregnancy and the fate of Sodom (18:1–33). Sarah appears to argue with God, denying that she laughed when she overheard that she would have a baby (18:9–15), then Abraham actively negotiates with God concerning the fate of Sodom (18:22–33). Indeed, prayer matters precisely because God is listening and is willing to respond to human beings with divine revelation and practical help. God's covenant with Abraham is thus revealed through genuine, relational, interactive conversations, resembling how Jesus reveals his own identity throughout the Fourth Gospel.

This typology describing God's revelation coming in the form of interactive conversations appears elsewhere in the Hebrew Bible as well. Jewish wisdom literature often personifies wisdom as a speaker. For example, the author of Proverbs 1:20–33 describes wisdom as a voice calling out to humanity, countering the voices of worldly temptation by inviting people to repent and walk faithfully. A similar pattern also appears in various prophetic texts. In Daniel 10, divine revelation comes as a slightly delayed response to Daniel's prayers; the angel says to Daniel, "Fear not, Daniel, for from the first day that you humbled yourself before your God, your words have been heard, and I come because of your words" (10:12). The revelation that follows thus demonstrates God listening and responding to Daniel's prayers. Shortly thereafter, Daniel is struck mute, and "one in the likeness of the children [son] of man touched my lips, and opened my mouth, and spoke" (10:15–16). Daniel was not asked to listen silently to God's revelation; instead, he had his speech restored by "one like the children [son] of man" so that he might engage with the revelatory vision. In the book of Habakkuk, God's revelation comes as a series of responses from the Lord (Hab 1:5–11; 2:2–20) to Habakkuk's complaining questions (Hab 1:1–4; 1:12–2:1). The structure of the entire book is an interactive exchange between an unhappy prophet and a responsive, gracious God, who teaches Habakkuk how to respond well to difficult circumstances (Hab 3:1–19). Jesus's willingness to hear and respond graciously to questions and his pattern of inviting further engagement thus echo Old Testament descriptions of a God who listens and responds to humanity, revealing divine purpose and character through relational conversations.

Identifying Jesus as *logos* in John 1:1 ties him even more closely to images of a speaking God, as seen in the Old Testament. Close connections between Jesus and Old Testament types surrounding the Word led Keener to propose that the *logos* in John 1:1–18 envisions Jesus as a personified Torah.[19] Usage patterns in the New Testament suggest differently. In both John's Gospel and the Septuagint, the most common Greek term used for Hebrew Scripture is *nomos*, which Keener concedes would suggest an embodied Torah to Jewish readers more naturally than *logos* does.[20] By contrast, the author of John consistently uses the term *logos* to describe spoken words, including the "*logos* of the woman's testimony" (4:39) and the "*logos* that you hear" (14:24). John 2:22 even distinguishes the *logos* that Jesus spoke from recorded Hebrew Scripture, while John 12:38 and 15:25 both use *logos* to point specifically to a spoken word that was later recorded in Hebrew Scripture.[21] Similar usage is common throughout the New Testament. James urges readers, "be a doer of the *logos* and not only a hearer" (Jas 1:22). The author of 2 Thessalonians uses *logos* to distinguish a spoken word from written letters (2 Thess 2:2, 15), as does Luke (Acts 15:27). It seems, then, that *logos* primarily points to a spoken word in the New Testament, connecting it to the typology of relational, revelatory conversations between God and humanity.[22] Its use in John 1:1 therefore does not suggest a written legal document so much as a relational interaction. Jesus in the Fourth Gospel appears as "God's Word . . . once more coming forth from the divine silence," marking a new phase in God's relationship with humanity.[23] As the Word made flesh, Jesus actively embodies a God who listens and responds to humanity.

Barth similarly describes the Word in terms of speech and hearing, which allows him to draw attention to key features of God's revealed nature. Barth insists that speech is the "only possible" translation of the *logos* of John 1, even though other terms like "mystery" and "act" might also be needed to explain the Word fully.[24] Barth writes:

> the Word of God is the Word that God spoke, speaks, and will speak in the midst of all men. . . . It is the Word of God's work upon men, for men, and with men. His work is not mute; rather, it speaks with a loud voice.[25]

Echoing John 1, Barth uses the image of a speaking God to clarify that the Word is tangible and effective, interacting with humanity in the past, present, and future. Barth insists that the expression "Word" must not be taken as mere metaphor either, writing,

> God's Word means that God speaks. Speaking is not a "symbol" (as P. Tillich, *Rel. Verwirkl.*, 1930, p 48 thinks). It is not a designation and description which on the basis of his own assessment of its symbolic force man has chosen for something very different from and quite alien to this expression.[26]

Barth thus makes clear that one cannot interpret the Word as mere human imagery created in an attempt to capture a transcendent God, since it points to the very nature of God's revelatory interactions with humanity. Barth also writes, "God's Word means the speaking God."[27] God's Word is not distinct from God's nature, and "the speaking God" underscores God's desire to actively engage with humanity. It is particularly important that Barth consistently frames God as speaker; this move allows Barth to emphasize God's own agency in revealing the Word. Barth adds that understanding the Word as speech attests to God's close relationship with humanity: "Speech, including God's speech, is the form in which reason communicates with reason and person with person. To be sure it is the divine reason communicating with the human reason and the divine person with the human person."[28] A spoken Word bespeaks the personhood of God and of humanity, which has been created in God's own image. Far from being mere metaphor, understanding God's Word as speech is central to Barth's theology because it attests to God's revealed character and to God's close relationship with humanity.

Barth's theology, though, also highlights a potential problem posed by understanding the Word as revealed through conversation with humanity: one might imagine that the Word requires a human conversation partner. Jenson's examination of triune conversations largely avoids any such concerns by emphasizing that the Trinity needs no outside conversation partner, but instead draws humanity into its own exchanges for humanity's benefit.[29] Barth himself responds to such concerns by insisting that the Word speaks "regardless of whether it is heard or not,"[30] and elsewhere writing, "Hearing man, as the object of the purpose of the speaking God, is thus included in the concept of the Word of God as a factual necessity, but he is not essential to it."[31] The Word of God might be directed to humanity, but the Word in no way requires humanity's hearing. When Jesus prays aloud in John 11:41–42 and says to the Father, "I knew you always hear me," Jesus indicates that Trinitarian conversations are ongoing, regardless of whether humans hear them or not. Eberhard Jüngel adds that God's speech uniquely requires no other conversation partner to give it form or content:

> No human being can speak from him or herself. But God is the one who does speak from himself. His word is the original expression of his being and the original form of address and, in the unity of both, the word that creates out of nothing.[32]

Just as God's Word can create *ex nihilo*, God alone can speak "from himself" and requires no human interlocutors to give divine conversation form or meaning. God's speech thus reflects the aseity of God. God's choice to speak to humanity is a matter of loving engagement, not ontological necessity.

As Jüngel's contrast reflects, comparing the Word to human speech poses an even more significant risk: anthropomorphizing a transcendent Trinity. Human communication can easily become confused, fraught, or incoherent, and reducing God's revelation to such an understanding risks minimizing the power of the Word. Luther consequently worries that "this analogy of our word is very inadequate and vague" because of the "wide gulf between the thoughts, discussions, and words of the human heart and those of God."[33] Barth similarly asks, "is the grace and the mystery of God . . . really the grace and mystery of the Word of God in the full biblical sense of the concept, if we think of it as reduced to this act of speaking?"[34] Like Jüngel and Luther, Barth draws a line between human and divine speech, writing, "God's speech is different from all other speech and God's action is different from all other action."[35] Barth also insists that "the self-presentation of God in His Word is not comparable with any other self-presentation."[36] Barth maintains that God's Word is distinct because it includes aspects of God's mystery through features like paradox and concealment.[37] This seems an artificial distinction, since human speech can include similar features, but it represents an important attempt to preserve the mystery and majesty of God's Word, which cannot be limited by human capacity to understand it. Understanding God's Word in terms of speech requires careful attention to God's unique and transcendent qualities, which human conversations will never encapsulate.

Understanding the Word made flesh in Christ as pointing to God's relational, revelatory conversations with humanity has significant implications for the operant missional ecclesiology of church planting, which will be explored more fully in the remainder of this chapter, and particularly in the next. A few preliminary observations, though, are in order. Jesus's actions as the embodied Word clarify why a missional church that seeks to proclaim the Word cannot content itself with offering "the transmission of verbal summaries of the Gospel from the distance of non-involvement."[38] The Word is not one-way communication, nor is it offered from a comfortable distance. Jesus's incarnation bespeaks vulnerability and God's ongoing, compassionate engagement with humanity. Churches seeking to proclaim the Word do not proclaim a distant, uninvolved God, but the Word made flesh, whose Spirit abides in and enlivens the church. The Word points to typology depicting a God who hears and answers human prayers, cares about human needs, and responds to spiritual crises and heartfelt questions. This picture of the Word gives new urgency to James's insistence that Christians must be "quick to hear and slow to speak" (Jas 1:19). Such a posture actively points to a God who listens, a model of patient compassion. Remembering that God speaks also reminds churches that God's voice deserves to be the first one consulted. As the writer of Hebrews warned, "See to it that you do not refuse him who is speaking" (Heb 12:25). Church planting requires a willingness to attend carefully to God's Word and to seek God's gracious guidance. God is speaking, listening, responding, and acting; in pointing to this reality, the Word offers planted churches very good news indeed.

Church as a Creature of the Word: The Nature of the Church

If church is a creature of the Word, as the Reformers taught, the church must somehow echo the relational, interactive nature of the revealed Word. Indeed, *ekklesia*, the Greek word most commonly translated as church, appears in the Gospels exclusively in contexts where the Word is revealed through conversational interactions. Descriptions of the early church in Acts further suggest that conversations are an important means by which the Spirit reveals the meaning of Word to the very first Christian congregations, effectively bringing the church to life. As we will see, churches have been called to reflect the interactive, relational engagement with God that characterized God's Word incarnate.

Reformation teachings clearly frame the church as a creature of the Word, a doctrine which became foundational for Protestant theology. Luther writes, "For since the church owes its birth to the Word, is nourished, aided, and strengthened by it, it is obvious that it cannot be without the Word. If it is without the Word it ceases to be a church."[39] Luther's phrasing suggests that this doctrine is "obvious," but it is important to recall that the context of his argument is a defense of the legitimacy of Protestant churches, whose pastors do not enjoy the blessing of Rome. The crux of Luther's argument is that a church's authority does not come from any human source, but from the authority of the Word that created and constitutes it. On the basis of this belief, Luther argues that the central ministry and "first office" of the church is the ministry of the Word, which is shared by all believers, not only those bearing papal blessings.[40] Calvin largely agrees with Luther on this point, writing,

> [I]t is necessary to remember, that whatever authority and dignity the Holy Spirit in Scripture confers on priests, or prophets, or successors of the Apostles, it wholly gives not to men themselves, but to the ministry to which they are appointed; or, to speak more plainly, to the word, the ministry to which they are appointed.[41]

It is significant that for Calvin, as for Luther, the only "authority and dignity" with which any Christian ministry can be conducted is that of the Word. Indeed, Calvin's description indicates that the ministry of the Word is the sole "ministry to which [Christians] are appointed." Luther and Calvin thus agree that the church's authority comes from the Word, and that the ministry of the Word is the church's central calling. The ministry of the Word thus became one of the primary marks of the true church in

Protestant theology; as Calvin puts it, "Wherever we see the word of God sincerely preached and heard, wherever we see the sacraments administered according to the institution of Christ, there we cannot have any doubt that the Church of God has some existence."[42] It is significant that for the church to have "some existence" in Calvin's mind, the Word must be both "sincerely preached and heard." It follows, then, that the Word must be not only spoken, but also received by listeners in order for a church to be truly present in a given place. Ensuring that the Word has been "heard" creates a compelling argument for reading Scripture in the vernacular, and for today's planted churches presenting the gospel using contemporary, clear language. It is thus the case that foundational elements of Protestant ecclesiology, from the church's independence from Rome to reading Scripture in the vernacular, rest on the idea that church is a creature of the Word.

Scripture thoroughly grounds the Reformers' instinctive understanding of church as a creature of the Word; references to "church" in the Gospels all appear in the context of conversations where people are actively trying to discern something about God. The term *ekklesia* (ἐκκλησία) rarely appears in the Gospels, but it does appear in Matthew 16:18.[43] After Peter proclaims Jesus as Messiah and Son of God (16:16), Jesus responds, calling Peter blessed (16:17) and saying, "You are Peter, and on this rock I will build my church [*ekklesia*], and the gates of hell shall not prevail against it" (16:18). The context of this exchange is important; Jesus draws out Peter's confession only after inviting the disciples to reflect on prior conversations they have had with others about Jesus's identity (16:13–14). Jesus insists that the Father revealed Jesus's identity to Peter (16:17), so Peter's declaration cannot be attributed solely to these prior conversations, but the sequence matters: the disciples hear others' impressions about Jesus, which leads them to a conversation with Jesus, which leads to a new revelation of Jesus's identity, which leads to a new articulation of the church's identity. It is also noteworthy that Peter's confession comes not because of one-way communication from Jesus, but in response to two questions that Jesus asks: "Who do people say that the Son of Man is?" and "But who do you say that I am?" (16:13, 15). Jesus's questions invite honest reflection on what others have said and an honest response from the disciples, which is articulated by their usual spokesperson, Peter.[44] The context of this foundational statement of ecclesial identity suggests that churches are called to echo the responsive, interactive qualities of the Word, listening to humanity and responding to God's searching questions.[45] The time, space, and energy which many planted churches devote to preaching belie a strong operant understanding of mission as primarily listening to God's Word and speaking to others about God. By contrast, Matthew 16 suggests that listening to others, including those outside the faith, and speaking to God are also part of the process by which the Spirit reveals Jesus's messianic identity to the church.

A similar pattern develops in Acts, which tells the story of how early Christians became the *ekklesia*. Acts is typically classified as an ancient historical or historiography text, genres that were less precise than modern academic histories.[46] Ancient histories or historiographies typically sought "to provide moral and political instruction" using "what they understood as the genuine past."[47] If the intention behind Acts is indeed to provide "moral instruction," then it is entirely reasonable to follow biblical interpreters who read Acts ecclesiologically, presupposing that its narratives are meant to guide later churches.[48] Some subtle details within Acts confirm the likelihood of such intentions. In Acts 2:17–18, there is a slight alteration to the phrasing of Joel 2:29, adding the phrase "and they will prophesy" to the end of the citation. This addition suggests that the quotation of Joel 2:29 is meant to "[look] both backward and forward," transforming the Pentecost narrative into a preview of subsequent church experiences.[49] Prominent church planting advocates therefore rightly turn to the Acts narratives for missional strategies and ecclesiological reflection.[50] Such moves must be made carefully, with due attention to differences between past and present and with due respect for the centuries of Christian thought that have occurred, but one need not overlook instructive elements of these foundational texts.

The Pentecost narrative (Acts 2) indicates that the Spirit's activity within the church first revealed itself through the speech of Christians. Luke describes the Spirit unexpectedly empowering Christians at Pentecost to converse with a much wider audience than they could have imagined, including many who were outside their fellowship (2:9–11). Peter's Pentecost sermon begins as a response to specific questions that people outside the Christian community began asking about their strange new speech (2:12–15). Peter's sermon offers an extensive explanation of Jesus's life and ministry (2:14–36), and it concludes by responding to questions that listeners ask about the implications of what he has just said (2:37–41). As a result of these exchanges, the church grows numerically and develops new patterns of practice (2:41–47). As in Matthew 16:13–20, the sequence is important: the church engages in conversations with people outside their fellowship; Peter acts as a spokesperson and articulates a new revelation of Jesus's identity; the church then develops a new self-understanding. Relational exchanges and a willingness to balance speaking, listening, and responding are central to the Spirit's revelatory process in forming the church and shaping its witness.

After Pentecost, the Acts narratives frequently describe the Spirit's activity within the church by detailing conversations that continue to clarify both the nature of the Word and the church's calling. Even hostile exchanges between Peter, John, and the Sanhedrin (4:1–22) lead the church to deepen its communal prayer life (4:23–30), strengthen communal practices (4:32–37), and receive additional revelations of the Spirit's presence in their midst (4:31). Philip, Peter, John, Paul, and Barnabas engage in a series of Spirit-led conversations with gentiles and Jews in a wide range of contexts (Acts 8–14). The pattern of these conversations clarifies the early church's relationship to Jewish law and its policies toward gentile believers (15:1–35). Peter and Cornelius, for example, each receive visions from God (Acts 10:1–23), but the Spirit does not reveal the meaning of their visions until they speak with one another about them (Acts 10:23–48). Peter later recounts his conversation with Cornelius to both the church (Acts 11:1–18) and the Jerusalem Council (Acts 15:8–11). It is only when speaking with the Jerusalem Council that Peter articulates the broader theological implications of his and Cornelius's visions for the wider church. Peter's interaction with Cornelius thus helps the entire church to discern God's character (15:8–9) and the meaning of Hebrew Scriptures (15:14–18). As a result, the church articulates a new missional ecclesiology (15:11, 19–31), one which includes gentiles. If the Acts narratives are intended to inform later church practices, churches must expect that internal and external conversations will be an important means by which the Spirit reveals God's ongoing work in their midst and deepens their corporate witness. No individual Christian has perfect insight into the Word, but in Acts, God speaks through the corporate body of believers, confirming and clarifying the Word as the Spirit guides the whole church to listen, speak, and respond.

This reading of Acts offers helpful insight into ways that the early Reformers understood and applied the doctrine of *sola scriptura*. As Tom Greggs has written, *sola scriptura* in its original formulations attests to the importance of the church's collective wisdom in discerning the Word.[51] This corporate understanding of *sola scriptura* has particular weight in a highly individualistic context like twenty-first-century America, where people might naturally assume that *sola scriptura* means something like, "Every church member is entitled to claim the label 'biblical' for their own personal position on an issue."[52] Against such individualistic understandings, Greggs clarifies, "It is the church's reading of Scripture which *sola scriptura* considers primarily."[53] According to Greggs, the Reformers used discussions of *sola scriptura* to affirm, "It is the very collectivity of the decisions of the pastors about the interpretation of Scripture that gives the decision weight, in comparison to the decisions and findings of a few individuals with regard to scriptural interpretation."[54] This understanding of *sola scriptura* accords well with accounts of the Jerusalem Council in Acts 15, where representatives of the entire church agreed together on the meaning of Hebrew Scriptures when articulating its implications for their missional ecclesiology. It is not only the "collectivity of the decisions of the pastors" that count, but the collective weight of the full community of believers.[55] Greggs helpfully clarifies that "the whole church engages together in judgment on the appropriate interpretation of texts,"[56] leaving space for people outside the clergy to participate in the process. If this were not the case, Protestants might inadvertently diminish the Spirit-empowered discernment of lay Christians. By contrast, in Acts 15, Peter and other leaders share personal narratives, but they also serve as spokespeople, recounting the stories of other believers, like Cornelius. As in the Jerusalem Council, it is still the case that "corporate interpretation of Scripture shapes the ecclesial identity of the church, and the ecclesial identity of the church shapes the way the church continues to read the Bible."[57] Churches' understanding of Scripture does not come in a vacuum but reflects the influence of centuries of traditions and teachings. For the church to discern and be formed by the Word in ever-changing contexts, it still needs the corporate wisdom of the full church body.

To discern and be formed by the Word, the church also needs the ministry of the Spirit, just as it did in Acts. Acts 1 frames the entire book that follows as demonstration of the Holy Spirit. Luke identifies Jesus's ministry as "through the Holy Spirit" (Acts 1:2), and Jesus's parting words to the disciples emphasize that they are to anticipate the Spirit's arrival, which will baptize them with power and inaugurate their witness (Acts 1:4–5, 8). Pentecost itself is an expression of the Spirit's own ministry within the community of believers, molding them into the church. The Pentecost narrative opens by describing the Spirit arriving within the gathered community "from heaven" with "a sound like a mighty rushing wind" (2:1). The Spirit appears in the form of "divided tongues as of fire" that "rested on each one of them" and empowered them to "speak in other tongues as the Spirit gave them utterance" (2:3–4). Upon closer examination, the exchanges at Pentecost reflect the very qualities of the Spirit that Jesus describes in the farewell discourse in John 13–16. Jesus indicates that the Spirit would remind believers what he had taught them (John 14:26), bear witness about him (15:26–27), "convict the world concerning sin and righteousness and judgment" (16:8–11), guide them into truth (16:13), and bring glory to God by declaring to them things of Christ (16:12–15). At Pentecost, Peter and the other believers recount Jesus's ministry (Acts 2:22–36), bear witness about him (2:32), see people "cut to the heart" and seeking repentance (2:37–41), are guided into the truth of Hebrew Scriptures (2:16–21, 25–31, 34–35) and glorify God, declaring the "the mighty works of God" in every language needed (2:11, 22). By an act of the Spirit, both the disciples and new converts thus realize their "corporate and communal identity in Christ" and so become re-ordered to God, to one another, and to those outside their fellowship.[58] This is why Paul insists that only by the Spirit could Corinthian believers hope to understand the things of God or become capable of teaching and interpreting the things of God (1 Cor 2:10–16). The exchanges of the church are revelatory and powerful only because of the Spirit's ministry, revealing the meaning and effect of the Word.

It is therefore important to examine ways that planted churches discern God's voice speaking in the midst of their exchanges. Echoing Jesus's statements about the authority of the early *ekklesia* in Matthew 16:18 and 18:15–20, Jenson reminds readers that ecclesial language reflects Christ's own speech, saying, "When the church pronounces absolution, this is Christ's absolution. When two or three gather as the church to petition the Father, there he is, praying with and indeed through them."[59] Jenson's reading of the Matthean texts is consistent with their plain meaning, emphasizing the voice of God speaking when Christians gather, listen, and respond. According to Jenson, Christian worship at its best echoes patterns of triune conversations:

> Christian speech to God is in the first instance addressed to the *Father*, with the Son and in the Spirit. But just so, we enter the triune converse itself, and may then sometimes be so located in its mutual exchanges that we address the Son, as in the primal liturgical cry, *Maranatha*, "Come, Lord," or the Spirit, as in the epicleses with which traditional liturgy is replete.[60]

It is significant that the forms of speech that reflect the voice of the Trinity are first and foremost moments of corporate prayer, when the church addresses God directly. It is also significant that in such moments the church speaks as one, not simply agreeing with one another, but echoing other Christian congregations that employ similar language. Liturgy and corporate prayer rightly include formulae that reflect the collective discernment of many generations of Christians who have actively wrestled with the same Word. One voice does not necessarily echo the Spirit, but when churches discern the Word together under the Spirit's leadership, the voice of God draws them into a unified symphony of praise and blessing.

Important initial implications arise for planted congregations from this understanding of church as a creature of the Word. The Spirit's work activating the wisdom and insights of a church body and revealing the meaning of the Word to believers requires much more from a congregation than passively listening to one speaker once a week. Churches that seek to discern the Word and witness to Christ's presence in their midst need time to speak together and wrestle with the meaning and application of Scriptures within their own context. The witness of the church began in a rich series of Spirit-led interactions, which quickly overflowed from their immediate fellowship to the surrounding community, where many were blessed. Spirit-led exchanges with others, including some who were not yet believers, proved to be a vital means by which the Spirit continued to form and instruct the church, revealing the truth of the Word and new ways they might embody the Word together. Conversations within and beyond the church matter deeply to the life and witness of a congregation. The power of corporate interactions also explains why, as we have seen, conversations in small groups or during prayer requests, particularly on sensitive, divisive issues, can shape the character of an entire congregation. By their corporate praise, churches can point others to a God who invites human response and reveals the beauty and majesty of the Word. By their corporate engagement and collective wrestling with Scripture, churches can better discern the Word, discovering its ongoing relevance to humanity. As churches respond to the Spirit together, they will find themselves well equipped as a body to proclaim the gospel to all who might seek Jesus.

Proclamation: Churches Making the Redemptive Word Audible

Of all a church's verbal exchanges, preaching deserves particular attention because of its prominence in American church planting movements. The operant missional ecclesiology in many planted congregations frames evangelistic preaching as a primary means by which seeking souls might receive revelation of the Word. This understanding of proclamation finds some support in Luther's own soteriology, which emphasizes the act of literally hearing the Word as carrying salvific importance. Barth, though, develops Lutheran ideas into a more complex theology of proclamation which understands revelation, preaching, and Scripture together revealing the Word, and argues that churchly proclamation encompasses much more than preaching. Together, these reflections offer considerable material to develop a theological interpretation of preaching in the context of the missional witness of a modern Protestant church.

Luther's soteriology offers some support to planted churches that frame preaching as central to their missional calling. Luther often describes human understanding of the Word in terms of hearing; for example, "the Word of God is perceived only by hearing. It is the nature of the Word to be heard."[61] In discussions of soteriology, Luther sees "hearing the Word" as central to developing a saving faith, and he interprets "hearing" very literally. In his exegesis of Hebrews, for example, Luther insists that "the ears alone are the organs of a Christian man."[62] He then adds: "If you ask a Christian what the work is by which he becomes worthy of the name 'Christian,' he will be able to give absolutely no other answer than that it is the hearing of the Word of God, that is, faith."[63] Becoming a Christian, for Luther, is functionally equivalent to "hearing the Word of God." Luther's emphasis on the ears as the sole "organs of a Christian man" obviates any possibility of reading his expression "hearing the Word" as mere metaphor. Timothy George therefore rightly concludes: "The hearing, the receiving, was primary for Luther. *Fides ex auditu*, 'faith out of hearing,' 'faith by means of listening,' is perhaps the best summary of his Reformation discovery."[64] Luther's soteriology so closely ties saving faith to physically hearing the Word that it even exposes Luther to charges of ableism. At one point, Luther expresses real concern that people who cannot physically hear might not be able to receive salvation.[65] Luther quickly resolves his concern,[66] but his soteriology offers justification to planted Protestant churches that invest substantial missional energy in preaching the Word and creating spaces where people might hear it.

It is important, though, to recall that in Luther's time, relatively few people were literate.[67] Indeed, for most of Christian history, many Christians could not read, and access to books and printed material was hardly universal. Not even all parts of gathered services would always have been accessible to the entire congregation; in medieval Europe, Bibles and liturgies were typically in Latin, but priests often delivered homilies in the vernacular, making preaching a particularly important means for lay Christians to access biblical texts.[68] Consequently, modern church planting ministries are hardly unique in emphasizing proclamation as a way for churches to participate in God's revelation of the Word. That said, in contemporary American settings, where written Bibles abound and literacy rates are relatively high, one might be tempted to overlook the theological significance of preaching.[69] This would be a mistake. In light of the consumeristic, individualistic culture that is common in twenty-first-century America, corporate faith experiences are well worth preserving. Preaching is a corporate faith experience, in which Christians gather together to hear the Word as a body. As a congregation gathers to hear a sermon, they are able to hear and see others who are also part of the body of believers that God addresses and redeems by the Word. By its very nature, then, the act of preaching and listening to a sermon reminds Christians that the same Word speaks to an entire church body even as it touches the hearts of individuals.[70] Preaching might have a different significance in contemporary American settings than it did in Luther's time, but it remains important to the life of a Christian faith community.

Barth's theology therefore rightly gives church proclamation serious attention. According to Barth, the three interrelated means by which the Word reveals itself are Scripture, revelation, and proclamation:

> The revealed Word of God we know only from the Scripture adopted by Church proclamation or the proclamation of the Church based on Scripture. The written Word of God we know only through the revelation which fulfills proclamation or through the proclamation fulfilled by revelation. The preached Word of God we know only through the revelation attested in Scripture or the Scripture which attests revelation.[71]

The essential interrelationship that Barth describes among proclamation, Scripture, and revelation loosely echoes the essential interrelationship among the persons of the Trinity.[72] Proclamation, according to Barth, requires confirmation by both revelation and Scripture to truly reveal the Word to human beings, and proclamation also helps Christians to discern Scripture and to recognize revelation. Proclamation is therefore vital to the church's discernment of the Word, but it cannot function on its own. One must therefore clarify exactly what "proclamation" means. Barth defines proclamation as "the preached Word of God," and later adds that proclamation "means the Word of God preached and the Word of God preached means . . . man's talk about God on the basis of God's own direction."[73] This definition of proclamation clearly envisions preaching, the most natural understanding of the term. If congregations understand proclamation as preaching and preaching as "talk about God on the basis of God's own direction," there is a significant risk: they might understandably conclude that a pastor's sermons are divinely inspired and carry the same authority as Scripture. Planted churches that elevate the status of a pastor too highly, or even substitute sermons for an official doctrinal statement, are more at risk of fostering this impression. Barth's three-part formulation, which balances preaching with Scripture and revelation in the discernment of the Word, helpfully counteracts these potential risks. Barth reminds us that Christian proclamation works only in concert with divine revelation and written Scripture to point people to the Word.

At times, Barth's own writing underscores the reality that Christians might easily assume that proclamation requires little more than passive repetition of something a preacher has heard, delivered to a passive audience, a one-way form of communication. For example, Barth says, "Not every man can speak God's Word. For not every man has heard it. But those who have heard it can and must repeat it."[74] He also says, "In the Acts and Epistles the preaching of the apostles is often regarded as equivalent to the Word of God itself. The active side of the function of these men has to be understood wholly and utterly in the light of the passive."[75] In this specific context, Barth is actually speaking about Scripture, clarifying that the authority of a biblical text derives from God, not its human authors. From Barth's analysis, though, it logically follows that preaching might seem more authoritative if it appears to be passive repetition. In one description of theology, Barth reinforces this image of human passivity, saying that with respect to the Word, theology

> can be only its human reflection, or mirroring (in the precise sense of "speculation"!); and its whole production can be only a human reproduction. In short, theology is not a creative act but only a praise of the Creator and of his act of creation—praise that to the greatest possible extent truly responds to the creative act of God.[76]

Barth adds that "theology shares with the biblical prophecy and apostolate a common concern for human response to the divine Word,"[77] suggesting that this category of "mirroring" also applies to other human responses to the Word, which might easily be understood to include preaching. Indeed, Barth frames the church as a site "where God has once spoken and is heard,"[78] with no reference to the church speaking back to God, potentially minimizing any human voices that might also be heard in a church. This understanding of revelatory human responses to God as simple hearing and repetition make it difficult to envision much other than one-way communication. Such descriptions frame Christians as appropriately reverent toward God, but silent about their own needs and potentially oblivious to the world's. Following such thinking, we could justifiably expect little of most Christians beyond passive reception of the Word, potentially justifying some of the entertainment industry practices that planted churches adopted. As Barth's analysis suggests, Protestant thought contains the genuine potential to envision church as little more than a site for passive reception of revelatory proclamation, not as a space for active engagement with a Word that hears, engages, and responds to humanity.

Helpfully, though, Barth also offers fuller descriptions of proclamation, making it clear that church proclamation indeed encompasses a wide range of interactive activities and practices that involve the entire church body. Barth writes:

> [The community] speaks, finally, by the simple fact that it prays for the world. . . . From the very beginning the community also expresses itself in spoken words and sentences by which, according to the summons of the Word, it attempts to make its faith audible. The work of the community consists also in its testimony through oral and written words, i.e., in the verbal self-expression by which it fulfils its commission of preaching, teaching, and pastoral counselling.[79]

Barth thus offers a clearer picture of how a church body might proclaim the Word corporately. Proclamation, according to Barth, also includes ministries like intercessory prayer, testimony, teaching, and counseling, which can involve oral or written words. This broader understanding of proclamation makes it clear how all Christians actively proclaim the Word, not only the teaching pastors or ordained preachers. Barth adds that everyone who has heard and believed the Word is called to proclaim it, writing, "'I believed, and so I spoke.' This attitude, taken over from the psalmist by Paul, indicates the situation peculiar to the entire community as such, and in the last analysis to each one of its members."[80] All Christians are part of the church "community" in Barth's thinking, and all are called to proclaim the Word which they have believed. This description of proclamation appropriately locates preaching within a wide range of church practices, all of which proclaim the Word. Barth thus creates safeguards against unduly elevating preaching or overlooking the callings of the rest of the congregation. Proclaiming the Word, like discerning the Word, is a corporate calling that includes the entire body.

Barth's fuller definition of proclamation also encourages churches to offer a more complete witness to the Word. Ministries like intercessory prayer and counseling position a church to hear and respond to human needs, pointing to a Word that also hears and responds to humanity. Jenson even argues that all Christian worship enacts "God's hearing of our word to him,"[81] helpfully reminding churches that gathering in faith to pray points to a God who hears and responds to prayer. At its best, churchly proclamation, in any form, is an active human response to God's own gracious Word. Jenson emphasizes how this response goes beyond mere repetition, writing, "What differentiates the worship of God from a religious relation to impersonal deity is that God must be spoken to."[82] For this reason, gathered Christian worship has long included a variety of verbal human responses to God's Word, and so participates in God's ongoing conversation with humanity. Jenson develops this understanding by defining a "person" of God as "one whom other persons may address in hope of response,"[83] adding,

> Humans, we may say, are those animals whose creation is not merely that God speaks *about* them but that he also speaks *to* them. Humans are those creatures who exist in that they are mentioned in the triune discourse *and* are called to join it. Humans are those creatures who not only exist by words that state God's moral will, but are given to hear and reply to those words.[84]

Human beings are created in the image of a responsive God who speaks with humanity,[85] and humans have an important calling to "hear and reply" to our Creator, who engages with humanity in a genuine relationship. This is an important reason why Christians cannot sacrifice worship for the sake of evangelistic preaching, as some churches have arguably done.[86] Nor can Christians be encouraged to behave as passive consumers of sermons. Participatory worship and active prayer are essential to proclaim the full richness of the Word, which hears human voices and invites human interlocutors to respond and engage with God.

Barth's fuller definition of proclamation as a corporate calling sits particularly well with key details in the Pentecost narratives of Acts 2. Peter's

Pentecost sermon receives considerable space in this narrative (2:14–36), and the responses to Peter's sermon confirm that the Spirit had indeed revealed the Word to a wider community (2:37–41). It is also important to recall that the occasion of Peter's sermon is the arrival of the Spirit within the Christian community (2:14–21), which reveals itself by a miracle of speaking in tongues (2:4–13). The nature of this miracle is not entirely clear, but it affects the speech of multiple members of the church community who corporately reflect the Spirit's presence (2:6–7, 11, 13, 15). Peter also quotes Joel's prophecy (Acts 2:17–18; Joel 2:28–32), which references a highly inclusive and diverse body of witnesses, including men and women, old and young, suggesting that the speech of more Christians than Peter must be acknowledged as revelatory. Blumhofer argues that the reference to "my male and my female servants" in Acts 2:17 indicates that the mass of Christians speaking in tongues at Pentecost became prophets, noting, "In the Old Testament, God rarely claims people as 'my servants'" but God "uses this title when addressing the prophets of Israel."[87] Barrett disagrees, citing the distinction in Acts 19:6 between prophesying and speaking in tongues, but acknowledges, "[Prophets] speak in a distinctive way that can be recognized as inspired; they function as servants of the church, comparable with teachers."[88] Barrett thus concedes that by the Spirit, unnamed church members came to "function as servants of the church, comparable with teachers" like Peter. Speaking in tongues was "a highly unusual phenomenon outside of Christian circles in the first century,"[89] and it bore witness to the work of the Spirit within the full corporate church. Peter's own proclamation, the Hebrew Scripture that he cites, and the Spirit's self-revelation through church members corporately witness to the Word. Acts 2 thus offers a powerful picture of how the Spirit reveals the Word to humanity when the full church participates in its proclamation, illustrating key themes of Barth's theology.

Acts 2 offers a beautiful picture of what church can be, but some planted American churches have been faced with scandals and shortcomings that dramatically limit their capacity to proclaim the Word. It is therefore vital to emphasize that the human voices which proclaim God's Word will always be flawed. Barth insists that the Word does not efface any human voice which proclaims it, writing,

> The willing and doing of proclaiming man . . . is not in any sense set aside in real proclamation. As Christ became true man and remains

> true man to all eternity, real proclamation becomes an event on the level of all other human events.[90]

The ever-present humanity in proclamation is therefore not something to be avoided or ignored; at its best, it transforms proclamation into an authentic sign pointing to the miracle of the incarnation.[91] By acknowledging the humanity of one proclaiming the Word, the miracle of humanity hearing God's Word becomes all the more striking, as Barth explains:

> But as Christ is not just true man, so it [proclamation] is not just the willing and doing of proclaiming man. It is also and indeed it is primarily and decisively the divine willing and doing. Precisely for this reason the human element is not set aside.[92]

The miracle of the Word speaking through human words becomes an important sign pointing to God's redemption of and work within flawed human beings.[93] This is why Barth reminds churches that it is not the human speaker, but the Word itself that gives proclamation its true value.[94] The reality of human speakers, though, also means that church proclamation will never be infallible, as Barth acknowledges:

> Even the most able speech of the most living faith is a human work. And this means that the community can go astray in its proclamation of the Word of God, in its interpretation of the biblical testimony, and finally in its own faith. Instead of being helpful, it can be obstructive to God's cause in the world by an understanding that is partly or wholly wrong, by devious or warped thought, by silly or too subtle speech. Every day the community must pray that this may not happen, but it must also do its own share of earnest *work* toward this goal.[95]

This understanding sits well with Luther's idea that church consists of people who are simultaneously justified and sinners.[96] Churches must indeed pray and work in order that their own ever-present humanity might point to God's redemptive mission in the world, not obscure it. Churches must also acknowledge the humanity of their preachers by granting them the accountability, discipleship, and encouragement that all Christians need, and by engaging together with the pastor in God's ministry among them. The Spirit's presence does not efface the human voices which proclaim the Word, and flawed human voices, including the preacher's, stand as ever in need of prayerful support and guidance. Only by the power of the Spirit can churches truly proclaim the Word, and faithful proclamation of the Word is essential to the witness of any church.

The *Sanctorum Communio*: Church Bodies Making the Redemptive Word Visible

A church's visible lived existence within a community along with its gathered worship and practical ministries attest wordlessly to God's redemptive work in the world. Bonhoeffer therefore devoted considerable energy to explaining why Christians must never reduce "church" to an abstract philosophical concept. Church, according to Bonhoeffer, is a gathering of real human beings who collectively become the visible body of Christ within a local community. Bonhoeffer's ecclesiology gives theological weight and revelatory importance to the embodied existence of churches. For this reason verbal proclamation, however Christians understand it, cannot be the only calling of any missional church, lest it offer an incomplete witness to the incarnation and to the Spirit's work in their midst.

Bonhoeffer broadly agrees with Barth that church is a place where God's revelation can occur. He writes, for example, "The church is founded on the revelation of God's heart."[97] For Bonhoeffer, though, it is not primarily proclamation so much as the church's embodied existence that reveals the Incarnate Word. He writes that in biblical descriptions of church as the "body of Christ," the term "body" "is not a concept referring to form but to function, namely the work of Christ."[98] Bonhoeffer's reading conflicts slightly with images of the church as body in 1 Corinthians 12 and Romans 12, which use the metaphor of "body" to emphasize that it is indeed formed from diverse individual members, much as a physical body is formed of many parts. His reading, though, accords well with descriptions of the church as "body" throughout the book of Ephesians (1:23, 4:12, 5:22–30), which emphasize the corporate body functioning together to point to the work of Christ. The author of Ephesians stresses that church is a body with Christ as its head (1:22; 4:15), an image that clarifies why church can never be separated from Christ, the one who is its unifying telos, its life, and its strength.[99] In Ephesians, church becomes a means of revealing God even to heavenly powers (Eph 3:10) because it is founded in God's eternal and unchanging purposes (Eph 1:3–14) by the work of the Spirit (Eph 2:22; 3:16; 5:18).[100] As the body of Christ, which Bonhoeffer called "Christ existing as church-community," the church's very existence points to the Word made flesh.[101] Church is therefore a work of the Spirit that points to God's self-revelation in Christ.

Bonhoeffer's descriptions of church as the body of Christ underscore another idea affirmed by theologians: church is an act of God that witnesses to God's redemption, not a human creation.[102] Only the work of the Spirit can transform a human gathering into a church, as the Pentecost narrative attests.[103] As Van't Slot rightly argues, in Bonhoeffer's ecclesiology, "'Church' cannot be considered as being built by those believers on themselves; it is formed by God, and by God alone, through his vocation and his binding together of believers."[104] This is a vitally important reminder to planted American churches, which sometimes seem functionally dependent on purely human strategies like the HUP, entertainment industry practices, or marketing research rather than the work of the Spirit. A living God alone can create new space for a church, as Bonhoeffer explains:

> One must confess that this place belongs to [God]. The order to make some historical place into God's place has not been confided to the church . . . for no human person, but God alone determines this place. The church which is aware of this waits for the word that transforms it into God's place in the world.[105]

Bonhoeffer's advice has particular relevance for American church planters. Christians who hope to plant a new church cannot simply create a new worship space on their own and expect God to bless it automatically. Instead, as Bonhoeffer says, Christians must "wait for the word that transforms" a local body of believers into "God's place in the world." Only God's own work through the Word and the ministry of the Spirit can truly create a church. In church planting, as in any divinely empowered human act, "Divine action is the condition of human activity; human activity is not the condition of divine activity."[106] Bonhoeffer therefore adds, "Waiting on God's choice, it avoids being established in some privileged place. Such a church has the promise of God."[107] Bonhoeffer rightly observes that fallen humans are all too prone to choose a strategic location to plant a new church, which risks connecting it more closely to centers of human power and privilege than to "the promise of God."[108] On one level, then, human beings cannot truly plant a church; only the Spirit's presence will transform a human gathering into the body of Christ. For this reason, the very existence of a Spirit-gathered and Spirit-led church points to the tangible work of God in human history.

It is important to stress that just as Christ was both fully divine and fully human, so the body of Christ, the *ekklesia*, is both a site of transcendent, eternal hope and a local gathering of human believers.[109] The humanity within churches is indeed an important component of their witness. Bonhoeffer is deeply concerned about what he calls a "docetic eschatology, derived from idealism" which reduces church to "an incorporeal concept."[110] The visible presence of real human beings within a church keeps it from becoming "docetic," as Bonhoeffer explains:

> A truth, a doctrine, or a religion needs no space of its own. Such entities are bodyless. They do not go beyond being heard, learned, and understood. But the incarnate Son of God needs not only ears or even hearts; he needs actual, living human beings who follow him. That is why he called his disciples into following him bodily. His community with them was something everyone could see.[111]

Christianity is neither mere "religion" nor a philosophy, which asks only to be heard and understood. It is faith in a living God who incorporates believers into a living body, which is called church.[112] Bonhoeffer therefore rightly insists that church is "not a community of common convictions or based on kindred spirits, but a community of love made up of real human beings."[113] Christians cannot simply follow Christ's teaching on their own, meditate individually on the Word, or restrict their engagement with Christianity to academic or philosophical musing. Nor can Christians be content to gather only with others like themselves, in groups where natural affinities abound. As Greggs writes, "The church is not simply a voluntary society of individual human wills which come together out of a shared or agreed sense of beliefs," nor is it "simply a place where humans are attracted to one another by virtue of a common or shared spirit."[114] God personally calls church into being, inviting its members to override their natural and normal human preferences and tribal allegiances under the headship of a common Lord.[115] The visible human bodies within the body of Christ, the church, thus point to the historical reality of Christ's incarnation and the ongoing redemptive ministry of the Spirit and the Word.

As a gathering of human beings, churches will resemble other human organizations. Even the New Testament word *ekklesia* could describe not only the church, but also a wide range of purely human organizations that also existed in antiquity, as illustrated by Acts 19:23–41. Describing an unruly mob in Ephesus, Acts 19:32 reads, "Now some cried out one thing, some another, for the assembly [*ekklesia*] was in confusion, and most of them did not know why they had come together." In response to the mob's agitation, a town clerk lists places where people might resolve their disputes and adds, "If you seek anything further, it shall be settled in the regular assembly [*ekklesia*]" (Acts 19:39). In antiquity, then, an *ekklesia* did not have to be religious, organized, or even remotely purposeful; it could describe a very loose and chaotic gathering of humans, or a regular assembly of local officials that had no ostensibly religious function. In other contexts, the same term *ekklesia* could describe voluntary trade associations which engaged in "rituals and communal meals," "frequently functioned as burial societies," and sometimes included "a community of goods, a required daily regiment, and strict taboos on diet and clothing."[116] Churches assumed many of the same practical functions that ancient trade unions once served, and so the shared term *ekklesia* seems natural. Much as Jesus's physical appearance matched that of other human beings, so churches have always resembled a wide range of purely human organizations, much as the Greek term *ekklesia* reflects.

For this reason, Bonhoeffer helpfully draws on sociological analysis to identify significant distinctions between churches and the purely human gatherings which they might resemble.[117] Bonhoeffer first insists that a church is not a "mass" of people where individual boundaries are lost.[118] Churches are therefore nothing like the unruly mob in Acts 19:32, nor are they cults that fail to respect the personhood of each member. Bonhoeffer adds that a church is also not a purpose-driven "society," which exists "only as a means to an end," whose "objective spirit . . . is not affirmed as a value in itself."[119] This is an important reminder for American church planting movements, whose operant missional ecclesiology has sometimes instrumentalized church for the sake of evangelistic ministries. Church is more than a simple means to an end, even an end as noble as evangelism. Church is not a glorified trade union, either, though some churches might minister very effectively to local people working in specific trades or businesses.[120] Neither is church like the "regular assembly" described in Acts 19:39, which exists solely for a defined purpose, like resolving disputes or keeping the peace in a local community. Instead, Bonhoeffer insists that church is a "community," which means it is valuable in its own right.[121] By its very existence, church demonstrates that "God simply wants community for its own sake, which really means for God's sake."[122] Church, like a beloved family or a gathering of dear friends, need not meet any measurable goals to matter deeply to its Creator.

Another important distinction between the *ekklesia* and other human gatherings is that its ministry extends well beyond the boundaries of its gathered worship spaces. Bonhoeffer writes:

> We must now ask whether spaces of proclamation and order are already sufficient to describe the visible form of the community of the body of Christ, or whether this community claims yet another space in the world. The answer of the New Testament is unambiguous. It holds that the church-community claims a physical space here on earth not only for its worship and its order, but also for the daily life of its members. That is why we must now speak of the living space [*Lebensraum*] of the visible church-community.[123]

Bonhoeffer rightly insists that church is called to do much more than provide "spaces of proclamation and order" for Christians. The visible church, as Christ's body, embodies its faith beyond the church's walls, testifying to Christ's transformative presence in the "daily life of its members." Bonhoeffer therefore worries that churches have largely forfeited their place in society, becoming irrelevant to many people's lives; he writes, "The present-day church is Christianity celebrating only from afar. It thereby stands at the periphery and not at the center of life."[124] Like Jesus venturing out to meet with Nicodemus and the Samaritan woman, and meeting fishermen at the shore when they return from a frustrating night of work, so churches are called to move outward, into the community, to meet people in the middle of the spaces where their lives are lived. Bonhoeffer rightly insists that church is not merely an institution which claims a single space, like the temple, but the body of Christ, whose members carry Christ's presence outward from gathered worship and into the wider world.[125] By contrast, the attractional model common in many planted churches risks creating the appearance that Christ's revelation is confined to physical "spaces of order and proclamation," which are not sufficient in and of themselves to witness to the cosmic, redemptive dimensions of the *missio Dei*.[126] For this reason, Bonhoeffer's reminder is vitally important: a church's witness must never be confined to designated worship spaces.

As the body of Christ moves into the world, it participates in God's own redemption of humanity. According to Bonhoeffer, the church's outward motion into the world attests, "The risen and exalted Christ has closed in on the world, in fact the body of Christ—in the form of the church-community—has broken into the very midst of the world itself."[127] The outward motion of the church points to God's own act of reaching into human history through the person of Christ, actively entering "into the very midst of the world itself." Bonhoeffer adds, "This visible church-community whose reality fully extends to all areas of life invades the world and snatches its children."[128] Bonhoeffer's descriptions of the church's movements, with images like "closing in," "breaking in," "invasion," and "snatching," can sound threateningly militaristic, but these actions describe not a military conquest so much as a loving rescue mission. This becomes most obvious in Bonhoeffer's description of a traditional "service of mourning" at the deceased's home, where the church community's movements attest to Christ's own presence:

> The community is making one final visit to the home of the deceased. This is a witness to the deceased (and the family) that he lived in a Christian home. . . . Christ comes in the guise of the congregation to the home, and in return, the house comes to Christ again, that is, at the funeral. . . . The congregation receives him from the family and brings him to the place where the community sleeps and awaits the coming of Christ.[129]

This beautiful picture of the ministry of a church to a grieving family makes clear that the physical movements of the congregation embody the loving ministry of Christ himself. These movements are clearly a rescue operation: the body of Christ goes to the home of the deceased and accompanies the deceased and the bereaved family to the church building and churchyard for the funeral. The church is thus able to "snatch its children" from despair, reminding them of the love of Christ, which enfolds all who believe, in life and in death. The church's movements in this moment are not ostensibly missional, but they visibly witness to Christ's ongoing care for humanity. The pastor alone cannot embody the same Christlike presence that the congregation embodies when it moves as one in Christ's name. Planted churches must therefore not neglect ordinary ministries of compassion for the sake of evangelism; normal, traditional congregational ministries have a powerful capacity to point human beings gently toward the redeeming love of the Word made flesh.

Bonhoeffer's insistent emphasis on the lived witness of congregations finds widespread resonance among later twentieth-century theologians. Barth, while committed to the importance of proclamation, was quick to add:

> The community does not speak with words alone. It speaks by the very fact of its existence in the world; by its characteristic attitude to

> world problems; and, moreover and especially, by its silent service to all the handicapped, weak, and needy in the world.[130]

Like Bonhoeffer, Barth also affirmed the importance of the lived witness of an entire congregation in "silent service" to the community, particularly those who are most vulnerable. These patterns of ministry and witness allow churches to offer what Jenson described as "visible words," the Word itself made visible.[131] Newbigin most emphatically agrees with Bonhoeffer that the embodied life of a congregation makes the gospel clear and visible to a community.[132] As Newbigin explains, true gospel witness "happens when the word is not a disembodied word, but comes from a community which embodies the true story, God's story, in a style of life which communicates both the grace and the judgement."[133] Newbigin therefore sees the whole congregation as enacting "Christ's priesthood," and frames gathered worship as an opportunity for the whole congregation to "renew its participation in Christ's priesthood."[134] Newbigin therefore insists that the church exercises Christ's priesthood "not within the walls of the church, but in the daily business of the world."[135] Like Bonhoeffer, Newbigin sees the lived presence of a congregation within "the daily business of the world" as profoundly missional. As a priesthood of all believers, the whole congregation shares in this missional calling, including "every member of the body."[136] Bonhoeffer's work thus accords well with subsequent threads in missional ecclesiological thought, encouraging planted churches to reflect on the many different ways that their corporate witness might be enacted within a local community.

Bonhoeffer's ecclesiology also includes a vitally important reminder that the theology of the cross must shape a church's relationship with the world. This facet of Bonhoeffer's ecclesiology likely reflects his experiences attending the Abyssinian Baptist Church in Harlem, New York, in 1930–31.[137] The Abyssinian Baptist Church, like many historically Black churches, identified with the suffering Jesus, not the triumphal Jesus, and so was quick to address social justice concerns within its community.[138] Unlike many American churches that Bonhoeffer visited, the Abyssinian Baptist Church allowed itself to "more closely assume the form of its suffering Lord."[139] Bonhoeffer's later theological writings reflect a similar ecclesial posture; in *Discipleship*, for example, he says:

> An idea requires fanatics, who neither know nor respect resistance. The idea is strong. But the Word of God is so weak that it suffers to

> be despised and rejected by people. For the Word, there are such things as hardened hearts and locked doors. The Word accepts the resistance it encounters and bears it.[140]

Bonhoeffer argues that churches must reflect the weakness of the Word, and be willing to suffer rejection, as Christ himself suffered, rather than risking triumphalism or coercion.[141] This is an important reminder to planted churches, which can easily become identified with their visible successes, like rapid growth, large networks, or impressive buildings. Rejection is also part of the witness of a Christlike church. In his prison writings, Bonhoeffer argues even more forcefully for churches to live sacrificially, writing:

> The church is church only when it is there for others. As a first step it must give away all its property to those in need. The clergy must live solely on the freewill offerings of the congregations and perhaps be engaged in some secular vocation. The church must participate in the worldly tasks of life in the community—not dominating but helping and serving. It must tell people in every calling what a life with Christ is, what it means "to be there for others." . . . The church's word gains weight and power not through concepts but by example.[142]

Bonhoeffer reminds churches why sacrificial living and identification with suffering, marginalized people will give "the church's word" real "weight and power." Christlike sacrifice requires churches to operate from a position of weakness, not strength. Churches must therefore avoid any ecclesiocentric missionary strategy that is primarily intended to strengthen the church's own position in society.[143] The richness of this theology also demonstrates why predominantly white planted churches would do well to follow Bonhoeffer's example and carefully attend to the teaching and traditions of Black churches. By allowing diverse Christian traditions to speak into gaps and blind spots that cultural conditioning can easily create, churches are better equipped to offer a more complete Christlike witness to the world.

Bonhoeffer's ecclesiology, though, also requires some critique, particularly in light of the experiences of American church planting movements. Bonhoeffer frequently describes church as the exclusive site of divine revelation, since he insists that the Spirit only operates within the church community.[144] Bonhoeffer therefore concludes, "Community with God exists only through Christ, but Christ is present only in his church-community."[145] He adds, "'to be in Christ' is synonymous with 'to be in the church-community.'"[146] To be in the presence of Christ, then, one must remain within the boundaries of the church. As Bonhoeffer insists, "*Extra ecclesiam nulla salus*. The question of church membership is a question of salvation. The boundaries of the church are the boundaries of salvation."[147] In practice this formulation risks, at minimum, exacerbating the ecclesiocentric missional vision shared by some planted churches. It is therefore important to hold such statements alongside Bonhoeffer's accounts of the church moving humbly outward into daily life as its members minister and bear witness to Christ's sacrificial love throughout their local community. The church in Bonhoeffer's vision is a community of believers, not a space.

It is also important to hold Bonhoeffer's statements about the presence of Christ in churches alongside his repeated cautions about the flawed human beings incorporated into the church. Like Barth, Bonhoeffer is acutely aware that sin will be ever present within the church, which he insists was "never pure," and will not realize its redemption fully until the eschaton.[148] Consequently, Bonhoeffer cautions that every church remains a "community of sinners" that "is fallible and imperfect as far as its understanding and will are concerned."[149] Ignoring the fallibility and imperfection of human beings within the church can lead people to expect an unrealistic and unattainable perfection from churches. For this reason, Bonhoeffer cautions, "Those who love their dream of a Christian community more than the Christian community itself become destroyers of that Christian community even though their personal intentions may be ever so honest, earnest, and sacrificial."[150] Church planters must therefore carefully weigh whether planting a new church is God's calling and not their own desire to realize some personal "dream of a Christian community." Theologians must similarly avoid crafting "blueprint ecclesiologies," visions of church that are so abstract and academic that they fail to acknowledge the human realities of ecclesial life.[151] Churches are unique and indispensable sites of divine witness in a local community, but they are not perfect.

Bonhoeffer's ecclesiology offers a powerful and theologically grounded set of reasons why God might lead Christians to participate in planting new churches as part of the *missio Dei*. Local congregations of gathered human beings matter deeply to God. For this reason, planted churches can hold Church Growth Theory more lightly without abandoning their sincere and deeply held missional commitments. They need not achieve any tangible growth goal to serve as effective witnesses to God's own loving desire for community. Indeed, churches that suffer rejection and weakness can become powerful witnesses to Christ's sacrificial love for humanity. Under the lens of Bonhoeffer's theology, one can more readily appreciate the importance of local churches. At the same time, Bonhoeffer's theology also offers valuable reminders and cautions to American church planting ministries. As Bonhoeffer insists, God alone is able to transform a human gathering into a living sign of Christ's own incarnation. Human growth strategies cannot possibly replace prayer and attention to the Spirit's work revealing the Word within a local congregation. Planted churches must also attend to their witness outside their own walls. Sometimes a church's most powerful witness is not evangelistic preaching, but tangible, loving service as a church body ministers within a community. Bonhoeffer makes it clear why neither the most effective traveling evangelist nor the most impressive media ministry can possibly replace the witness of a local church body. As Bonhoeffer reminds Christians, churches have a unique calling to exist as a visible sign of Christ's incarnation and God's redemptive, transformative love.

Theological Interpretations for Planted American Churches: Key Findings

The importance that American church planting ministries have placed on local church communities is entirely justified by Protestant Christian tradition, which takes seriously the significance of local churches within the *missio Dei*. Jenson, Barth, and Bonhoeffer each insist that the Spirit gathers congregations together in order to offer the world a unique witness to God's relational Word. The act of planting churches can thus be understood as participation in the *missio Dei*, a response to God's call to make the Word visible and audible within local communities. It is vitally important, though, that church planting movements heed Bonhoeffer's counsel and wait prayerfully on the Word, which alone can transform an ordinary human gathering into the *sanctorum communio*. The true goal of church planting cannot be increasing membership numbers; at its best, church allows a corporate faith community to point humanity to a relational God who listens, speaks, and responds. In light of Jesus's ministry and Protestant theological traditions, planted churches are not simply called to speak the gospel, but to listen and respond faithfully, much as Jesus did. Consequently, community life within the church matters, as does faithful, patient engagement with God and the wider world.

The theological interpretations of church offered by Jenson, Barth, and Bonhoeffer are drawn from threads of Protestant thinking that many planted churches would readily espouse. They include a number of helpful challenges and reminders for planted American churches that seek to draw their practices into closer alignment with their beliefs. By reflecting theologically on the nature of the Word and considering what it means to be a creature of the Word, churches are well positioned to enact their missional calling. Theological interpretations of missional church challenge planted churches to take their ministries and corporate identity seriously as they participate with God in making the Word known. Following Christ, churches have the capacity to speak to God in prayer, engage relationally within and outside their fellowship, and witness to the miracle of the incarnation as the Spirit reveals the Word to humanity. America's planted churches need a tangible example of missional church planting that embodies listening and responding, as well as a theologically sound means of assessing praxis. Protestant Christian theology has produced ample helpful resources to guide American church planting movements as they participate tangibly in the Spirit's work calling sustainable, theologically grounded missional churches into being. Out of this understanding of identity and callings, it is possible now to reflect more fully on actual practices and consider how churches might assess and, where needed, adjust them.

5
Practical Ways Forward for American Church Planting Movements

"We know that what we're doing isn't working, but we're not sure what else to do." My conversation with one church planter had taken a moving turn. As we spoke, the pressures and frustrations of his ministry felt as palpable as the lovely Florida breeze gracing our shaded outdoor table that afternoon. Attendance at his church had not recovered to pre-pandemic levels, and there were growing concerns about the budget. A recent staff meeting had been devoted to reviewing attendance statistics and discussing ways the church had operated in the past, hoping to find something, some idea, some strategy, some catchphrase, anything that might recreate former successes. This was a different time, though, which called for new ideas, he felt, but where to find them? Hearing him speak, I remembered a time when I was researching the history of church planting and examining the common instinct to turn to earlier models for inspiration. In response, an academic mentor said something that has haunted me ever since: "God doesn't lead his people 'back.' He leads them forward, and on to the day of the Lord." Learning from the past is a wise and valuable exercise; trying to recreate the past is a different impulse. Like the nation of Israel wandering in the Sinai desert, some American church planters have been tempted to go back, particularly in the complicated post-pandemic world. Many, though, like the one I spoke with, are really searching for concrete ways forward, for theologically grounded praxis that responds well to the present moment, embodies the hope of Christ's redemption, honors lessons learned, and moves practices closer to the beliefs and callings they hold most dear.

As we have seen, the Word indeed speaks, and it also listens and responds. As a creature of the Word, church bodies share a call to discern and proclaim the Word together in order that they might point humanity to Jesus's redemption. Planted churches have certainly taken their missional call to heart. Many operated out of a culture and operant missional ecclesiology that led them to favor an attractional missional model, where the chief attraction was a gathered service featuring high production values and an accessible sermon. The practical outcomes have been mixed, with compelling innovations in style developing alongside mounting pressure on pastors and mounting consumerism within the congregation. Under the influence of Church Growth Theory, churches have sometimes struggled to assess their ministries theologically or to identify more effective, theologically grounded forms of praxis.

This chapter will consider practical ways forward for planted churches and those who research them. Within Michael Moynagh's accounts of Fresh Expressions of Church, a UK-based church planting movement, we will begin to see a complementary model of missional church planting that takes seriously the relational dynamics of a God who speaks, listens, and responds to humanity.[1] Moynagh combines an insider's account of church planting praxis with theological reflection on their experiences.[2] His primary focus is the United Kingdom rather than the United States, but the postmodernist, post-Christendom context he envisions is very similar to the contexts many American churches hope to serve. Moynagh thus offers a practical, theologically grounded approach to church planting that honors the missional commitments of American church planting ministries. He describes churches as a nexus of four relational conversations: internal conversations within a local church, conversations between the church and God, conversations among churches, and conversations between the church and the world.[3] These four conversations sit well with the four Nicene marks of the church (one, holy, catholic, and apostolic), an important connection that Moynagh's published work has not explored to date.[4] Holding Moynagh's four conversations alongside the four Nicene marks of the church creates a helpful framework for evaluating missional ecclesial praxis in light of traditional Christian understandings of church. It is therefore possible for researchers and church planting ministries to assess the spiritual development of planted congregations by considering the extent to which each of a church's four defining relationships might be moving toward its corresponding Nicene mark. As we will see, this assessment framework is grounded in a more theologically robust missional ecclesiology than Church Growth Theory, and it also produces a more comprehensive and actionable picture of congregational life and praxis.

This chapter will address Osmer's fourth task of theological reflection: the pragmatic task.[5] Osmer intends for the pragmatic task to facilitate positive, practical changes in congregations in light of insights developed during the first three tasks of theological reflection.[6] To be truly practical, any recommendations must acknowledge churches' history, account for the context in which they minister, and be consistent with their theological traditions. Consequently, this chapter will develop practical implications of the theology that chapter 4 examined with an eye to the specific challenges and contextual features of American church planting movements that chapters 2 and 3 identified. This chapter will also offer initial evaluations of some common patterns in current American church planting praxis. By reexamining established patterns of praxis, evaluating a promising complementary approach to church planting, and describing a theologically grounded assessment method, this chapter will equip planted American churches and those who research them with resources that are truly practical.

One of the challenges inherent in Osmer's fourth task is that his overall method focuses on the experience of being "brought up short," which "tends to focus on occasions when there are problems in a pastoral context."[7] This is an important critique. By focusing on problems rather than healthy patterns of praxis, Osmer's method has "a tendency to dislocate theological reflection from the ordinary ways in which the Christian church is continually engaged in theology and practice."[8] Healthy churches cannot ignore problems, and some problems we have seen in recent years have been tragic indeed. Problems underscore the need that planted churches have for theologically grounded praxis that will empower them to function as healthy, life-giving missional congregations. Consequently, the aim of this chapter is not simply to address problems, but also to describe theologically grounded, well-researched, practically feasible ways forward for planted American congregations. As Osmer rightly indicates in his description of the pragmatic task, enacting transformative change requires courageous leadership.[9] This chapter will therefore highlight key implications for church leaders alongside broader recommendations for congregations as a whole. Planted churches can indeed move forward together in hope, honoring both their ecclesial identity and their missional callings as the Spirit leads them to minister in ever-changing contexts.

A Complementary Approach: Planting Fresh Expressions of Church

The church is a creature of God's relational Word, and, as chapter 4 explored, New Testament accounts describe the church emerging in dynamic moments of speaking, listening, and responding relationally. Fresh Expressions of Church, a church planting movement that originated in the United Kingdom, offers a glimpse into how contemporary congregations might embody this understanding of missional church identity. Moynagh's accounts of the operant missional ecclesiology of Fresh Expressions frame the practice of church planting squarely within the context of relational conversations with God, one another, and humanity. We will therefore consider Moynagh's theological reflections on missional church praxis and identify helpful resources it offers that honor American planted churches' callings and convictions.

Fresh Expressions of Church originated in the United Kingdom around the turn of the millennium as a church planting and renewal movement, primarily but not exclusively operating within the Church of England.[10] The term "Fresh Expressions" first appeared in *Mission-Shaped Church*, a 2004 report on missional churches in England.[11] One early and widely quoted description of the movement explained that Fresh Expressions of Church aimed to offer "a form of church for our changing culture established primarily for the benefit of people who are not members of any church."[12] This formulation is highly consistent with the missional vision of planted American churches, which similarly hope to offer freshly contextualized forms of church with a particular eye to unchurched people.[13] The authors of *Mission-Shaped Church* note that they chose to call this movement "Fresh Expressions of Church" in the hopes that this name would "carry less baggage" than another term in common use: "Emerging church."[14] This note underscores important similarities between Fresh Expressions of Church and the ECM. Fresh Expressions and Emerging churches are roughly contemporaneous, and both attend to the particularities of planting churches within postmodernist, post-Christendom cultures.[15] The most important difference is that Fresh Expressions primarily took shape within an existing denomination of established state churches, while the ECM was far less institutionalized. Fresh Expressions congregations have become relatively common in the United Kingdom, so much so that it has been said that "no self-respecting diocese is without one, and in most cases, each will have several."[16] By contrast, Fresh Expressions has been much slower to take root within the United States, while the ECM found more traction.[17] In spite of these differences, Fresh Expressions of Church substantially parallels recent developments within American church planting movements, underscoring potential compatibilities in terms of approach and internal culture.

The term "Fresh Expressions of Church" bears further examination because it offers important insights about the operant missional ecclesiology of the movement as a whole. *Mission-Shaped Church* argues that one marker of a missional church is "inculturation," defined as a "three-way conversation" in which

> [t]he conversation partners are: the historic gospel, uniquely revealed in Holy Scripture and embodied in the Catholic creeds; the Church, which is engaging in mission, with its own particular culture and history; the culture within which the gospel is being shared.[18]

Fresh Expressions of Church thus defines itself as a conversational interaction, much as the implicit metaphor in the term "Expression" suggests. The "Fresh" in Fresh Expressions has rightly worried some critics of the movement, who fear that it belies little more than an unhealthy attraction to novelty or a desire to chase fast-moving trends.[19] In light of Fresh Expressions' implicit conversational metaphors, though, a "fresh expression" instead points to the active engagement, flexibility, and improvisational dynamics inherent in any genuine conversation.[20] When a healthy conversation develops, participants expect each other to offer something "fresh" that both moves the exchange forward and maintains logical consistency with what has already been said. Merely repeating previously spoken words rarely serves as an adequate conversational response; instead, thoughtful listening and responding calls for something "fresh" to be spoken as conversation partners continue to engage with one another. The conversational dynamics implicit in the term "Fresh Expressions" thus encourage "freshness" not for the sake of novelty, but to underscore their interest in responding at once to the gospel, their own ecclesial traditions, and their surrounding culture. Fresh Expressions is an approach to church planting that takes Christian tradition seriously while also encouraging creative contributions that empower congregations to respond faithfully to ever-changing contexts. Creative relational exchanges are at the heart of their operant missional ecclesiology.

Michael Moynagh has developed the most extensive articulation of the operant missional ecclesiology of Fresh Expressions to date, further clarifying the initial picture of the movement that *Mission-Shaped Church* offered. Moynagh describes church as "an event in the context of four sets of relationships," namely the church's relationships "to the Godhead, between members of the local church, to the world, and between each part and the whole body."[21] At times, Moynagh tellingly shifts from describing four "relationships" to describing four "conversations." For example, he writes, "The *conversations* that make up the church are with the Trinity, with the world, between different parts of the wider church and within each ecclesial gathering."[22] These four conversation partners are identical to the four categories of relationships that Moynagh cites as defining a missional church. Moynagh also writes that the church's four sets of relationships are "joined together in the community's sequence of conversations."[23] For this reason, he then insists: "The kingdom-shaped church is in perpetual conversation about the kingdom and with the world. These conversations are part of an ongoing series of interactions that are not just at the heart of church, but constitute its very existence."[24] The connections Moynagh draws between a church's relationships and its conversations are never fully articulated, but they are intuitively logical. Conversations are a common, practical means of building relationships and a helpful barometer of how relationships are evolving. Moynagh's missional ecclesiology thus identifies four categories of relationships that define a church and ties them to four conversations that shape ecclesial life and mission.

Conversations are not just a metaphor; they inform much of the actual missional ecclesial praxis within Fresh Expressions of Church. Those seeking to start a new Fresh Expression of Church are called to prioritize listening in tangible ways. The authors of *Mission-Shaped Church* cited the "principle of listening" as foundational to their own research and described Fresh Expressions of Church as an act of "double listening," attending at once to God and to their local context.[25] According to Moynagh, planting a church requires "listening to God and to the people the founding community feels called to serve."[26] Fresh Expressions therefore adopts a "serving first" model, in which the first step in planting a new church is lovingly listening to people within a local area.[27] For this reason, Fresh Expressions generally begins not by identifying or opening a worship space, but by creating space for actual conversations to develop between Christians and those outside the church. This often involves an ongoing activity that fosters regular interactions between Christians and others in their community; examples include a café for parents dropping off children at a church-run school, a community book club, or a father-son football league at a local park.[28] Listening, according to Moynagh, is an actively receptive process that requires building healthy relationships over time.[29] By creating space and time for genuine conversations to unfold, the hope is that Christians will not only build relationships with others, but that eventually spiritual conversations, discipleship, and even acts of worship might arise organically, giving birth to a new church.[30] One need not adopt Moynagh's approach fully to appreciate the missional value he assigns to Christians engaging in regular conversations that build relationships between a church and a wider community. Indeed, some American churches have even been planted out of projects that began as parachurch organizations offering loving service to people within local communities.[31] Moynagh's "serving first" model faithfully sends the church out into the world, pointing others to a Word that hears and responds to humanity.

The operant missional ecclesiology at work within Fresh Expressions is somewhat different from that shared by many planted American churches, which have typically focused on creating sites for attractive, relevant gospel preaching and gathered worship.[32] The missional motion of American church planting has often been attractional, focused on drawing people into church, while that of Fresh Expressions is more incarnational, with a focus on carrying the Word outward and into a community. Indeed, one early description of a "Fresh Expression of Church" specified that it "will come into being primarily through the principles of listening, service, incarnational mission and making disciples."[33] This description emphasizes that a church's prayers for and service to a community are central to its missional witness and identity, much as Barth and Bonhoeffer insisted.[34] As chapter 4 argued, the Gospel of John shows Jesus repeatedly engaged in real, relational conversations with others outside his immediate band of disciples; Fresh Expressions' approach similarly aims to listen and engage with people in a wider community so that they might encounter Christ's transformative love within their own contexts. The aims are thus similar to those of many planted American churches, but the process and sequence look somewhat different.

Moynagh's account of Fresh Expressions' operant missional ecclesiology has important qualities that make it potentially helpful to American church planters. Moynagh's vision of a missional church specifically accounts for its own internal relationships as well as its relationships with God and with other churches, helpfully encouraging planted churches that they are called to more than just evangelism.[35] The balance Moynagh describes between these four relationships obviates a common temptation within planted American churches: instrumentalizing other ecclesial relationships for the sake of evangelism. Moynagh's ecclesiology enacts important theological insights from Bonhoeffer and Newbigin, who similarly insisted that the "community of saints" must never become a means to an end, even if the end is as noble as evangelism.[36] As Barth reminded readers, gospel preaching cannot alone reveal the Word to humanity; preaching instead works together with Scripture, revelation, and other forms of churchly proclamation to reveal the Word.[37] For this reason, a missional church that hopes to participate in the revelation of God's Word will benefit by empowering its congregation to understand, discern, and proclaim the Word together, much as Moynagh's model encourages. The Jerusalem Council in Acts 15 demonstrates how listening to other Christians can indeed reveal important insights about the Word and give churches better guidance on how they might embody the Word within a particular missional setting. Within Fresh Expressions of Church, American congregations find important reflections on the significance of honoring the church body and developing balanced ministries that make the Word both audible and visible in local communities.

By framing his vision of missional church in terms of relational conversations, Moynagh also avoids "blueprint ecclesiologies," understandings of church that are so idealistic or abstract that they cannot address the human realities of ecclesial life.[38] Barth and Bonhoeffer insisted that churches testify to the reality of Christ's incarnation by combining the Spirit's ministry with genuinely human speech and actions.[39] Moynagh's emphasis on conversations helps to ground his ecclesiology within tangible human contexts. Conversations are a practical experience that most people understand well. Conversations can take a variety of forms, depending on the participants and the context in which they occur. To engage in a genuine conversation, one must be prepared to listen to the other and respond to what is said. A conversation is not wholly scripted, though some established cultural patterns will guide the interaction. Like relationships, conversations can be healthy or unhealthy at any given moment. The same conversation might even feel fruitful to one partner and frustrating to another, requiring careful attention to all participants. Many of these same dynamics are at play within planted churches, where specific forms vary, cultural patterns guide ministry, and a variety of participants contribute and respond to a shared dynamic experience. Moynagh's missional ecclesiology thus has the advantage of drawing attention to God's relational Word and also to the concrete and varied experiences of human beings within churches. This ecclesiology does not unduly idealize churches; it implicitly encourages them to assess their core relationships, be aware of varied participants and contexts, and recall that both human and divine agents are involved in their fellowship.

It is also important to acknowledge that Fresh Expressions' operant missional ecclesiology has some limitations. Much like Luther's emphasis on physically hearing the Word, Fresh Expressions' implicit emphasis on conversation risks ableism.[40] Churches that adopt it must therefore remain sensitive to the variety of methods, verbal and nonverbal, by which people communicate and build relationships. Emphasizing conversation also risks minimizing the significance of nonverbal sacraments. Moynagh argues that even nonverbal rites like the Eucharist must be understood in the context of a church's verbal exchanges:

> Understanding church in terms of practices—of gathering round the word, celebrating the sacraments and other expected behaviours—fails to do justice to how any one practice originates in conversation, is constantly being defined through conversation, and has a meaning that varies, if only in tiny degrees, from one conversation to another.[41]

By drawing attention to what people say and hear around the sacraments, Moynagh rightly reminds Christians that sacramental practices do not exist in a verbal vacuum. A church's liturgy generally includes specific explanations and declarations that differentiate ordinary washing from baptism, or ordinary bread and wine consumption from the Eucharist. Moynagh, though, arguably diminishes the nonverbal, embodied qualities of the sacraments, which have their own significance. Jenson even called them "visible words" that attest tangibly to the Spirit's work within the church.[42] Churches must therefore attend thoughtfully to ways that verbal communication affects people's experience of sacraments and ecclesial relationships without overlooking the significance of nonverbal communication or embodied sacramental practices. In other words, verbal and nonverbal elements of church are both significant, and neither can be safely ignored.

Another critique of Moynagh's missional ecclesiology is that it risks reinforcing ecclesiocentrism.[43] The four conversations that Moynagh describes do not include God's own conversations with the world, leaving one to imagine that all interactions between humanity and God are mediated by the church. On one level, this is consistent with Bonhoeffer's emphasis on the idea *extra ecclesiam nulla salus*.[44] It also sits well with many missional church advocates, who seek to preserve a place for churches within the *missio Dei*.[45] Hoekendijk, though, rightly criticizes ecclesiocentric missions, reminding churches that God is always at work in the world and insisting that a church's mission must always point to God's redemption of the entire cosmos.[46] Important threads of Hoekendijk's critique have become surprisingly palatable to American church planters in recent years. Canadian SBC-affiliated church planter Henry Blackaby similarly insisted that God is always at work in the world, and a Christian's calling is therefore to discern God's own work and participate in it.[47] Blackaby's widely read popular works thus effectively repackaged key components of Hoekendijk's critique in a form that American church planters have widely embraced. Churches must not overestimate human agency in mission, nor underestimate God's capacity to speak to people who are outside a church's fellowship, inviting them to receive the redemptive Word. God calls churches to participate in mission, but they must always remember that it remains the *missio Dei*.

A more significant disadvantage of Moynagh's missional ecclesiology is that it minimizes important differences that distinguish the various conversation partners. Moynagh's model makes no distinction between ordained leaders and lay church members, subsuming both under the broad category "conversations within each ecclesial gathering."[48] This move risks obscuring genuine power imbalances that have at times created serious problems within planted American congregations.[49] In order to address such situations, we must remain alert to their potential. Secular studies have widely acknowledged that leaders' words are perceived differently than others, and biblical texts rightly encourage churches to select their leaders with care.[50] By contrast, Moynagh adds that while the church's four conversations "can be demarcated for analytical purposes . . . in real life . . . they are deeply entwined and enrich each other."[51] Moynagh thus suggests that the four conversation partners that comprise a church can easily be conflated. Under this perspective, it becomes far too easy to imagine, for example, that a pastor speaks with God's own voice, a perception that can lead to spiritual abuse.[52] It is therefore vitally important that churches remain mindful of power imbalances and aware of the ever-present human frailty within churches. The four conversation partners, and those comprised within various categories, are not identical.

Perhaps the most problematic feature of Moynagh's missional ecclesiology is that it risks minimizing the church's most important conversation partner: the triune God. Moynagh insists, "One set of relations must not take precedence over the others, not even direct relations with the Trinity."[53] It would be right to say that none of a church's relationships should be neglected, but if the Holy Spirit sustains churches, which exist as the body of Christ for the glory of God, then surely interactions with a triune God deserve precedence. Even Moynagh eventually acknowledges that what makes church "distinct from other organisations is that it is embraced within the conversations of the Trinity."[54] This reality is particularly evident in Acts, where the Spirit infuses all four categories of the early church's conversations: conversations within the local church (Acts 2:4), prayerful exchanges with God (Acts 4:31), interactions with other churches (Acts 8:14–17), and evangelistic conversations with people outside the church (Acts 2:4–13, 17–18; 4:8; 7:55; 8:29). It is therefore essential to emphasize the defining importance of a church's conversations with God, which give a distinctive character, power, and purpose to all of a church's relationships.

While not without limitations, Fresh Expressions of Church offers American church planters a helpful example of how they might embody a balanced missional ecclesiology. Moynagh's account of Fresh Expressions of Church reframes the practice of planting churches as a set of relationships which everyday conversations will build and sustain. Moynagh describes a balanced operant missional ecclesiology that is replete with reminders of how and why churches must listen well. As Fresh Expressions' methodology reflects, Jesus went out from his immediate fellowship of disciples to hear and engage with others, and missional churches are called to do likewise. This approach offers a helpful way forward to planted churches that have overemphasized gathered services and assigned too much of their missional focus to preaching alone. Moynagh's accounts of Fresh Expressions also remind churches that they need not choose between developing their own fellowship and building life-giving relationships with people who are unchurched. A conversation, after all, requires a healthy balance of speaking, listening, and responding, and so does participation in a missional church. Times of prayer and listening can be at least as valuable to the community as preaching. Indeed, simply listening to God and to others, as Fresh Expressions encourages, frees planted churches from having to intuit fresh ways to remain "relevant" in ever-changing contexts. This approach is about relationships, not performances, and so it offers a helpful counterbalance to some of the more challenging realities that have developed within the operant missional ecclesiology shared by many planted American churches.

Assessment Beyond the Numbers: Ecclesial Relationships and the Nicene Marks

Planted American churches have implicitly enacted the spirit of the Reformers' charge *ecclesia semper reformanda* by refining the look and feel of their gathered services, seeking ever more effective ways of communicating the gospel in a rapidly changing culture. Unfortunately, without clear operant understandings of what "church" actually is or how God calls churches to engage in the *missio Dei*, planted churches may struggle to identify and evaluate effective reforms. Church Growth Theory offered a metric that promised to identify effective praxis: church attendance. Though this metric has proved to be methodologically and theologically questionable, its tantalizing clarity transformed attendance statistics into a de facto measure of effectiveness in many American congregations. The desire to assess current praxis and reform it as needed was a healthy one; the specific changes that Church Growth Theory encouraged were not always. As chapter 2 explored, focus on attendance growth placed unsustainable pressure on pastors to draw crowds, and serious problems sometimes resulted. Planted churches need a better way to assess praxis, one which is more consistent with Christian theological understandings of a church's identity and callings. As we will see, Moynagh's account of Fresh Expressions offers resources for developing precisely such an assessment.

Moynagh derives the four relationships that are central to a church's identity from a passage in *Mission-Shaped Church*, which identifies four "directions" along which a missional church will "journey."[55] The authors of *Mission-Shaped Church* write that a missional church will move "up" toward God in holiness, "in" toward one another in Christian unity, "out" toward the world in mission, and "of" or from other churches in catholicity.[56] Tellingly, the authors of *Mission-Shaped Church* derive these movements from reflection on the four Nicene marks: oneness, holiness, catholicity, and apostolicity.[57] The four categories of relationships that Moynagh identifies as central to a church's identity thus stem indirectly from reflection on the four Nicene marks of church. Moynagh's work accurately identifies the most natural ways that planted missional churches will embody the four Nicene marks, but it overlooks the value of reflecting on the marks themselves. As previous research has also proposed, the four Nicene marks of church can offer a helpful, theologically grounded focus for assessing praxis within planted churches.[58] While no congregation will embody the four marks perfectly, every congregation can move toward them as they actively work to foster oneness, holiness, catholicity, and apostolicity. The question then becomes where to look within a planted church to spot possible movement toward or away from each of the Nicene marks. The four conversations that Moynagh identifies as central to a planted church's identity offer a helpful place to look: a church's actual interactions within its own fellowship, with God, with other churches, and with those outside the faith. Together, the four Nicene marks and Moynagh's four-conversation model of missional church create a practical, theologically grounded framework for developing a qualitative evaluation of church planting praxis.

Using this framework, the four Nicene marks of church clarify the qualities which healthy churches aim to cultivate, while Moynagh's four sets of relational conversations identify specific places to observe and foster the development of each quality. Conversations within a church bring members into healthy Christian relationships with one another, moving the congregation toward oneness. Conversations with God remind the church of its connection to a holy God, who sanctifies and sustains them, moving them toward holiness. Conversations with other churches develop a shared understanding that every congregation participates in a global body of Christians, moving them toward catholicity. Conversations with the world make the Word visible and audible within local communities, moving the church outward and fulfilling its apostolic calling. Combining the Nicene marks with Moynagh's four conversations thus gives direction and precision to a church's assessment of its own key relationships. In assessing the church's oneness, for example, a congregation can attend to its own internal conversations and consider how well they are fostering unity. If people are engaging constructively with one another despite differences, then the congregation is moving toward oneness. If, by contrast, the church's internal conversations are splintering into smaller, mutually exclusive circles of interaction, more work is needed to foster congregational unity. By interweaving discussions of a church's four relationships with language about "four conversations," Moynagh's work indirectly suggests formal and informal methods that might be used to assess the ministries of planted churches.

This assessment framework offers tangible, research-based methods for assessment and practical, theologically grounded remedies for any challenges it identifies. In recent years, theologians, practical theologians, and secular analysts of organizational dynamics have drawn helpful attention to the importance of actual conversations.[59] Indeed, much qualitative research depends on attentive conversations, as researchers engage directly with people in specific communities and observe their shared practices and speech patterns. Such methods are uniquely well suited to examining missional church ministries. As the previous chapter highlighted, the church is a creature of the Word, which does more than speak: the Word made flesh in Christ also listened and engaged with humanity, much as a thoughtful conversation partner would do. Because church is a creature of the Word, churches since the time of Acts have depended on conversations within and outside their fellowship to discern the Word. Consequently, it benefits both churches and those who research them to consider who a church's current conversation partners are and how their conversations are developing. If one conversation partner is saying too much without listening, or perhaps listening without speaking or responding, restoring a healthy balance of speech, response, and listening will often prove helpful. Conversations can be revelatory, and fostering healthy conversations can identify important challenges and move relationships forward.

Of all the church's conversation partners, the most important is God. We must accept, though, that conversations with God cannot be assessed using exactly the same methods we use to assess human conversations, marking a practical limitation of this method. For example, Moynagh describes qualitative researchers studying conversations within one missional gathering to determine whether or not it had become a mature, fully formed church.[60] Such studies will often yield helpful information about human interactions, but qualitative research by itself cannot capture every dimension of God's interactions with a congregation. Fortunately, Jesus promised the gift of the Spirit, who would reveal God's truth to believers, speak God's own words for God's glory (John 16:13–15), and remind believers what God has already said and done in Christ (John 14:26). As chapter 4 argued, the Spirit's activity at Pentecost brought the church into being (Acts 2). The Spirit's work includes conviction of sin and righteousness (John 16:8–11). Missional churches that take seriously the idea of *ecclesia semper reformanda* will find the soundest partner in the Holy Spirit, who actively empowers churches to discern God's voice and identify areas where change is needed.

The subsections that follow will illustrate how this assessment method works by reexamining common patterns within the operant missional ecclesiology of American church planting movements, as described in chapters 2 and 3, in light of Moynagh's four conversations and the four Nicene marks of the church. This material will be organized according to the traditional order of the four Nicene marks: one, holy, catholic, and apostolic. Each subsection will briefly explain the Nicene mark, then examine the corresponding relationship from Moynagh's model to consider ways planted American churches have and have not been moving toward the mark. As we will see, this assessment framework offers the potential for comprehensive evaluation and points to practical ways forward.

Credo unam ecclesiam: *Conversations Within the Local Church*

The Nicene quality of oneness speaks to the unity of a local congregation. Oneness does not mean that congregations are uniform. In any healthy congregation, there will be different opinions, perspectives, and gifts, much as the biblical metaphor of one body with many different parts implies.[61] The book of Ephesians offers particularly clear support for the idea that churches include people of different racial, political, and/or spiritual backgrounds who become "one body," with "one Spirit," "one hope," "one Lord," "one faith," "one baptism," and "one God" (4:4–5).[62] Though this language of oneness in Ephesians might be at least partly aspirational, Bonhoeffer actively borrowed from Ephesians 4:4–7 when explaining to American congregations why the Christian bonds they share are more substantive than the national identities which divided them in wartime.[63] Elsewhere, Bonhoeffer even defines church unity as a "multiplicity and community of its members," using body imagery from 1 Corinthians 12 to stress that "each retains its own identity" even though "they all have an identity of their own only as members of one body."[64] In looking for evidence of oneness within a church's internal relationships, then, one does not expect uniformity. Healthy relational conversations indeed presume some diversity among participants. As Pattison rightly says, in any conversation there is a presumption that "participants start from very different assumptions and understandings."[65] By its nature, "[the] concept of conversation does not necessarily imply that participants end up agreeing on every point," either.[66] In seeking unity, then, the hope is to find evidence that a diverse body of Christians is actively engaging with one another as members of a shared fellowship.

The expectation of inherent diversity among members of one local body of Christ creates a powerful argument against planted churches adopting the HUP. Dividing the church according to demographics, or allowing natural, fallen human affinities to foster a homogeneous congregation sets a dangerous precedent: allowing believers to remake a church community according to their own image.[67] As we have seen, in some planted churches, individualistic consumerism creates an environment where people who are not part of a "target" audience or prevalent demographic group could easily feel out of place. By contrast, God's own redemptive mission invites every tribe, nation, and tongue to unite in a chorus of praise (Rev 7:9). Congregational diversity also attests to the reality of Christ's redemption at the cross, creating a new community where genuine differences can be reconciled (Eph 2:11–22). Where there is only one perspective, true Nicene oneness will remain aspirational. Where genuine diversity of thought, giftedness, perspective, and/or background flourishes, a congregation's oneness makes God's own redemption evident in a powerful way.

In light of Nicene unity, the emphasis on small group ministries that has become prevalent in many planted congregations bears some reexamination. In planted American churches, particularly larger ones, members often find the most opportunity to build relationships within small group ministries.[68] If there is little opportunity for members to interact with church members outside of their small groups, the oneness of the church can easily struggle. For this reason, Bonhoeffer wrote with concern about the rise of "small private gatherings" within churches for "prayer, scripture reading, receiving the sacraments, as well as exercising church discipline."[69] Indeed, many of these have been common functions of small group ministries, particularly in larger congregations, where volunteer small group leaders often assume responsibilities for pastoral care and discipleship. Such groups, Bonhoeffer noted, can foster or exacerbate divisions within a congregation,[70] effectively becoming exclusive cliques. This risk seems particularly acute in planted churches which apply the HUP by organizing demographically homogeneous small groups.[71] As Barth says of churches in a different context,

> There is no justification theological, spiritual, or biblical for the existence of a plurality of churches genuinely separated in this way and mutually excluding one another internally and therefore externally. A plurality of churches in this sense means a plurality of lords, a plurality of spirits, a plurality of gods.[72]

Demographically homogeneous small groups risk creating precisely this impression of a "plurality of churches" within a single congregation, which remain "genuinely separated" and "mutually excluding [of] one another." At some point, planted churches need opportunities for meaningful relationships to form beyond small groups, particularly if small groups are homogeneous. Regular fellowship meals or social gatherings where members can interact more widely will foster congregational oneness, as will mission, ministry, and service teams that prioritize heterogeneity. By creating substantive opportunities for members from different backgrounds to develop ongoing relationships, congregations will move toward Nicene oneness.[73]

It is also important that planted churches consider carefully the design of gathered worship spaces, which might unintentionally discourage people from forming relationships within the congregation. Some planted churches have either adapted or borrowed space from cinemas, for example, while many others have integrated elements from entertainment venues, like projection screens or advanced lighting.[74] Such features create familiar, comfortable environments for many modern Americans, but as chapter 3 explained, they also carry cultural baggage. A movie theater, for example, is designed to actively discourage conversations, which are deemed a distraction; at best, people might chat with those they accompanied to the theater before or after a film. People generally do not make new friends at the cinema, nor do they expect any substantive connections with the people they see on screens. In such a setting, it is hard to imagine either fruitful internal conversations or a spirit of oneness among those gathered. Planted churches, particularly those that hope to welcome Americans with little church background, must therefore weigh carefully the design and cultural associations of these spaces. If a space indeed appears to discourage interactions, churches might need to do more to actively encourage them. Something as simple as reminding people to greet one another or pray with others during a worship service can foster helpful interactions. A robust coffee hour before or after services can contribute substantially to ecclesial life. Planted churches have long been mindful of barriers that might keep people from attending, and rightly so.[75] It is now equally important to attend to unintended cultural cues that create barriers against Nicene oneness.

In describing congregational oneness, the first Nicene mark does not distinguish pastors from the congregation, nor does Moynagh's missional ecclesiology. While churches must remain aware of potential power imbalances, Nicene oneness also carries the helpful reminder that pastors are included within the church's one fellowship. The pastoral office does not obviate any Christian's need for the care, mutual accountability, encouragement, and spiritual discernment of a church body. American church planting movements have rightly taken measures to remove any perception of ceremonial isolation around pastors, such as eschewing robes and clerical titles and encouraging informality in services.[76] Their overemphasis on preaching, though, unwittingly raised even more substantive barriers between pastor and congregation. As churches gradually reassigned pastoral care and relational responsibilities to other staff or volunteer leaders, pastors effectively became distant speakers, with fewer opportunities to build relationships within their congregation. Spaces and practices that framed pastors as professional entertainers only furthered the growing divide between pastor and congregation, making it even harder for pastors to access the support and accountability that all Christians need. By contrast, in allowing pastors of planted congregations opportunities to share preaching duties with other staff and/or lay volunteers, churches create time for pastors to build relationships. Pastors certainly need time to hear and respond to the cares and concerns of the congregation, much as Christ's own pattern of ministry reflects. When pastors regularly interact with their congregation, and relationships of mutual trust and concern form, communal discernment of the Word in the spirit of *sola scriptura* becomes far more realistic and natural. Ministry thus becomes more sustainable and more effective when pastors enjoy regular, healthy, relational conversations with their congregation.

Rick and Kay Warren have told a personal story that illustrates what this might look like in the context of a large planted church.[77] As the Warrens tell it, on the day they lost their son to suicide, members of their small group physically surrounded them.[78] These loving people were there the moment the Warrens heard the awful news and stayed with them overnight, sleeping on sofas and floors so that they would not feel alone.[79] As Rick Warren recalls, "it was their ministry of presence," and it helped sustain the couple when they were in the deep pain of fresh grief.[80] Their story echoes Bonhoeffer's description of a church body's movements during a service of remembrance, when "Christ disguised as the church" comes to the home of a bereaved family and becomes a tangible sign of God's loving presence among them.[81] It is remarkable that the Warrens had a small group that felt authorized to minister to them so intimately. Were they simply seen as distant celebrity speakers, others would have surely felt awkward coming to them in such a moment. The immediate care and compassion that the Warrens received bespeaks long-standing relationships built through many honest mutual conversations. All pastors need the care and compassion of a church, and not only in tragic moments. When the church body functions as one caring community, it enfolds everyone involved, including the pastor, and points humanity toward the ever-present love of Christ.

Planted churches cannot allow the oneness of their body to be reduced to cliquishness or subsumed by consumerist entertainment models. All Christians need time and space to interact within their church as they corporately discern God's voice and encourage one another in faithfulness. In some cases, reconfiguring physical spaces or rethinking small group ministries might encourage better relationships and in turn promote oneness. Allocating time for pastors to listen and engage with others as part of a unified church body makes their ministry more sustainable and creates space for corporate discernment to develop. Attending to a church's internal conversations will reveal practices that are drawing them into one body or drifting away from true oneness. Congregations need ongoing reminders to attend and care for one another, as part of one body moving toward Nicene unity.

Credo sanctam ecclesiam: *Conversations with God*

Nicene holiness is not a function of human beings within the church, but reflects the presence of a holy God, who creates and sustains the church.[82] God is therefore the church's most significant conversation partner. Planted churches that espouse this belief have sometimes focused attention nevertheless on more humanly inspired approaches to church like marketing and branding strategies or growth statistics. These other voices have created tremendous, inappropriate pressure on many churches, and the unintended consequences have at times led to a serious compromise of their corporate witness. By contrast, attending to God's voice will foster congregational holiness, reminding planted churches of the power of the Spirit's ministry within their midst.

Churches particularly need to attend to God's voice when initially planting a new congregation. As Bonhoeffer explains, God alone gives the "order to make some historical place into God's place," adding, "The church which is aware of this waits for the word that transforms it into God's place in the world."[83] "Waiting for the word" requires prayerful patience and listening in order to discern God's hand at work in a local community. As Bonhoeffer rightly insists, by "waiting on God's choice" when deciding where to plant a new church, a congregation "avoids being established in some privileged place."[84] By contrast, strategic analysis of potential new sites has become common in church planting literature. Identifying areas with "receptive populations" where churches might expect to grow quickly was a thread of McGavran's work which found wide resonance.[85] Cities, for example, have long been cited as a particularly promising strategic location for planting churches.[86] Unfortunately, these applications of Church Growth Theory often appear functionally atheistic, focusing more on sociological research or marketing studies than the Spirit's voice. David Olson critiqued this approach, concerned that it risks unduly aligning Christian churches with wealthy, educated, and influential urban populations while neglecting struggling and rural communities.[87] Lesslie Newbigin and Michael Green similarly worried about the potential for Western churches to develop a "Constantinian Captivity" to spheres of cultural and political influence.[88] Such concerns are well founded; seeking a fast-growing, "receptive," or influential population risks reinforcing existing patterns of privilege found in the wider culture, potentially compromising the church's holiness. It is therefore important to reassure planted churches that the Spirit leads congregations. Humans might labor to plant or nurture a church, but church is ultimately a creation of the Spirit, something that only God can truly establish or grow.[89] Planted churches that misattribute their identity to a founding pastor are missing important opportunities to celebrate God's own presence. Repentance and faith in any individual heart is properly understood as the work of the Spirit, not the product of human strategies or persuasion.[90] Patiently listening for the Spirit's voice locates the project of church planting within God's holy, redemptive mission and reminds individuals and congregations to remain in regular conversation with a holy God.

Churches moving toward Nicene holiness need regular interactions with God. This means that planted churches cannot sacrifice Christian worship, not even for the sake of evangelistic mission.[91] Worship is central to the life of any church, drawing the congregation into corporate interactions with God through time-honored liturgies, readings, and prayers. Participatory sung worship and responsive prayers engage the whole congregation in these interactions. Such practices enrich a church's proclamation by demonstrating that God indeed listens and invites Christians to "approach the throne of grace with confidence" (Heb 4:16).[92] Jenson adds that the beauty of sung worship points to God's own creativity, writing:

> That the proclamation and prayer of the church regularly bursts into beauty, indeed seems to insist on music and choreography and

> setting, is not an adventitious hankering to decorate. A congregation singing a hymn of praise to the Father is doubling the Son's praise, and the surge of rhythm and melody is the surge of the Spirit's glorification of the Father and Son.[93]

According to Jenson, such moments not only mark human response to God, but echo the Son and Spirit's own praises of the Father.[94] Corporate worship thus creates an audible reflection of God's majesty and creativity. Participatory worship also allows humans to respond to God, as Christians together demonstrate their "enjoyment of God" and "are taken into the triune singing. Perhaps we may say we are allowed to double the parts."[95] The beauty of such an exchange is palpable, and points to the beauty of the Word, by whom all things were created. This is why Warren rightly insists that people who are not Christians can experience something of God's presence by observing Christian worship.[96] As Christian worship draws a church into conversation with a holy God, it allows the church to echo God's own voice and respond together to the beauty and creativity of God's grace.

The rise of ancient-future practices in planted congregations, as discussed in chapter 2, marks a commendable effort to strengthen churches' conversations with God. Ancient-future practices draw heavily on meditative, contemplative practices and so create space for individuals to listen to God.[97] Teaching people how to attend to God's voice is an important function of any church. In *Sanctorum Communio*, Bonhoeffer reminds readers that the Spirit addresses individuals within a church, leading them into a place of solitude before God.[98] Churches encourage this kind of healthy solitude even during gathered services by including time for silent individual prayers. Bonhoeffer describes the importance of an individual's relationship with a holy God, writing, "Whoever cannot be alone should beware of community."[99] Individual experiences with God empower corporate faith, offering the church a tangible witness to God's sustaining grace.[100] Bonhoeffer adds, though, "Whoever cannot stand being in community should beware being alone."[101] Individual times of prayerful conversation with God are vitally important. Allowing time for individuals to share what they have heard from God through ancient-future practices, or any other means, creates equally important opportunities for congregations to practice corporate discernment. Like the Jerusalem Council demonstrates, individual encounters with God often make more sense when Christians discuss them together.[102] Patterns within individual encounters help a congregation to discern the Spirit's leading, as they did in Acts 15, identifying new areas of missional calling and fruitful applications of scriptural truth. These need time and space to be discerned well. Ancient-future practices therefore may be helpful, particularly when churches also create space to discern and celebrate God's voice together.

Preaching has long been an important means by which churches encourage people to engage with the Word. The space and time many planted congregations devote to preaching is staggering. Some churches have equipped their buildings with elaborate multimedia "stages" in place of pulpits and built "auditoriums" in place of sanctuaries.[103] Mars Hill Church is an extreme example; weekly sermons there were simulcast across multiple locations and could last well over an hour.[104] Mars Hill, though, was not an outlier so much as an exaggeration of a common pattern. Willow Creek's Seeker Sensitive services, for example, largely followed Billy Graham's pattern and designed the entire meeting to heighten responses to an evangelistic sermon.[105] In such a context, pastors might easily feel like a one-man or one-woman band, performing in order to draw a crowd. In reality, the full church body shares a calling to proclaim the Word. As we have seen, proclamation includes preaching, and it also includes prayer, service, and other acts of listening and responding to human needs.[106] By devoting more time in gathered services to prayer and contemplation, planted churches subtly reinforce a belief that most would readily espouse: all Christians are called to attend to God's voice. Testimonies and stories from the wider congregation create space for planted churches to discern the Spirit's hand working in their midst. Even something as simple as praying for the pastor before the start of the sermon subtly reminds everyone, including the pastor, that she or he depends on the Spirit to make the Word audible. Under the Spirit's leadership, churches hope to collectively discern and proclaim the Word, as chapter 4 explained. Shifting some of the focus from the pastor's voice to God's returns attention to its rightful place.

A missional ecclesiology that prioritizes the church's corporate conversations with God will begin to approach the pastoral office somewhat differently than many planted churches have. As Newbigin writes, "The priesthood of the ordained ministry is to enable, not remove, the priesthood of the whole church."[107] Churches that embody a shared belief in a priesthood of all believers will come to treat their pastor less as a solo speaker and more as a discussion moderator. A moderator is often very helpful, especially in conversations with multiple partners. Moderators encourage everyone to attend to the variety of voices present and draw out any that might have gone quiet. A moderator is never expected to carry the whole interaction. In the same way, pastors cannot carry the entire weight of a church's interactions, but can encourage church members to attend to one another and to God. Another helpful analogy is to imagine the pastor not as a one-man or one-woman band, but as an orchestra conductor. A conductor is essential to an orchestral performance. Conductors coordinate the timing and expression of all the musicians, drawing their individual performances together into a single harmonious concert. The art of conducting therefore requires listening carefully to those present, and also minding the music written by the composer. The conductor is not the composer, any more than the pastor is the author and sustainer of a church. Nor is the conductor the only person expected to attend to the composer's work; everyone in the orchestra must actively read the music and consider how each of them might perform it best. These understandings of congregational leadership take seriously the agency of the Word in founding the church. They remind churches that they are the body of Christ, consisting of many members, each of whom is empowered by the Spirit to contribute to the common good (1 Cor 12). They also discourage congregational passivity, a subtle temptation that has accompanied the entertainment practices visible in many planted churches. In times of struggle or leadership transition, framing the pastoral office as one part of a larger body safeguards the congregation. Churches need to be reminded that they are more than a pastor's "brand" or style, just as an orchestra is more than its conductor and a discussion is greater than its moderator. Leaders contribute to the healthy functioning of a church, but they are not solely responsible for a congregation's relationship with God.

It is also important to recall that biblical accounts do not suggest that congregations must always remain silent before God; indeed, Christians have been invited to "approach the throne of grace with confidence" as they pray.[108] As we saw in chapter 4, Old Testament accounts of people who engaged with God frequently described intercessions on behalf of others, even those who were outside the faith. Like Abraham pleaded with God for the people in Sodom, so churches today embody their corporate priesthood when they pray for God's mercy and grace within their own communities. Daniel's encounter with God in Daniel 10 followed many years of faithful prayers for his exiled nation in Babylon.[109] Long before God answered Daniel's prayers, the prophet Jeremiah had sent a letter to this same group of exiles which urged them to "build houses" and "plant gardens" in their new community, to give their children in marriage, and most importantly, to "seek the peace and prosperity of the city into which I have carried you in exile. Pray to the Lord for it, because if it prospers, you will prosper, too."[110] Planted churches that enact Christ's own priesthood will similarly intercede for their communities, praying for God's peace and blessing to reveal itself in tangible ways. Conversation with God requires listening, and it also encourages church bodies to speak to God on behalf of others, crying out for the needs and concerns around them.

As planted congregations attend to God's voice, they will grow in holiness. Most would readily espouse this belief. Similarly, Protestant congregations often espouse the idea that the church is a priesthood of all believers. Nonetheless, in practice, some have placed far too much pressure on the priesthood of the ordained clergy. As planted churches return to a right focus on God's own voice, they remind one another of their shared calling to engage with the Word together and to offer priestly intercessions for others. Attending to God's voice also reminds planted churches why their worship matters and encourages them to use strategies like ancient-future practices effectively. Restoring the church's most important conversation partner, God, to God's rightful place brings all other ecclesial relationships into proper balance.

Credo catholicam ecclesiam: *Conversations Between Churches*

Churches express Nicene catholicity when congregations engage well with one another. Catholicity describes the reality that each local congregation is part of the one Church universal, which means that recognizably Christian expressions will appear in every local church.[111] Each local church is part of a global and historic fellowship of Christian faith and can draw strength and inspiration from that fellowship by participating in the larger story that God is telling through the Church Universal. Unfortunately, in planted American churches, the catholicity of the church at times feels aspirational, and the rugged congregationalism evident in many church planting movements has at times obscured this important Nicene mark. That said, plurality of local congregations itself offers churches an invitation to renew Christian catholicity. Bonhoeffer felt that America's theological and cultural diversity would actually encourage "a certain modesty" in local churches by creating an ever-present awareness that "the church is something beyond the denominations."[112] As Bonhoeffer concluded, "The concept of the church invisible cannot be far away."[113] Conversations between churches subtly remind Christians that their faith is indeed in something much bigger than any one local congregation and so moves churches toward greater catholicity.

We must frankly acknowledge that the act of planting churches has at times created more divisiveness than catholicity. Hybels, for example, began Willow Creek only after conducting a survey to learn why people did not attend church already; his survey concluded that proclamation in most area churches seemed unclear, insensitive, and/or irrelevant to many people.[114] Such a finding hardly seems charitable to other local churches. Hybels by no means suggested that he coordinated this survey with other congregations, questioned the accuracy of this finding, or even shared the results privately with other churches before publishing this account of them. As a result, his memory of this survey reads like little more than a complaint about existing churches. Church planters have often been vocal critics of existing church praxis, for good and for ill. This is in part because many espouse faith in Church Growth Theory, which concludes that any church which is effective will grow.[115] Lack of visible growth thus makes it far too easy for planted congregations to critique other area churches that are not growing. Some churches might justifiably suspect that the very act of planting a new church is an implicit critique of their own ministry, a thought that hardly encourages healthy relationships between local congregations.[116] Widespread perceptions that planted churches compete with existing churches for a limited pool of members only exacerbate such tensions.[117] Warren, for example, has had to emphasize repeatedly that Saddleback Church actively encourages Christians who are already church members to remain in their current church.[118] Sometimes the term "church planting" even papers over something better understood as a church split, when leaders with very different missional or ecclesial visions go their separate ways, amicably or not.[119] One researcher found that over 20 percent of the church planters he interviewed reported conflict within a church as a major motivation for starting a new church.[120] In such circumstances, one hardly expects to see many healthy ongoing exchanges between congregations, much less consistent movement toward catholicity.

Nonetheless, among planted American churches, conversations between local congregations have occurred and at times have been very constructive. The Lausanne Congress of 1974 offers a healthy model of international missional engagement between congregations, even those from very different cultural and/or confessional backgrounds.[121] Planted churches like Saddleback and Willow Creek have long operated training networks, and Acts 29 fosters a similar network of global church planting partners.[122] These networks create space for healthy interactions between representatives from very different congregations. American church planting leaders frequently read and cite one another's work, focusing on common missional visions rather than confessional differences.[123] As the rise of interdenominational networks and literature attests, church planters are often very eager to learn from one another. These interactions between churches are highly encouraging and deserve praise.

Inter-church conversations, though, still bear further development, even among planted churches. In practice, a sizeable share of recent American church planting efforts have occurred within denominations that are congregationalist, like the SBC, or among loose "networks" of independent churches, like Acts 29.[124] These organizations do not always have the same formal mechanisms that denominations use to call regular meetings, nor is there always a clearly defined expectation for interaction between local congregations. Some missional church networks meet very infrequently; for example, since its inception in 1974, the full Lausanne Congress has only met four times to date, though there have been additional smaller meetings within regional subgroups.[125] Even when church planting networks meet, they typically focus much of their energy on addressing pragmatic concerns like marketing strategies or trends in praxis; corporate theological reflection is rarer.[126] Perhaps more problematically, some church planting networks and training events function in hierarchical ways. When training is focused on the praxis of high-profile churches like Saddleback or Willow Creek, they risk amplifying the perceived importance of these congregations and their founding pastors' personal celebrity. Billing them as "training" events for all but the host church further frames the exchange as asymmetrical. Leaders of planted churches sometimes engage with multiple networks in the hope of attracting financial and/or logistical support for their congregation.[127] Patrons, though, are not partners, and such arrangements between churches can stifle helpful mutual exchanges and beneficial critiques. In addition, most church planting networks and training conferences only include pastors, offering lay Christians far less opportunity to engage with others outside their own congregation. Consequently, the opportunity for genuine conversations between planted churches can be more limited than we might assume.

There are now opportunities to dramatically expand conversations between churches. Holy Trinity Church Brompton, in London, UK, for example, offered free online training for churches around the world that use their Alpha Courses in 2021 and 2022.[128] The format of these events permitted little interaction among participants, but it highlighted the potential of new technologies to increase engagement between congregations. Online meetings offer affordable and convenient ways to supplement in-person conferences whenever travel is expensive, inconvenient, or unavailable. This reality means that meetings between local church leaders can feasibly become more frequent. It also has the potential to widen participation and include individuals and churches who cannot travel as easily. As congregations continue to navigate the new realities that the Covid-19 pandemic and post-pandemic culture have created, widened access to online meeting technologies offers clear potential to help local churches engage better with other congregations around the world. Such technologies hold great promise to move churches toward catholicity, building relationships and increasing awareness of shared challenges, blessings, and ties with a Holy God.

Within local communities, even more engagement between churches is feasible. Many planted churches have similar interests, like offering a community food pantry, ministering to speakers of other languages, or supporting local schools. Shared holidays like Easter create opportunities for joint services, such as sunrise services in a local cemetery or other public space. Joint services and prayer meetings, shared social events, and common community ministry projects all create helpful opportunities for meaningful exchanges among people from different congregations. Billy Graham's own ministry indeed offered ways to unite local missional churches, as volunteers and congregations came together to plan ways to support the event and the people who would come to faith as a result. Whenever churches foster engagement between their congregations, they subtly disrupt any perception that planted churches are in competition with one another for members. They also offer substantial benefits to the many planted American churches that are racially and/or politically homogeneous. As one leading qualitative researcher of planted American churches discovered, "Ongoing conversation is in itself a mechanism or a strategy to maintain a plurality of identities and positions within emerging congregations."[129] Predominantly white planted congregations, for example, can fruitfully follow Bonhoeffer's example and learn from the missional theology and praxis of predominantly Black congregations.[130] Such an interaction reportedly happened when Billy Graham and Tony Evans spoke informally after a joint missional event and discussed their different operant understandings of "mission."[131] Even in the face of real theological differences, Moynagh insists, "It is by engaging with . . . differences that the denomination will better understand its Lord, its mission, and itself. Members must be open to critique."[132] As churches interact with one another in substantive ways, they grow to appreciate varied expressions of a recognizably shared Christian faith. In time, such interactions might even lead to more healthy diversity within local congregations and more accessible forms of praxis, making an even wider variety of seekers feel welcome. At minimum, they offer homogeneous planted churches a practical first step toward that worthy goal.

It is also important to stress that planted congregations need healthy dialogue with existing churches, particularly those within their local community. Tim Keller and his associate Stefan Paas argue that planted churches are uniquely positioned to bless other local churches by serving as a "laboratory" or "haven" for those interested in experimenting with new forms of praxis and training new leaders.[133] Paas and Keller's vision is commendable, but it presupposes meaningful ongoing collaboration among local churches. For their vision to work, local churches would need to agree on specific practices to try or innovations to study, set the parameters of the experiment, and discuss the results honestly and openly together. For planted churches to be an effective training vehicle for new leaders, congregations would also need to agree on mutually acceptable methods for identifying, recruiting, and training leaders. Such discussions alone could move participating congregations toward greater catholicity, apart from any other benefits their shared research or training might generate. As churches work together to identify effective leaders and practices, they acknowledge their shared values and vision even as they learn from the different perspectives each brings to the task.

Planted churches' operant missional ecclesiology has historically emphasized the local congregation, but planted churches have also taken important steps toward catholicity by engaging with one another across confessional and geographic divides. As this research has demonstrated, there are many visibly shared patterns of praxis among planted American congregations, which point to the reality of Christian catholicity. Church planting networks have created opportunities for Christians to share hard-won insights and support one another's efforts, and still fuller and richer collaboration remains possible. As planted churches move toward catholicity, their members gain a clearer vision of their calling and enjoy richer fellowship with other believers around the world. Missional Christians are co-laborers, not competitors, and Christianity is far bigger than any one local congregation.

Credo apostolicam ecclesiam: *Conversations with Those Outside the Church*

The apostolic mark of church is particularly important to define, since the term has meant very different things to different churches. Barth defines it as consistency with the faith of the apostles,[134] while others describe it in terms of a formal apostolic succession of leaders,[135] or even a specific ministerial office.[136] It is important to recall that the word "apostle" is a transliteration of a Greek word which literally means "sent out." The apostles were so named because they were called to carry the Word outward, to "Jerusalem, Judea, Samaria, and the ends of the earth" (Acts 1:8). The outward motion of the apostles from Jerusalem to the "ends of the earth" reflects the strong missional commitment of most planted American churches. Consequently, some church planting advocates have even used the term "apostolic" to denote any pioneering missional church.[137] When churches engage with those outside of Christian fellowship, they move toward apostolicity and honor the apostles' calling to "send out" the Word into a wider world.

Missional commitment has been one of the most consistent hallmarks of planted American churches. From the 1960s to the present, planted churches have thought carefully and creatively about how to express the gospel clearly to those who are not already Christians. Their most common missional model, though, has generally been attractional. Attractional approaches sometimes make it difficult to move members outside of what Bonhoeffer called churches' "spaces of proclamation and order,"[138] since the stated aim is often to make those very spaces more inviting, comfortable, and welcoming. As Bonhoeffer writes, a church moving toward apostolicity "claims yet another space in the world," a space that is "not only for its worship and its order," but is tied to "the daily life of its members."[139] This is where the missional approach of Fresh Expressions of Church offers a powerful complement to the work American church planters are already doing. Unlike many planted American churches, Fresh Expressions' missional model intentionally sends lay Christians outward, promoting regular and substantive engagement between church members and people within their local communities. This is an approach well worth further consideration.

One important guideline is that churches must always promote genuine and ethical relationships. Fresh Expressions' method of planting churches involves "tangible acts of service," but according to Moynagh, the aim is to offer "a love that serves people not by creating dependency, but by enabling individuals to flourish."[140] Consequently, Moynagh envisions "acts of kindness" not as one-way charity but as a group activity where Christians and non-Christians work together to serve one another and their wider community.[141] In practice, this looks less like a food bank solely operated by a church and more like a community kitchen, where everyone involved shares meals, recipes, fellowship, and acts of kindness. Christians thus do not position themselves as distant patrons dispensing charity, but as friends who are willing to be vulnerable when they give and receive from others.[142] The simple act of listening requires a similar posture; Levinas defines listening as an ethical form of receiving from the Other, writing:

> To approach the Other in conversation is to welcome his expression, in which at each instant he overflows the idea a thought would carry away from it. It is therefore to *receive* from the Other beyond the capacity of the I, which means exactly: to have the idea of infinity. But this means also: to be taught.[143]

Listening "welcomes" the Other's full being, attending to and learning from the Other rather than simply looking for ideas that "a thought would carry away from" a conversation. Listening is a particularly ethical way to engage because it allows the Other to reveal him/herself on his/her own terms.[144] In the process of genuinely listening, Christians learn more about their neighbors and gain important insights about their shared context. In much the same way, Fresh Expressions looks for ways to encourage people outside the church to engage naturally and authentically with Christians. Receptivity is as crucial to an ethical relationship as listening is to an authentic conversation, and Fresh Expressions offers countless practical examples of how missional Christians might demonstrate receptivity as they move beyond their church fellowship and out into their community.

By prioritizing the loving witness of a church within a community over time, Moynagh's missional ecclesiology resembles another stream of church planting known as incarnational church planting.[145] The incarnational approach to church planting attests to an important theological truth: the lived presence of Christians as a church in a community points to the miracle of the Word made flesh and dwelling among us (John 1:14).[146] For this reason, some American church planters have adopted approaches that prioritize engagement within local communities. For example, Jay Pathak and Dave Runyon have written compellingly about the importance of being a good neighbor, encouraging Christians to get to know their actual neighbors and build substantive fellowship within their immediate communities.[147] Similarly, Christopher James defines roughly a quarter of the church planters he interviewed in greater Seattle as following a "Neighborhood Incarnation" model that has "distinctive emphases on the local parish, extra-congregational forms of ecclesial life, and an approach to mission centered in hospitality and service."[148] Consequently, these churches meet in carefully crafted "community spaces" and "third places" like coffee shops where church members can interact meaningfully with others in their local neighborhood.[149] There is much that is beautiful and commendable in this approach to apostolicity. The potential risk, which is shared with Fresh Expressions, is placing all the emphasis on loving human presence in a community without pointing to the gospel itself. Incarnational missions must always point to the incarnation. For this reason, the Spirit might rightly guide some planted churches to complementary missional approaches that emphasize apologetics or worship more strongly.[150] Incarnational or relational approaches to mission, though, are broadly consistent with Bonhoeffer's observation that the church cannot be contained with the "spaces of order and proclamation," but must also extend outward, into the center of community life and everyday work.[151] It is therefore important that churches honor their apostolic calling and allow the Spirit to send them out beyond gathered services and into courageous conversations with a wider world.

The vulnerability associated with Fresh Expressions and other similar missional church models might prove uncomfortable for some American Christians. Like Billy Graham, many planted congregations have adopted a pretribulationist eschatology and so tend to see themselves and "the world" as completely separate.[152] Under the lens of this eschatology, "the world" can appear either threatening or so different from Christianity that genuine conversation between church and the world does not seem feasible. As Keller explains, this kind of operant theology means that missional American churches are often more effective and comfortable "reaching" people with some Christian background than those with a different faith or no faith.[153] Percy worries that even Fresh Expressions of Church risks unintentionally creating "a sect that sees itself as engaged with but apart from society."[154] This is a serious concern shared by the authors of *Mission-Shaped Church*, who remind planted churches that "the gospel can only be proclaimed in a culture, not at a culture."[155] If Christians cannot lovingly befriend those outside their faith, acknowledging a common humanity and a shared need for Jesus's redemption, it will be impossible to evangelize well, no matter how hip or relevant gathered services might be. Furthermore, Moynagh rightly notes that there is an undeveloped sense that "time and time again it is the *world* that has been good for the *church*."[156] As Moynagh explains, "Outside pressure groups, for example, make the churches sensitive to ecological and social issues and stir Christians' consciences."[157] Christians can justifiably approach the world not as a frightening threat nor solely as a potential source of converts, but as a dialogue partner. Like any good dialogue partner, those outside the church will at times offer helpful perspectives, questions, and even critiques. In Matthew 16 and throughout the book of Acts, the Spirit moved as Christians engaged with outside dialogue partners, who ultimately helped the church understand Jesus better, discern their own callings, and refine their understandings of the Word.[158] Churches need not fear the world as they courageously follow Jesus outward, openly and honestly engaging with people beyond their immediate fellowship.

It is also important to clarify that engaging ethically with those outside the faith does not require Christians to remain silent about differences between the gospel and contemporary culture.[159] As Moynagh writes, the church must "do more than embrace visible signs of the kingdom" that it may find in the world, it must also "critique their absence and point to salvation in Christ."[160] Newbigin similarly insists that proper missional engagement

> is neither withdrawal from the world into a religious sanctuary; nor is it engagement with the world on the world's terms. . . . It is a totally uncompromising yet totally vulnerable challenge to the powers of evil in the name and in the power of the kingship of God present in the crucified and risen Jesus.[161]

The church is called to both speak and act as a sign of the redemption of Christ, in full confidence that Christ has overcome the world, however troubled the world might be (John 16:33). Newbigin therefore advocates a balance between evangelistic proclamation and social justice ministry in the name of Christ.[162] Similarly, Bevans argues that mission can best be understood as prophetic dialogue, a willingness to engage relationally and also to confront problems.[163] Authentic relationships create space for honest conversations, where differences can be explored and even challenged in healthy ways.[164] When planted churches take Bevans's call to prophetic dialogue seriously, they find themselves even closer to the heart of the Lausanne Covenant, which similarly balances evangelistic proclamation and social engagement.[165] This balance will often look like courageous conversations with the world, asking challenging questions and speaking honestly about problems.

Fresh Expressions of Church and other similar models offer practical examples of how planted congregations might embody Jesus's own pattern of listening, speaking, and responding to others. This incarnational approach complements the emphasis of many planted American churches, which have traditionally focused on inviting people to come to church and listen to evangelistic preaching. By contrast, Fresh Expressions and similar models send Christians out into their community. These missional churches teach Christians how to engage well with others as they partner with their neighbors in friendship and in shared service to a community. From the relationships that form, acts of worship, new faith communities, and prophetic responses to injustice can develop, giving added credibility to a church's evangelistic preaching. This pattern is not without limitations, but it offers planted American churches practical ways to move further toward apostolicity and to proclaim the Word well, making Christ audible and visible in local communities.

A Way Forward: Aligning Beliefs and Practices

In the Christian life, it is far too natural for espoused beliefs and operant theology to drift slowly out of alignment, particularly when unexamined cultural influences weigh heavily. Self-assessment can detect and remedy such drift, but it has not always been clear what, beyond attendance statistics, would offer a helpful means of assessing missional church praxis. This chapter has aimed to identify ways to draw the operant missional ecclesiology of church planting into closer alignment with espoused theology, offering an assessment framework that encourages planted churches and those who research them to evaluate missional congregational ministries in light of their espoused callings. Both the example of Fresh Expressions of Church and the Nicene assessment framework modeled in this chapter empower planted churches to identify sustainable ways forward which will balance theological clarity with feasible praxis, in the spirit of the Reformation concept *ecclesia semper reformanda*.

Planted congregations have espoused a strong commitment to mission, but their attractional models and accommodation of the HUP at times risked turning their missional focus inward, onto the church itself.[166] Fresh Expressions of Church illustrates a series of concrete practices that reorient missional churches, practically turning their attention outward in light of their apostolic calling to carry the gospel beyond the immediate church fellowship. Furthermore, Moynagh's implicit emphasis on conversations points to specific practical strategies for improving praxis where appropriate. Churches are called to listen as well as speak, and in assessing the quality of their four key relationships, churches must be willing to consider whether more needs to be said in some contexts, and whether they might need to listen more carefully in others. By simply taking time to speak, listen, and respond thoughtfully, churches will at once strengthen important relationships and point more clearly to the compassionate ministry of the Word made flesh in Christ.

The widespread influence of Church Growth Theory has meant that planted churches have too often seen attendance growth or decline as a de facto measure of missional and ecclesial effectiveness. Even academic research has been drawn to larger churches, devoting considerable attention to the implications of Church Growth Theory and to the study of "megachurches."[167] At times, a twin focus on size and growth has caused serious theological drift, generating unsustainable pressures and allowing problems to hide behind impressive numbers. Planted churches and those who research them have needed better methods to assess their praxis than the seductively simple metrics that Church Growth Theory offers. The assessment described here empowers both researchers and planted churches to look beyond membership statistics and to weigh praxis against long-standing theological understandings of a Christian church. As the Covid-19 pandemic made clear, sudden declines in attendance are not always under a church's control, nor are they necessarily a mark of flawed praxis. In the same way, rapid growth in churches requires equally thoughtful examination, since not all growth is healthy, and large congregations will also experience challenges. In times of growth, churches need to understand how their congregation is changing, consider which voices remain audible in their midst, and attend to any that have gone silent. Understanding church attendance patterns requires careful theological reflection, which the Nicene marks encourage.

Examining core relationships in light of the four Nicene marks of the church also yields a more comprehensive and theologically grounded evaluation of current praxis than simple membership statistics ever could. Churches can conduct this assessment formally, in partnership with academic researchers, or informally, as congregations reflect together on their own ministries. As praxis evolves, this assessment framework will empower planted churches to weigh proposed methods not against attendance, but against their identity and their sacred callings. The four Nicene marks identify key directions in which a church will move. While no congregation will embody any mark perfectly, they can check their directions of travel against the four compass points of the Nicene marks and redirect energy where needed.

The aim of this chapter has been to encourage churches to notice God's work in their midst, to celebrate positive developments, and to move together toward the aims and callings they rightly hold dear. The missional commitment that led Christians to plant churches included much that was commendable. Planted congregations have had challenges, but they have also brought ideas of mission home to many ordinary Christians. The example of Fresh Expressions of Church is only one of many viable approaches that can helpfully complement the good work American church planters are already doing. When congregations have a clear understanding of their calling and identity as Christian churches, they will be better able to identify additional helpful examples. Paul once wrote to a church that he had helped to plant, saying he was "confident in this, that he who began a good work in you will carry it on to completion until the day of Christ Jesus" (Phil 1:6). Planted American churches are not complete yet, but neither is the Spirit's ministry. Churches can therefore be confident and creative in all their ecclesial relationships, trusting God to carry on with the *missio Dei* until the day of Christ Jesus and to build the church "into a holy temple in the Lord," "a dwelling place in which God lives by his Spirit" (Eph 2:21–22).

Conclusion

Coda: The Spirit's Ministry Within the *Sanctorum Communio*

Church planting invites Christians to attend to the Spirit's ministry as they watch new congregations come to life. When congregations begin today, Christians still expect to see the same Spirit that arrived in Acts 2 at work, albeit in unpredictable ways. An episode from Newbigin's own experience illustrates this pattern and presents a practical, hopeful illustration of how the Spirit will work through Christians to reveal the Word and bring communities to faith. While he was serving as a bishop in Madurai, India, Newbigin once received a request to baptize twenty-five families in a rural village outside his own diocese.[1] When this request came, neither Newbigin nor the bishop overseeing that village were aware of any "evangelistic work in that area."[2] Newbigin traveled to the village, listened to the villagers, and pieced together the story of how they came to faith, which he called "a drama in four acts":

> Act I saw the visit of a team of development workers who helped them to put down a well, install an electric pump, and get a clean water supply. The leader of the team was a Christian engineer, a good man but not much of a communicator. He told them he was a Christian, and they saw that he was a good man. That was all. End of Act I.
>
> Next, a few months later, one of the villagers went to the neighbouring town to make some purchases and a colporteur sold him a copy of the Gospel of St Mark. He began to read it, became interested,

> and started discussing it with his neighbours who gathered round to hear him read. End of Act II, with no visible change.
>
> Some months passed, and an independent evangelist paid a visit to the village. As is the manner of his tribe, he preached a fiery sermon, stayed the night in the village, and left behind a tract that said: "If you die tonight, where will you go?" The villagers decided that the matter was more serious than they had thought and that further investigation was called for. So (and this is Act IV) they sent word to a village five miles away where there was a Christian congregation. "Will you please tell us," they asked, "what is all this about this man Jesus?" It happened that one of the members of the congregation (all of them landless labourers) had had an accident and was unable to do field work. The congregation decided to send him over to the other village, to spend a month with them answering their enquiry.
>
> The result was a group of twenty-five families as ready for and as eager for baptism as any that I have seen.
>
> The point of the story is obvious. If you had assembled the engineer, the colporteur, the evangelist and the coolie for a seminar on missionary methods, they would probably have disagreed with each other—perhaps violently. Unknown to each other, each had done faithfully the work for which the Holy Spirit had given the equipment. The strategy was not in any human hands.[3]

And so, in a drama of four acts, a new community of people came to faith.

When I discussed Newbigin's story with a group of church leaders in training recently, I asked them, "Who is the evangelist?" They enthusiastically responded, "All of them." They meant the four human beings whose action Newbigin described, and of course they were right. We all need to remember, though, that the most important partner in church planting is the one that can be hardest to glimpse: the Holy Spirit. People in this village came to faith not because of any human strategy, but by the faithful ministry of the Spirit, guiding and directing everyone who participated in this drama. As Newbigin says, "The strategy was not in any human hands." This new faith community did not appear because of "a seminar on missionary methods," but because of an unpredictable series of events that the Spirit flawlessly orchestrated over time. This pattern explains why Paul refrained from using human strategies like "lofty" or "persuasive" speech, conveying only the Spirit and God's own power to those under his care, in order that their faith might be directed rightly to God alone (1 Cor 2:1–5). Planted churches need not rely on marketing strategies or clever, well-crafted preaching to make the gospel known. The Spirit will bring people to faith in God's own good time and according to God's own gentle, patient Word. Only by the Spirit can the Word truly be revealed, and the Spirit's ministry is trustworthy.

As Newbigin makes clear, the revelation of God's Word is often a slower process than some might imagine, and patience is essential for those who participate. Planted American congregations that have seen scores of people stream down an aisle at the end of a Billy Graham crusade or read accounts of rapid growth in a newly planted church have come to expect that faithful ministry yields visible, immediate conversions. Newbigin's account, though, offers an encouraging reminder that the Spirit often takes a longer, slower path to bringing new Christians to faith. In this story, the Spirit worked through multiple people faithfully witnessing to Christ's redemption over time. Newbigin does not indicate whether any of them saw the fruit of their witness; since the process took "some months," perhaps only the injured laborer ever caught a glimpse of the new faith community coming into being. Each participant in this drama had to trust in the Spirit's work before and after their own involvement. This is an important reminder, particularly for planted American churches laboring under the influence of Church Growth Theory.[4] Year-to-year attendance growth cannot always be expected, nor is it the only mark of faithful witness. As Newbigin explains, "Mission in Christ's way will not be a success story as the world reckons success."[5] After all, witnessing to Christ means pointing to one who was despised and rejected by many.[6] As Bonhoeffer rightly reminds churches,

> The Word of God is so weak that it suffers to be despised and rejected by people. For the Word, there are such things as hardened hearts and locked doors. The Word accepts the resistance it encounters and bears it.[7]

In Jesus's name, planted churches will sometimes be called to bear rejection and to face "hardened hearts and locked doors" faithfully. Even when the results of witness are more encouraging, churches often need to wait faithfully while the Spirit gently, graciously draws new believers into Christian community. This is why churches must assess their practices according to theological understandings of ecclesial identity and missional callings, not according to short-term results. Patient and thoughtful assessment of praxis leaves the Spirit space to draw forth fruit in God's own time.

Newbigin's account also illustrates ways that the Spirit invites the full body of Christ to participate in the revelation of the Word. The Spirit worked through extended conversations between the injured laborer and the villagers as well as one relatively brief exchange between a villager and a bookseller. The active kindness of the Christian engineer, who was "not much of a communicator," mattered at least as much as the fiery preaching of a visiting evangelist. Written texts like the gospel and the tract were as significant as verbal exchanges. The villager who purchased the Gospel of Mark immediately wanted to discuss it with others, and so the Spirit included even those who were not yet Christians in the process of revealing the Word to this community. This story illustrates how all believers can be empowered to act according to their gifts in order to build up the body of faith (1 Cor 12). Pastors cannot bear the weight of witness alone. Newbigin's task as an ordained church leader was primarily to attend to all of these stories and draw them into a unified, harmonious account of God's grace unfolding through the faithful ministry of many. Conversations between Newbigin and this new community of faith thus drew out a beautiful picture of God's own work, which Newbigin's writing shared with Christians outside their local area. The Spirit blesses a variety of witnesses and involves the full body of a missional church in making the Word known.

Another arguably more subtle participant in Newbigin's story was the visible body of Christ in the neighboring village. Newbigin does not say how long these faithful Christians had maintained a church, but they were visible enough that even people in the next village knew where to go when questions arose about Jesus. Newbigin saw little pattern in the process by which people came to faith during his service in India, but he saw one common factor:

> The presence of a believing, worshipping, celebrating congregation of people deeply involved in the ordinary life of their neighbourhood. . . . It was the work of the Spirit . . . flowing out through the faithful words and deeds of its members.[8]

Bonhoeffer therefore rightly argues that the visible presence of a church body within a community points others to the historic reality of the incarnation, just as the Spirit's work in this faithful unnamed congregation did.[9] There is no indication whether or not any of the new Christians in the next village ever joined their church, and this church's membership might not have increased at all, but their ministry still mattered. As churches minister faithfully to those under their care, their wordless, sacrificial service gives the Word weight and power, demonstrating that Christ is present whenever even two or three of them gather.[10] People have been won to faith after witnessing a church's ministry to families in hospitals, offering little more than meals and loving presence.[11] As Bonhoeffer described it, even a traditional funeral service powerfully demonstrates the hope of Christ, embodying the loving embrace of God that enfolds grieving families and departed souls alike.[12] By its very presence, a healthy, balanced church makes the love of Christ visible and audible to the world. As churches honor the Spirit's calling and faithfully minister to those under their care, the Spirit will reveal the hope of Christ's redemption. Churches can bless one another by their very presence, much as this nameless church blessed their neighbors, fostering a beautiful conversation about faith that the Spirit used to help reveal the truth of the gospel. Planting a church can be a powerful and faithful act of witness, making the Word more visible and audible to local communities.

Twenty-first-century America differs significantly from the context described by Newbigin, but the same Spirit ministers in American planted churches today. The Spirit reveals the Word through a variety of acts of witness and faithful ministry, and so missional churches need the active participation of their full congregation. Attending to only one conversation partner or moving toward only one of the four Nicene marks is not enough. The Spirit works through churches to witness to Jesus's redemption as they heed the Spirit's call to speak, listen, and respond well, attending to God's voice and the voices of those around them. A church's missional ecclesiology and assessment of its own praxis must leave the Spirit space and time to bring faith to life. The *missio Dei* is bigger than any local church. The Spirit can be trusted to reveal the Word in God's own time.

New Directions for Further Research

The account of church planting developed here, like much work in practical theological reflection, is a necessary starting point, offered in the hope of empowering further contributions from scholars and church planting practitioners. Missional and ecclesiological patterns observed in planted American churches have had a substantial influence on wider American Christian expressions and on planted congregations around the world, which all bear further study. Now that broad patterns in the operant missional ecclesiology of American church planting have been identified, additional voices will be able to fruitfully develop and complexify these patterns in a variety of helpful ways. The focus of this research was limited to congregations and church planting networks that originated in the United States, but many church planting networks have also engaged with global partners outside the United States. Furthermore, American church planting literature and training materials have been widely exported, as is most evident in Willow Creek's global training network and Rick Warren's internationally best-selling books. Some communities outside the United States also have long-standing experience with North American missionaries planting churches in their own communities; these congregations have therefore been influenced by American church planting paradigms and patterns as well. It is now important to examine how patterns of operant missional ecclesiology common to American church planting networks have been received, adapted, or changed altogether in different cultural contexts. Insights from scholars and churches outside the United States are particularly valuable, since they are better placed to identify culturally specific features of the patterns described here that might not be immediately obvious to American eyes. People from diverse cultural backgrounds will also bring important perspectives to bear on operant missional ecclesiology and will articulate approaches to the task of planting churches that differ fruitfully from those profiled here.

This book has also found that much of the current literature and praxis of church planting has been centered on pastoral leadership, with far less to guide the corporate ministries of lay congregants. Laypeople constitute the vast majority of most congregations, making it vitally important to expand the picture of congregational identity and praxis that chapters 4 and 5 of this study offered. The individualism and consumerism that have been observed within American church planting movements point to broader cultural patterns which make it more difficult to appreciate what it means to be a cohesive faith community, one church which corporately discerns and proclaims the Word. This is another area where global perspectives have much to contribute. Concepts like *ubuntu* which stem from cultures that prioritize community offer a helpful corrective to consumerist American individualism. American congregations need a fuller understanding of what it means to live in fellowship with one another and more examples that reveal how Christians might participate well in a shared worshiping community. By articulating the nature and practices of congregations, churches will be further empowered to witness faithfully to God's relational Word and to enjoy richer Christian fellowship.

A significant gap which this book could not address fully is the lack of research on church planting in historically Black churches, immigrant churches, and other monoracial congregations. Church planting has certainly happened outside predominantly white congregations, as we have seen. Monoracial planted congregations deserve far more study and theological reflection, which will benefit churches and communities in many contexts. As chapter 3 briefly mentioned, Black theologians have already described patterns of operant missional ecclesiology which differ fruitfully from those seen in many of the planted congregations described here. Given the rich Christian theology and compelling commitment to holistic mission many of these churches advocate, understanding how and why church planting functions in monoracial congregations will offer helpful insights into complementary practices and alternative possibilities for church planting. Some promising research has already been offered on multiracial church planting, and more such research is both welcome and important.

In addition, the structure and nature of church planting networks bear further study. As the practice of church planting has proliferated within the United States, so has the range of training and support networks available to planted congregations. The structure of these networks varies widely. Some provide little more than financial support to affiliated churches, while others provide comprehensive training, pastoral screening, oversight, and ongoing leadership support. Church planting networks like the SBC's Send Network are specialized organizational entities embedded within wider denominational structures. Other networks, like Acts 29 and the Willow Creek Association, arose from the ministry of a specific planted church. Still others, like the informal networks that are common among independent charismatic planted churches, arose organically among congregations with similar confessional backgrounds and affinities. Many planted churches look to networks to provide local congregations support, oversight, and credibility, making it all the more important to understand how they function and what kinds of operant missional ecclesiology they facilitate. As this book explained, catholicity is itself an important mark of churches, and conversations between congregations are vital, making these networks an important potential means of helpful connections. Not all church planting networks offer local churches equal relational support. Fuller studies of the variety of networks that exist will offer helpful insights to both scholars and practitioners, revealing additional features of the organizational structures and operant theology within church planting movements.

In this season, when so much in society is changing, when the realities of the Covid-19 pandemic have challenged long-held understandings of gathered worship and embodied community, one must expect church planting movements to adapt. As they do, it will be important to revisit the findings presented here and consider how planted American congregations continue to develop their operant missional ecclesiology. As long as planted churches continue to respond creatively to cultural changes, church planting researchers will have new insights, experiences, and approaches to explore. Cahalan and Nieman helpfully remind practical theologians that the practice of theological reflection "will necessarily remain incomplete" because human beings "cannot fully anticipate the outcomes of even their most faithful actions."[13] Consequently, they add, "practical theology must remain open to God's future."[14] It is therefore with hope for the possibilities of church planting in America, confidence in the ongoing contributions of researchers, and abiding faith in the Spirit's abiding ministry that this research concludes.

Notes

Introduction

1 David T. Olson, *The American Church in Crisis* (Grand Rapids: Zondervan, 2008), 120.

2 The SBC's 2021 Annual Convention Report predicts a decrease in new church starts for the next few years, as the Covid-19 pandemic caused their leadership training for church planters to slow; see SBC Executive Committee, *Annual of the 2021 Southern Baptist Convention* (Nashville, TN: Southern Baptist Convention, 2021), 133, 247, 55, accessed March 28, 2021, https://www.sbc.net/wp-content/uploads/2021/09/2021-SBC-Annual.pdf.

3 E.g., Lynne Hybels and Bill Hybels, *Rediscovering Church: The Story and Vision of Willow Creek Community Church* (Grand Rapids: Zondervan, 1995); Global Leadership Network, "Who We Are," accessed November 1, 2021, https://globalleadership.org/who-we-are/; Purpose Driven Church, "Where Healthy Churches Are Built," accessed November 1, 2021; Richard Warren, *The Purpose Driven Church: Growth Without Compromising Your Message and Mission* (Grand Rapids: Zondervan, 1995).

4 *Christianity Today*, "*Christianity Today*'s New Hit Podcast, 'The Rise and Fall of Mars Hill,' Stirs Evangelical Soul-Searching," news release, August 13, 2021, https://www.christianitytoday.org/media-room/news/2021/christianity-todays-new-hit-podcast-rise-and-fall-of-mars-h.html.

5 Less than two months after its first episode was released, over 2.5 million listeners had downloaded it. Download figures reflect comparably

large audiences in the United Kingdom and Canada. See "*Christianity Today*'s New Hit Podcast."

6 Dale Chamberlain, "Hillsong Atlanta Pastor Sam Collier Announces Resignation, Cites Recent Scandals as Reason," *Church Leaders*, March 23, 2022, https://churchleaders.com/news/420312-sam-collier-resignation-hillsong-atlanta.html; Roxanne Stone, "A Pair of Hillsong Docuseries Planned, Examining the Megachurch's Culture, the Fall of Carl Lentz," Church Leaders, June 25, 2021, https://churchleaders.com/news/400260-a-pair-of-hillsong-docuseries-planned-examining-the-megachurchs-culture-the-fall-of-carl-lentz.html.

7 Olson, *American Church in Crisis*, 122–24; Edward Stetzer and Warren Bird, "The State of Church Planting in the United States: Research Overview and Qualitative Study of Primary Church Planting Entities," *Journal of the American Society for Church Growth* 19, no. 2 (2008): 5, https://place.asburyseminary.edu/jascg/vol19/iss2/2/. Stetzer and Bird rightly note that some church planting practitioners claim that as many as 70–80 percent of new churches close within five years, though the evidence for this claim is unclear; Stetzer and Bird, "State of Church Planting," 37, note 4. As Richard Pitt explains, Stetzer and Bird's numbers do not include churches planted outside traditional evangelical denominations and networks, which often lack the support denominational churches enjoy. Pitt adds that some new Christian fellowships may function as a church for years before they call themselves a church. These factors suggest that some nascent church plants can easily come and go unnoticed by even diligent researchers like Stetzer and Bird; see Richard N. Pitt, *Church Planters: Inside the World of Religion Entrepreneurs* (New York: Oxford University Press, 2022), 311–12, notes 42–43.

8 E.g., Warren, *Purpose Driven Church*; Ed Stetzer, *Planting Missional Churches* (Nashville: Broadman & Holman, 2006); David V. Garrison, *Church Planting Movements: How God Is Redeeming a Lost World* (Monument, CO: WIGTake Resources, 2004).

9 E.g., Hybels and Hybels, *Rediscovering Church*; Warren, *Purpose Driven Church*.

10 E.g., G. A. Pritchard, *Willow Creek Seeker Services: Evaluating a New Way of Doing Church* (Grand Rapids: Baker Books, 1996); Gerardo Martí, *A Mosaic of Believers: Diversity and Innovation in a Multiethnic Church* (Bloomington: Indiana University Press, 2005); Gerardo Martí, *Hollywood Faith: Holiness, Prosperity, and Ambition in a Los Angeles Church* (New Brunswick, NJ: Rutgers University Press, 2008); James S. Bielo, *Emerging Evangelicals: Faith, Modernity, and the Desire for Authenticity* (New York: New York University Press, 2011); Christopher James, *Church Planting in Post-Christian Soil: Theology and Practice* (Oxford: Oxford University Press, 2017); Jessica Johnson, *Biblical Porn:*

Affect, Labor, and Pastor Mark Driscoll's Evangelical Empire (Durham, NC: Duke University Press, 2018).

11 Donald McGavran, *Understanding Church Growth* (Grand Rapids: Eerdmans, 1970); Charles Van Engen, "The Growth of the True Church: An Analysis of the Ecclesiology of Church Growth Theory" (doctoral thesis, Vrije Universiteit, Amsterdam, 1981).

12 Scott Thumma, *Twenty Years of Congregational Change: The 2020 Faith Communities Today Overview* (Hartford, CT: Hartford Institute for Religion Research/Faith Communities Today, 2021), 5, 11–17, https://faithcommunitiestoday.org/fact-2020-survey/.

13 E.g., the Acts 29 Network; Sarah Eekhoff Zylstra, "How Acts 29 Survived—and Thrived—After the Collapse of Mars Hill," The Gospel Coalition, December 5, 2017, https://www.thegospelcoalition.org/article/how-acts-29-survived-and-thrived-after-the-collapse-of-mars-hill/.

14 Gerardo Martí, "The Global Phenomenon of Hillsong Church: An Initial Assessment," *Sociology of Religion: A Quarterly Review* 78, no. 4 (2017); Mark Hutchinson, "'Up the Windsor Road': Social Complexity, Geographies of Emotion, and the Rise of Hillsong," in *The Hillsong Movement Examined: You Call Me Out upon the Waters*, ed. Tom Wagner and Tanya Riches (Cham, Switzerland: Palgrave Macmillan, 2017); Thomas Wagner, "Branding, Music, and Religion: Standardization and Adaptation in the Experience of the 'Hillsong Sound,'" in *Religions as Brands: New Perspectives on the Marketization of Religion and Spirituality*, ed. Jean-Claude Usunier and Jörg Stolz, Ashgate AHRC/ESRC Religion and Society (London: Routledge, 2014).

15 Damian O. Emetuche, *The Future of Church Planting in North America*, American University Studies, Series VII, Theology and Religion 342 (New York: Peter Lang, 2014).

16 Lesslie Newbigin, *The Gospel in a Pluralist Society* (Grand Rapids: Eerdmans, 1989), 141–54; David J. Bosch, *Transforming Mission: Paradigm Shifts in the Theology of Mission*, 20th anniversary ed., American Society of Missiology Series 16 (Maryknoll, NY: Orbis, 2011), 430–42.

17 Dana L. Robert, "Historiographic Foundations from Latourette and Van Dusen to Andrew F. Walls," in *Understanding World Christianity: The Vision and Work of Andrew F. Walls*, ed. William R. Burrows, Mark R. Gornik, and Janice A. McLean (Maryknoll, NY: Orbis, 2011), 152.

18 Dietrich Bonhoeffer, "Protestantism Without Reformation," in *Theological Education Underground, 1937–1940*, ed. Victoria J. Barnett, trans. Victoria J. Barnett et al., vol. 15 of *Dietrich Bonhoeffer Works* (Minneapolis: Fortress, 2012), 441–42, 445–46.

19 Scott Thumma, "The Megachurch Phenomenon: Reshaping Church and Faith for the Twenty-First Century," in *The Cambridge History of Religions in America*, vol. 3, ed. Stephen Stein (Cambridge: Cambridge

University Press, 2012), 579; Justin Wilford, *Sacred Subdivisions: The Posturban Transformation of American Evangelicalism* (New York: New York University Press, 2012), 7.

20 Thumma, "Megachurch Phenomenon," 582.

21 Tom Wagner, *Music, Branding, and Consumer Culture in Church: Hillsong in Focus*, Routledge Studies in Religion (London: Routledge, 2020), 59.

22 E.g., audio clips reflect Driscoll's insistence that he founded the Mars Hill Church with little support or mentoring from other churches, a claim that is demonstrably untrue. Mike Cosper, host, *The Rise and Fall of Mars Hill*, podcast, "Bonus Episode: Boca Raton's Church Planting O.G.," *Christianity Today*, October 19, 2021, https://www.christianitytoday.com/ct/podcasts/rise-and-fall-of-mars-hill/mars-hill-podcast-driscoll-david-nicholas.html.

23 Donald E. Miller, *Reinventing American Protestantism: Christianity in the New Millennium* (Berkeley: University of California Press, 1997), 19; Wagner, *Music, Branding, and Consumer Culture*, 30–31.

24 Mike Cosper, host, *The Rise and Fall of Mars Hill*, podcast, "Episode 2: Boomers, the Big Sort, and Really, Really Big Churches," *Christianity Today*, June 28, 2021, https://www.christianitytoday.com/ct/podcasts/rise-and-fall-of-mars-hill/mars-hill-podcast-boomers-big-sort-hybels-warren-driscoll.html; Mike Cosper, host, *The Rise and Fall of Mars Hill*, podcast, "Episode 1: Who Killed Mars Hill?" *Christianity Today*, June 22, 2021, https://www.christianitytoday.com/ct/podcasts/rise-and-fall-of-mars-hill/who-killed-mars-hill-church-mark-driscoll-rise-fall.html.

25 Cosper, "Bonus Episode: Boca Raton's Church Planting O.G."; Mark Wingfield, "Acts 29 Ups the Ante by Offering Church Planters $50,000 Apiece," *Baptist News Global*, January 14, 2022, https://baptistnews.com/article/acts-29-ups-the-ante-by-offering-church-planters-50000-apiece/.

26 Cosper, "Episode 2: Boomers, the Big Sort"; Cosper, "Episode 1: Who Killed Mars Hill?"; Mark Driscoll, "Born Again to Follow Jesus," in video sermon series Follow Me: What It Means to Be a Disciple of Jesus, Saddleback Church, June 9, 2013, https://saddleback.com/watch/follow-me/born-again-to-follow-jesus?autoplay=true; Wingfield, "Acts 29 Ups the Ante."

27 Cosper, "Episode 2: Boomers, the Big Sort"; Cosper, "Episode 1: Who Killed Mars Hill?"

28 Eddie Gibbs and Ryan K. Bolger, *Emerging Churches: Creating Christian Community in Postmodern Cultures* (Grand Rapids: Baker Academic, 2005), 24.

29 Timothy Keller, "Why Plant Churches?" (2002/2009), accessed October 7, 2021, http://download.redeemer.com/pdf/learn/resources/Why

_Plant_Churches-Keller.pdf. Cf. Timothy Keller, "Why Church Planting?" Acts 29, January 9, 2012, https://www.acts29.com/why-church-planting/.

30 Keller, "Why Plant Churches?" 2–4, 6.

31 Stefan Paas, *Church Planting in the Secular West: Learning from the European Experience*, The Gospel and Our Culture (Grand Rapids: Eerdmans, 2016), 10–31.

32 Perhaps the best recent example of this is David Garrison, though, tellingly, even he includes the ministries of Rick Warren and Bill Hybels under the heading "church planting movement"; Garrison, *Church Planting Movements*, 167.

33 Paas, *Church Planting*, 32–33.

34 Bonhoeffer, "Protestantism Without Reformation," 439–46; Paas, *Church Planting*, 31–49.

35 Stuart Murray, *Church Planting: Laying Foundations* (Scottsdale, PA: Herald Press, 2001), 88–89, 97–103. At times, US church planters also engage in what Murray called "replacement planting," starting churches in order to renew Christianity in areas where it has declined, or "sectarian planting," starting churches that express a particular denominational tradition; Murray, *Church Planting*, 88, 91–94.

36 Roland Allen, *Missionary Methods: St. Paul's or Ours?* (Cambridge: Lutterworth Press, 2006), 83, 124–25, 42–47; Roland Allen, *The Spontaneous Expansion of the Church—and the Causes Which Hinder It* (Cambridge: Lutterworth Press, 2006), 3.

37 Michael Moynagh, *Church for Every Context* (London: SCM, 2012), 197–221.

38 Moynagh, *Church for Every Context*, 206–8.

39 E.g., the seventh article of the Augsburg Confession; John Calvin, *Institutes of the Christian Religion*, trans. Henry Beveridge, vol. 4 (Edinburgh: Calvin Translation Society, 1846), 1.9, 21ff. The adverb "rightly" begs important questions about how a congregation proclaims the gospel and administers the sacraments. Chapter 4 will consider the theology of proclamation operant in many planted US churches. Sacramental theology, though, is slightly beyond the scope of this research, in part because planted American churches do not emphasize it as strongly as they do the ministry of the Word.

40 These are two of the criteria that have been established by researchers to define "new churches" in the United Kingdom; Sheila Akomiah-Conteh, "The Changing Landscape of the Church in Post-Christendom Britain: New Churches in Glasgow, 2000–2016" (PhD diss., University of Aberdeen, 2019), 125–36.

41 This is another criterion established by researchers examining "new churches" in the United Kingdom; Akomiah-Conteh, "Changing Landscape," 125–36.

42 Warren, for example, served for more than four decades at Saddleback, in part because his own research indicated that "healthy, large churches" are more likely to have one lead pastor serving for a long tenure. If Warren's findings are true, they bespeak a greater probability that planted churches which share Warren's vision will either have or seek a lead pastor willing to serve for many years. See Warren, *Purpose Driven Church*, 30–31. Tellingly, Pitt's analysis of current data on churches found, "The median age of founder-led congregations, across denominations, is about 25 years; 60% have been in existence for more than 20 years" (Pitt, *Church Planters*, 24). While not all founder-led churches will identify as "plants," some planted churches remain under the leadership of a founding pastor for many years.

43 Helen Cameron et al., *Talking About God in Practice: Theological Action Research and Practical Theology* (London: SCM, 2010), 54.

44 Cameron et al., *Talking About God in Practice*, 54.

45 John Swinton and Harriet Mowat, *Practical Theology and Qualitative Research*, 2nd ed. (London: SCM, 2016), 5. Swinton and Mowat attribute this idea to Margaret Mead.

46 Cameron et al., *Talking About God in Practice*, 14.

47 Swinton and Mowat, *Practical Theology and Qualitative Research*, 20.

48 Jeff Astley, *Ordinary Theology: Looking, Listening and Learning in Theology*, Explorations in Practical, Pastoral, and Empirical Theology (London: Routledge, 2017), 70–72.

49 Astley, *Ordinary Theology*, 71.

50 Astley, *Ordinary Theology*, 63–64.

51 Roger Finke and Rodney Stark, *The Churching of America, 1776–2005: Winners and Losers in Our Religious Economy*, rev. ed. (New Brunswick, NJ: Rutgers University Press, 2005).

52 The present researcher, for example, is technically a lay Christian.

53 Richard R. Osmer, *Practical Theology: An Introduction* (Grand Rapids: Eerdmans, 2008), 26.

54 Osmer, *Practical Theology*, 25–26.

55 Osmer, *Practical Theology*.

56 Osmer, *Practical Theology*, 27–29.

57 Osmer, *Practical Theology*, 28, 31–78.

58 Osmer, *Practical Theology*, 5.

59 Osmer, *Practical Theology*, 28–29, 79–128.

60 Osmer, *Practical Theology*, 8–9, 29, 129–74.

61 Osmer, *Practical Theology*, 29, 175–218.

62 Osmer, *Practical Theology*, 29, 175–218.

63 Osmer, *Practical Theology*, 17.

64 E.g., Johnson, *Biblical Porn*; Jessica Johnson, "The Fall of Mars Hill Church in Seattle: How Online Counter-Narratives Catalyzed Change," in *The Demise of Religion: How Religions End, Die, or*

Dissipate, ed. Michael Stausberg, Stuart A. Wright, and Carole M. Cusack (London: Bloomsbury Academic, 2020); Cosper, "Episode 1: Who Killed Mars Hill?"

65 Osmer, *Practical Theology*, 18–25.

66 Kathleen A. Cahalan and James Nieman, "Mapping the Field of Practical Theology," in *Life Abundant: Practical Theology, Theological Education, and Christian Ministry*, ed. Dorothy C. Bass and Craig Dykstra (Grand Rapids: Eerdmans, 2008), 84–85; Pete Ward, *Introducing Practical Theology: Mission, Ministry, and the Life of the Church* (Grand Rapids: Baker Academic, 2017), 100–102.

67 Osmer, *Practical Theology*, 1–29, 219–41.

68 Osmer, *Practical Theology*, 1–29, 219–41.

69 Cahalan and Nieman, "Mapping the Field," 84–85.

70 Jeff Astley, "The Analysis, Investigation, and Application of Ordinary Theology," in *Exploring Ordinary Theology: Everyday Christian Believing and the Church*, ed. Jeff Astley and Leslie J. Francis, Explorations in Practical, Pastoral and Empirical Theology (London: Routledge/Taylor & Francis, 2016), 3.

71 Paas, *Church Planting*, 3.

72 Osmer, *Practical Theology*, 18–20.

1 A Prehistory of Modern Church Planting

1 For a discussion of Allen's influence, see Craig Ott and J. D. Payne, eds., *Missionary Methods: Research, Reflections, and Realities*, Evangelical Missiological Society Series 21 (Pasadena: William Carey Library, 2013). For discussions of McGavran's influence, see Gary L. McIntosh, "Donald McGavran: Life, Influence and Legacy in Mission," in *The State of Missiology Today: Global Innovations in Christian Witness*, ed. Charles E. Van Engen, Missiological Engagements (Downers Grove, IL: InterVarsity Press, 2016); Charles E. Van Engen, "Innovating Mission: Retrospect and Prospect in the Field of Missiology," in Van Engen, *State of Missiology Today*.

2 Allen, *Missionary Methods*, 83, 124–25, 42–47; Allen, *Spontaneous Expansion*, 3.

3 Allen, *Missionary Methods*, 81, 141–45; Allen, *Spontaneous Expansion*, 5, 18–25, 32–33, 41–42.

4 Allen, *Missionary Methods*, 81, 111–25; Allen, *Spontaneous Expansion*, 43–59.

5 Allen, *Spontaneous Expansion*, 144–46.

6 Allen, *Spontaneous Expansion*, 144–46.

7 Rob S. Hughes, "Roland Allen's Understanding of the Spirit's Centrality in Mission," in Ott and Payne, *Missionary Methods*; C. Peter Wagner, *Church Planting for a Greater Harvest: A Comprehensive Guide* (Ventura, CA: Regal, 1990).

8 Allen, *Missionary Methods*, 81, 141–45; Allen, *Spontaneous Expansion*, 5, 18–25, 32–33, 41–42.
9 Allen, *Missionary Methods*.
10 E.g., Eddie Gibbs, *The Rebirth of the Church: Applying Paul's Vision for Ministry in Our Post-Christian World* (Grand Rapids: Baker Academic, 2013).
11 Cf. Eckhard J. Schnabel, *Paul the Missionary: Realities, Strategies and Methods* (Downers Grove, IL: InterVarsity Press, 2008), 13–14.
12 Robert L. Gallagher, "Missionary Methods: St. Paul's, St. Roland's, or Ours?" in Ott and Payne, *Missionary Methods*, 5, 11–12.
13 Allen, *Missionary Methods*.
14 Darrell Guder, *Be My Witnesses: The Church's Mission, Message, and Messengers* (Grand Rapids: Eerdmans, 1985); Darrell Guder, "Ecclesiology and Witness," in *The T&T Clark Handbook of Ecclesiology*, ed. Kimlyn J. Bender and D. Stephen Long (New York: T&T Clark, 2020); Lesslie Newbigin, *Mission in Christ's Way: Bible Studies* (Geneva: World Council of Churches Publications, 1987), accessed June 21, 2021, https://newbiginresources.org/wp-content/uploads/2016/12/87mcw.pdf; Gibbs and Bolger, *Emerging Churches*, 47–64.
15 Guder, *Be My Witnesses*; Gary Corwin, "From Roland Allen to Rick Warren: Sources of Inspiration Guiding North American Evangelical Missions Methodology, 1912–2012," in Ott and Payne, *Missionary Methods*, 84–88.
16 James W. Thompson, *The Church According to Paul: Rediscovering the Community Conformed to Christ* (Grand Rapids: Baker Academic, 2014), 247–48.
17 Thompson, *Church According to Paul*, 247–48.
18 Gibbs, *Rebirth of the Church*, 25–26.
19 Gibbs, *Rebirth of the Church*, 25–26.
20 Gibbs, *Rebirth of the Church*, 26.
21 Donald McGavran, *How Churches Grow: The New Frontiers of Mission* (London: World Dominion Press, 1959), 67–76.
22 Donald Anderson McGavran, *The Bridges of God: A Study in the Strategy of Missions* (London: World Dominion Press; New York: Friendship Press, 1955), 50–55.
23 McGavran, *Bridges of God*, 53.
24 McGavran, *Bridges of God*, 50–55.
25 McGavran, *Bridges of God*, 52–53; McGavran, *Understanding Church Growth*, 260–77.
26 McGavran, *How Churches Grow*, 67–76, 81, 113–21.
27 Lesslie Newbigin, *The Household of God: Lectures on the Nature of the Church* (London: SCM, 1953; New York: Friendship Press, 1954), 168–70. Newbigin was addressing a different missiology in this specific

context, but his concerns about instrumentalizing church for the sake of evangelism are wholly applicable to McGavran's work.

28 Johannes C. Hoekendijk, "The Call to Evangelism," *International Review of Mission* 39, no. 154 (1950); Johannes C. Hoekendijk, "The Church in Missionary Thinking," *International Review of Mission* 41, no. 3 (1952).

29 Newbigin, *Mission in Christ's Way*, 9–13; Newbigin, *Gospel in a Pluralist Society*, 118, 130–42; Bosch, *Transforming Mission*, 390–98, 402–30; Dale T. Irvin, "For the Sake of the World: Stephen B. Bevans and Johannes C. Hoekendijk in Dialogue," *International Bulletin of Mission Research* 44, no. 1 (2020), https://doi.org/10.1177/2396939319839291; Donald McGavran, "Essential Evangelism," in *Eye of the Storm: The Great Debate in Mission*, ed. Donald McGavran (Waco: Word, 1972).

30 E.g., Guder, *Be My Witnesses.*

31 Allen specifically laments that this had not yet happened; Allen, *Missionary Methods*, 142.

32 McGavran, *Bridges of God.*

33 Lesslie Newbigin, *The Other Side of 1984: Questions for the Churches* (Geneva: World Council of Churches Publications, 1983), https://newbiginresources.org/1983-the-other-side-of-1984-questions-for-the-churches-with-a-postscript-by-s-wesley-ariarajah/.

34 Hoekendijk, "Call to Evangelism," 163.

35 Hoekendijk, "Call to Evangelism," 163.

36 Hoekendijk, "Call to Evangelism," 166.

37 Thompson, *Church According to Paul*, 247–48.

38 Eric S. Fife and Arthur F. Glasser, *Missions in Crisis: Rethinking Missionary Strategy* (Chicago: InterVarsity Press, 1961), 72–107. Arthur Glasser was himself expelled from China in 1951 after five years of missionary service.

39 Hoekendijk, "Church in Missionary Thinking." Hoekendijk specifically cites India (p. 327) and Indonesia (p. 330) as places he thought likely to experience missionary expulsions in the near future, similar to those that had occurred in China.

40 Fife and Glasser, *Missions in Crisis*, 65, 67, 79, 82–83, 87–90, 147–52; Jordan Bishop, "Numerical Growth—An Adequate Criterion of Mission?" *International Review of Missions* 57, no. 227 (1968): 286; Marie-Louise Martin, "Does the World Need Fantastically Growing Churches?" *International Review of Missions* 57, no. 227 (1968).

41 Bishop, "Numerical Growth"; Ronan Hoffman, "Conversion and the Mission of the Church," *Journal of Ecumenical Studies* 5, no. 1 (1968); Avery Dulles, "The Changing Nature of Mission," in McGavran, *Eye of the Storm.*

42 Hoffman, "Conversion and the Mission of the Church."

43 Mark A. Noll, *The New Shape of World Christianity: How American Experience Reflects Global Faith* (Downers Grove, IL: InterVarsity Press, 2009), 20.

44 Dulles, "Changing Nature of Mission"; Ralph Winter, "The Highest Priority: Cross-Cultural Evangelism," in *Let the Earth Hear His Voice: Official Reference Volume, Papers and Responses*, ed. J. D. Douglas (Minneapolis: World Wide Publications, 1974).

45 E.g., Olson, *American Church in Crisis*; Noll, *New Shape of World Christianity*, 20. One of the earliest examples of this view of mission appeared in 1946, arguing that France had become a mission field; Henri Godon, Yvan Daniel, and Georges Guérin, *La France, pays de mission?* (Lyon: Les Éditions de l'Abeille, 1943). While rare, there have been challenges to the widespread perception of declining church attendance in the United States; see Finke and Stark, *Churching of America*.

46 Gibson Winter, *The Suburban Captivity of the Churches: An Analysis of Protestant Responsibility in the Expanding Metropolis* (New York: Macmillan, 1962).

47 Jürgen Schuster, "Karl Hartenstein: Mission with a Focus on the End," *Mission Studies* 19, no. 1 (2002).

48 Herwig Wagner, "Hartensteins Beitrag zum Aufbruch in der Missionstheologie 1945–1960," in *Karl Hartenstein—Leben in weltweitem Horizont Beitrage zu seinem 100 Geburtstag*, ed. Fritz Lamparter (Bonn: Verlag für Kultur und Wissenschaft, 1995), 133; quoted in Schuster, "Karl Hartenstein," 66.

49 Hoekendijk, "Call to Evangelism"; Hoekendijk, "Church in Missionary Thinking"; Schuster, "Karl Hartenstein," 75.

50 Irvin, "For the Sake of the World," 26.

51 Charles Van Engen, *Mission on the Way: Issues in Mission Theology* (Grand Rapids: Baker Books, 1996), 154–55; Irvin, "For the Sake of the World."

52 Timothy C. Tennent, "Lausanne and Global Evangelicalism: Theological Distinctives and Missiological Impact," in *The Lausanne Movement: A Range of Perspectives*, ed. Margunn Serigstad Dahle, Lars Dahle, and Knud Jørgensen, Regnum Edinburgh Centenary Series 22 (Oxford: Regnum Books International, 2014), 50.

53 Van Engen, *Mission on the Way*, 154–55.

54 Tennent, "Lausanne and Global Evangelicalism," 46. It is worth noting that Tennent's essay, quoted here, is reproduced in full on the Lausanne Movement's website (https://lausanne.org/content/lausanne-and-global-evangelicalism-theological-distinctives-and-missiological-impact, accessed May 13, 2021). The Lausanne website states, "The author is writing in a personal capacity and the views do not necessarily represent those of the Lausanne Movement,"

though its prominence on both the Lausanne Movement website and in the edited volume *The Lausanne Movement* suggest that Tennent's understanding of the Covenant has wide resonance.

55 Tennent, "Lausanne and Global Evangelicalism," 46. See also John Stott's commentary on the first article of the Lausanne Covenant; John Stott, "The Lausanne Covenant: An Exposition and Commentary," Lausanne Movement, Lausanne Occasional Papers 3 (1975), https://lausanne.org/occasional-paper/lop-3.

56 Stott, "Lausanne Covenant."

57 Efiong S. Utuk, "From Wheaton to Lausanne: The Road to Modification of Contemporary Evangelical Mission Theology," *Missiology: An International Review* 14, no. 2 (1986): 214; Tennent, "Lausanne and Global Evangelicalism," 50. See especially Howard Snyder's spirited defense of "church-centered evangelism"; Howard Snyder, "The Church as God's Agent in Evangelism," in Douglas, *Let the Earth Hear His Voice*, 329.

58 Utuk, "From Wheaton to Lausanne," 215–16.

59 Donald McGavran, "The Dimensions of World Evangelization," in Douglas, *Let the Earth Hear His Voice*.

60 See the following chapters in McGavran, *Eye of the Storm*: Donald McGavran, "Will Uppsala Betray the Two Billion?"; John Stott, "Does Section Two Provide Sufficient Emphasis on Evangelism?"; Alan Tippett, "For Uppsala to Consider"; and Ralph Winter, "Further Comment on 'Drafts for Sections.'"

61 Samuel Escobar, "Evangelism and Man's Search for Freedom, Justice, and Fulfillment," in Douglas, *Let the Earth Hear His Voice*.

62 Escobar, "Evangelism and Man's Search," 315.

63 McGavran, *Bridges of God*, 52–53; McGavran, *Understanding Church Growth*, 260–77; McGavran, "Will Uppsala Betray the Two Billion?"

64 Snyder, "Church as God's Agent in Evangelism"; Stott, "Lausanne Covenant"; Utuk, "From Wheaton to Lausanne."

65 Tennent, "Lausanne and Global Evangelicalism," 57.

66 Darren Dochuk, "Lausanne '74 and American Evangelicalism's Latin Turn," in *Turning Points in the History of American Evangelicalism*, ed. Heath W. Carter and Laura Rominger Porter (Grand Rapids: Eerdmans, 2017), 247.

67 Dochuk, "Lausanne '74," 247.

68 Lausanne Movement, "What Global Leaders Were Saying About Cape Town 2010," accessed November 5, 2021, https://lausanne.org/gatherings/related/what-global-leaders-were-saying-about-cape-town-2010.

69 Brad Christerson and Richard Flory, *The Rise of Network Christianity: How Independent Leaders Are Changing the Religious Landscape*,

Global Pentecostal and Charismatic Christianity (New York: Oxford University Press, 2017), 29.

70 Lausanne Movement, "Movement Day and Lausanne," accessed November 4, 2021, https://lausanne.org/content/lga/2016-05/movement-day-and-lausanne. Tim Keller gave two plenary addresses at the 2010 Lausanne Congress in South Africa, recorded and posted to the Lausanne Movement website; Timothy Keller, "Why Cities?" (paper presented at the Third Lausanne Congress on World Evangelization, Cape Town, South Africa, October 20, 2010), accessed November 4, 2021, https://lausanne.org/content/world-faiths-what-is-gods-global-urban-mission-tim-keller; Timothy Keller, "How Do You Reach Cities?" (paper presented at the Third Lausanne Congress on World Evangelization, Cape Town, South Africa, October 22, 2010), https://lausanne.org/content/how-reach-cities.

71 Tennent, "Lausanne and Global Evangelicalism," 45, 57–58; Stott, "Lausanne Covenant," preface; Utuk, "From Wheaton to Lausanne," 215, 217.

72 "The Lausanne Covenant Statement of Faith," Acts 29, accessed November 4, 2021, https://www.acts29.com/the-lausanne-covenant-statement-of-faith/.

73 McIntosh, "Donald McGavran"; Van Engen, "Innovating Mission."

74 McGavran, *Bridges of God*, 109–25, 143–49; McGavran, *How Churches Grow*, 73–76, 144–54; McGavran, *Understanding Church Growth*.

75 McGavran, *Understanding Church Growth*, 103–42, 284–85. It is worth noting that *Understanding Church Growth* was revised and republished twice, in 1980 and 1990.

76 McGavran, *How Churches Grow*, 144–54.

77 Allen, *Spontaneous Expansion*.

78 Warren, *Purpose Driven Church*, 13–16, 21, 29–31.

79 Stetzer, *Planting Missional Churches*, 24.

80 Van Engen, "Growth of the True Church."

81 McGavran, *Understanding Church Growth*, 85.

82 McGavran, *Understanding Church Growth*, 290.

83 McGavran, *Understanding Church Growth*, 289–91.

84 Michael O. Emerson and Christian Smith, *Divided by Faith: Evangelical Religion and the Problem of Race in America* (Oxford: Oxford University Press, 2000), 135–52.

85 Lyle E. Schaller, *44 Questions for Church Planters* (Nashville: Abingdon, 1991), 77–78.

86 Michael Moynagh, *Church in Life: Innovation, Mission and Ecclesiology* (London: SCM, 2017), 219–36.

87 Hybels and Hybels, *Rediscovering Church*; Gibbs and Bolger, *Emerging Churches*.

88 Warren, *Purpose Driven Church*, 174–75.

89 Rodney Stark and Roger Finke, *Acts of Faith: Explaining the Human Side of Religion* (Berkeley: University of California Press, 2000); Finke and Stark, *Churching of America.*
90 Finke and Stark, *Churching of America.*
91 Emerson and Smith, *Divided by Faith*, 135–36; Finke and Stark, *Churching of America*, 249–51.
92 Finke and Stark, *Churching of America*, 72–116, 156–96, 235–83.
93 Paas, *Church Planting*, 127–46.
94 Stark and Finke, *Acts of Faith*, 114–39.
95 McGavran, *Bridges of God*, 109–25; McGavran, *How Churches Grow*, 67–76; McGavran, "Will Uppsala Betray the Two Billion?"; Wagner, *Church Planting*, 11; Keller, "Why Plant Churches?" 1; Stetzer, *Planting Missional Churches*, 32.
96 Paas, *Church Planting*, 146–80.
97 Paas, *Church Planting*, 170–77.
98 Warren, *Purpose Driven Church*, 33. Bethany Moreton argued that Southern California was a popular destination for evangelicals relocating for economic reasons in the early to mid-twentieth century; Bethany Moreton, *To Serve God and Wal-Mart: The Making of Christian Free Enterprise* (Cambridge, MA: Harvard University Press, 2009), 24–35.
99 Stefan Paas, "Church Renewal by Church Planting: The Significance of Church Planting for the Future of Christianity in Europe," *Theology Today* 68, no. 4 (2012): 473, https://doi.org/10.1177/0040573611424326.
100 Paas, *Church Planting*, 156.
101 Paas, *Church Planting*, 111–80.
102 McGavran, *Understanding Church Growth*, 69–84; Finke and Stark, *Churching of America*, 12–22.
103 Roy Wallis and Steve Bruce, "The Stark-Bainbridge Theory of Religion: A Critical Analysis and Counter Proposals," *Sociological Analysis* 45, no. 1 (1984); Steve Bruce and Roy Wallis, "Homage to Ozymandias: A Rejoinder to Bainbridge and Stark," *Sociological Analysis* 46, no. 1 (1985); Steve Bruce, "Religion and Rational Choice: A Critique of Economic Explanations of Religious Behavior," *Sociology of Religion* 54, no. 2 (1993); Steve Bruce, *Choice and Religion: A Critique of Rational Choice Theory* (Oxford: Oxford University Press, 1999).
104 Finke and Stark, *Churching of America*, 72–116, 156–96, 235–83.
105 Bruce, *Choice and Religion*, 42–43.
106 Bruce, *Choice and Religion*, 42–43.
107 Bruce, *Choice and Religion*, 42–43.
108 Steve Bruce, "The Pervasive World-View: Religion in Pre-Modern Britain," *British Journal of Sociology* 48, no. 4 (1997).
109 Van Engen, "Growth of the True Church."
110 Van Engen, "Growth of the True Church," 454–507.

111 Lesslie Newbigin, *The Open Secret: An Introduction to the Theology of Mission*, rev. ed. (Grand Rapids: Eerdmans, 1995), 135–80; Newbigin, *Mission in Christ's Way*, 35–37.
112 Newbigin, *Mission in Christ's Way*, 35–37.
113 Newbigin, *Mission in Christ's Way*, 35–37.
114 McGavran, *Understanding Church Growth*, 198, 278–95.
115 Bosch, *Transforming Mission*, 391, 408, 442; cf. Matthew John, "Evangelism and the Growth of the Church," *International Review of Missions* 57, no. 227 (1968).
116 Bishop, "Numerical Growth," 288.
117 Newbigin, *Open Secret*, 131, 44–47, 57; Newbigin, *Gospel in a Pluralist Society*, 146, 151.
118 Wagner, *Church Planting*, 11. A few examples of this statement being cited by current church planting advocates include Keller, "Why Plant Churches?"; Keller, "Why Church Planting?"; Stetzer, *Planting Missional Churches*, 32.
119 Keller, "Why Plant Churches?" 1. It is worth recalling that this essay is cited on the Acts 29 website as part of its statement of faith; Keller, "Why Church Planting?"

2 Developing Operant Theology Within American Church Planting Movements

1 E.g., Hybels and Hybels, *Rediscovering Church*; Warren, *Purpose Driven Church*; Pritchard, *Willow Creek Seeker Services*; Bielo, *Emerging Evangelicals*; Wilford, *Sacred Subdivisions*; James, *Church Planting in Post-Christian Soil*; Johnson, *Biblical Porn*.
2 Osmer, *Practical Theology*, 4–6, 31–78.
3 Cahalan and Nieman, "Mapping the Field," 83–84.
4 Osmer, *Practical Theology*, 5–6, 11, 31–78.
5 Cahalan and Nieman, "Mapping the Field," 80–81.
6 Ward, *Introducing Practical Theology*, 27.
7 Pritchard, *Willow Creek Seeker Services*, 16.
8 Pritchard, *Willow Creek Seeker Services*, 16.
9 Lauren Winner, *The Dangers of Christian Practice: On Wayward Gifts, Characteristic Damage, and Sin* (New Haven: Yale University Press, 2018).
10 Ward, *Introducing Practical Theology*, 27–28.
11 Swinton and Mowat, *Practical Theology and Qualitative Research*, 13; Ward, *Introducing Practical Theology*, 103–4.
12 Astley, "Analysis, Investigation, and Application of Ordinary Theology," 3.
13 Miller, *Reinventing American Protestantism*, 20; Mark A. Noll, *Protestants in America*, Religion in American Life (Oxford: Oxford University

Press, 2000), 116–17, 122–29; Christerson and Flory, *Rise of Network Christianity*.

14 Miller, *Reinventing American Protestantism*.

15 Miller, *Reinventing American Protestantism*, 19.

16 Miller, *Reinventing American Protestantism*, 19; Christerson and Flory, *Rise of Network Christianity*, 18–26.

17 Miller, *Reinventing American Protestantism*, 19; Noll, *Protestants in America*, 116–17.

18 C. Peter Wagner, "Mission and Church in Four Worlds," in *Crucial Dimensions in World Evangelization*, ed. Arthur F. Glasser et al. (Pasadena: William Carey Library, 1976), 278–80.

19 Wagner, "Mission and Church in Four Worlds," 279; Miller, *Reinventing American Protestantism*, 20; John Fletcher, *Preaching to Convert: Evangelical Outreach and Performance Activism in a Secular Age* (Ann Arbor: University of Michigan Press, 2013), 234.

20 Miller, *Reinventing American Protestantism*, 20–22.

21 Miller, *Reinventing American Protestantism*, 20, 22–23.

22 Escobar, "Evangelism and Man's Search."

23 McGavran, "Dimensions of World Evangelization."

24 Miller, *Reinventing American Protestantism*, 33–35.

25 Miller, *Reinventing American Protestantism*, 48.

26 Warren, *Purpose Driven Church*, 33; Mark T. Mulder and Gerardo Martí, *The Glass Church: Robert H. Schuller, the Crystal Cathedral, and the Strain of Megachurch Ministry* (New Brunswick, NJ: Rutgers University Press, 2020), 39–50.

27 Dochuk, "Lausanne '74," 271; Mulder and Martí, *Glass Church*, 39–50, 55–56; Moreton, *To Serve God and Wal-Mart*, 24–35.

28 Miller, *Reinventing American Protestantism*, 33–35.

29 Miller, *Reinventing American Protestantism*, 161–62.

30 Miller, *Reinventing American Protestantism*, 16–19, 35–37.

31 Christerson and Flory, *Rise of Network Christianity*, 14, 19–20; Miller, *Reinventing American Protestantism*, 19, 50–51.

32 Miller, *Reinventing American Protestantism*, 50–51.

33 Miller, *Reinventing American Protestantism*, 50–51.

34 Christerson and Flory, *Rise of Network Christianity*, 14, 42.

35 Allen, *Missionary Methods*, 81, 141–45; Allen, *Spontaneous Expansion*, 5, 18–25, 32–33, 41–42.

36 C. Peter Wagner, *Apostles Today: Biblical Government for Biblical Power* (Ventura, CA: Regal, 2006), 23; quoted in Christerson and Flory, *Rise of Network Christianity*, 9.

37 Miller, *Reinventing American Protestantism*, 20.

38 Christerson and Flory, *Rise of Network Christianity*, 11.

39 Miller, *Reinventing American Protestantism*, 134–56.

40 Wagner, *Apostles Today*, 23; quoted in Christerson and Flory, *Rise of Network Christianity*, 9.
41 Christerson and Flory, *Rise of Network Christianity*, 11.
42 Miller, *Reinventing American Protestantism*, 37.
43 Christerson and Flory, *Rise of Network Christianity*, 11.
44 Warren, *Purpose Driven Church*, 38–39; Wilford, *Sacred Subdivisions*, 14; Kimon Howland Sargeant, *Seeker Churches: Promoting Traditional Religion in a Nontraditional Way* (New Brunswick, NJ: Rutgers University Press, 2000), 2.
45 Sargeant, *Seeker Churches*, 202–5; Wilford, *Sacred Subdivisions*, 169–71.
46 Pritchard, *Willow Creek Seeker Services*; Sargeant, *Seeker Churches*; Wilford, *Sacred Subdivisions*; Fletcher, *Preaching to Convert*, 220–61.
47 Warren, *Purpose Driven Church*, 32.
48 Warren, *Purpose Driven Church*, 38–39.
49 Emetuche, *Future of Church Planting*, 15.
50 This number includes "replants" of existing churches, new campus locations added to existing churches, and existing churches that choose to join the SBC. Nonetheless, the stated hope was that most will be genuinely new church plants, with a stated goal of at least six hundred entirely new churches planted per year; SBC Executive Committee, *Annual of the 2021 Southern Baptist Convention*, 247.
51 Hybels and Hybels, *Rediscovering Church*, 26–42.
52 Hybels and Hybels, *Rediscovering Church*, 46–55.
53 Hybels and Hybels, *Rediscovering Church*, 52, 206.
54 Pritchard, *Willow Creek Seeker Services*, 27.
55 Cf. Sargeant, *Seeker Churches*, 171–72.
56 Warren, *Purpose Driven Church*, 273. Cf. Wagner, "Mission and Church in Four Worlds," 279; Miller, *Reinventing American Protestantism*, 20.
57 Hybels and Hybels, *Rediscovering Church*, 32–42; Miller, *Reinventing American Protestantism*, 20.
58 Pritchard, *Willow Creek Seeker Services*, 28, 116–21; Miller, *Reinventing American Protestantism*, 20; Wilford, *Sacred Subdivisions*, 1.
59 Wilford, *Sacred Subdivisions*, 7–8, 169–70.
60 Hybels and Hybels, *Rediscovering Church*, 208; Wilford, *Sacred Subdivisions*, 5.
61 Warren, *Purpose Driven Church*, 46; Wilford, *Sacred Subdivisions*, 5.
62 Hybels and Hybels, *Rediscovering Church*, 206–7.
63 Warren, *Purpose Driven Church*, 50.
64 Wilford, *Sacred Subdivisions*, 3.
65 Saddleback Church, "Made New," accessed November 24, 2021.
66 Warren, *Purpose Driven Church*, 29–32.
67 Warren, *Purpose Driven Church*, 16, 30.
68 Warren, *Purpose Driven Church*, 15–16.

69 Allen, *Spontaneous Expansion.*
70 Warren, *Purpose Driven Church*, 251–53.
71 Warren, *Purpose Driven Church*, 254–55.
72 Hybels and Hybels, *Rediscovering Church*, 57–58, 205.
73 Hybels and Hybels, *Rediscovering Church*, 57–58.
74 Saddleback Church, "Connect," accessed November 7, 2021, https://saddleback.com/connect.
75 Schaller, *44 Questions*, 57–58; Saddleback Church, "Connect"; Fletcher, *Preaching to Convert*, 240–45.
76 Schaller, *44 Questions*, 56–57; Saddleback Church, "Connect."
77 Warren, *Purpose Driven Church*, 45–46; Saddleback Church, "Connect."
78 Noll, *Protestants in America*, 128–29.
79 Hybels and Hybels, *Rediscovering Church*, 208–9.
80 Fletcher, *Preaching to Convert*, 241.
81 Newbigin, *Gospel in a Pluralist Society*, 141–54; Bosch, *Transforming Mission*, 430–42.
82 Wilford, *Sacred Subdivisions*, 14.
83 Hybels and Hybels, *Rediscovering Church*, 207–8.
84 Warren, *Purpose Driven Church*, 294–302; Fletcher, *Preaching to Convert*, 236–37.
85 Hybels and Hybels, *Rediscovering Church*, 57–59, 205; Warren, *Purpose Driven Church*, 197ff.
86 Newbigin, *Gospel in a Pluralist Society*, 141–54. Cf. Bosch, *Transforming Mission*, 438.
87 Newbigin, *Gospel in a Pluralist Society*, 152.
88 Newbigin, *Gospel in a Pluralist Society*, 152.
89 Pritchard, *Willow Creek Seeker Services*, 223.
90 Fletcher, *Preaching to Convert*, 251.
91 Wilford, *Sacred Subdivisions*, 15–16; Fletcher, *Preaching to Convert*, 254–55.
92 Greg Hawkins and Cally Parkinson, *Reveal: Where Are You?* (Barrington, IL: Willow Creek Resources, 2007).
93 Pritchard, *Willow Creek Seeker Services*, 25.
94 Hybels and Hybels, *Rediscovering Church*, 172–177.
95 Pritchard, *Willow Creek Seeker Services*, 188–89.
96 Jill Stevenson, *Sensational Devotion: Evangelical Performance in Twenty-First-Century America* (Ann Arbor: University of Michigan Press, 2013), 221.
97 Warren, *Purpose Driven Church*, 80.
98 Warren, *Purpose Driven Church*, 103, 239–49.
99 Warren, *Purpose Driven Church*, 239–42.
100 Wilford, *Sacred Subdivisions*.

101 Warren, *Purpose Driven Church.*

102 Pritchard, *Willow Creek Seeker Services,* 12.

103 Hybels and Hybels, *Rediscovering Church;* Warren, *Purpose Driven Church.*

104 Purpose Driven Church, "Where Healthy Churches Are Built"; Global Leadership Network, "Who We Are"; Hybels and Hybels, *Rediscovering Church,* 142–44.

105 Sargeant, *Seeker Churches,* 202–5.

106 Pritchard, *Willow Creek Seeker Services,* 12–13.

107 Sargeant, *Seeker Churches,* 7–8.

108 Wilford, *Sacred Subdivisions,* 7–10, 169–71.

109 Wilford, *Sacred Subdivisions,* 7.

110 E.g., Newbigin, *Open Secret,* 135–80; Bosch, *Transforming Mission,* 391, 408, 425, 430; Garrison, *Church Planting Movements,* 24–25.

111 D. A. Carson, *Becoming Conversant with the Emerging Church: Understanding a Movement and Its Implications* (Grand Rapids: Zondervan, 2005), 11–44.

112 Carson, *Becoming Conversant with the Emerging Church,* 25–36; Gibbs and Bolger, *Emerging Churches;* Bielo, *Emerging Evangelicals.*

113 Mark Driscoll and Gerry Breshears, *Vintage Church: Timeless Truths and Timely Methods* (Wheaton, IL: Crossway, 2008), 53; Mark Driscoll, *Religion Saves + Nine Other Misconceptions* (Wheaton, IL: Crossway, 2009), 209–10.

114 Carson, *Becoming Conversant with the Emerging Church,* 11–44.

115 E.g., Chris Morton, "Eulogizing the Emergent Church and Defining a Missional Movement," *Growth and Mission,* February 21, 2013.

116 Robert E. Webber, *The Younger Evangelicals: Facing the Challenges of the New World* (Grand Rapids: Baker Books, 2002), 115–17; Robert E. Webber, ed., *Listening to the Beliefs of Emerging Churches: Five Perspectives* (Grand Rapids: Zondervan, 2007); Driscoll and Breshears, *Vintage Church;* Johnson, *Biblical Porn;* Johnson, "Fall of Mars Hill"; Zylstra, "How Acts 29 Survived—and Thrived."

117 Other recognizably Emerging churches in Seattle which were more theologically liberal took considerable pains to define themselves as distinct from Mars Hill, some even framing Mars Hill as a foil to their own missional church praxis; James, *Church Planting in Post-Christian Soil,* 122.

118 Craig Van Gelder, *The Ministry of the Missional Church: A Community Led by the Spirit* (Grand Rapids: Baker Books, 2007), 87, 102, 107; Driscoll, *Religion Saves,* 216; Bielo, *Emerging Evangelicals,* 11–12.

119 Lesslie Newbigin, *Foolishness to the Greeks: The Gospel and Western Culture* (Grand Rapids: Eerdmans, 1988); Newbigin, *Gospel in a Pluralist Society.* Evidence of Newbigin's influence is perhaps most visible

in the opening pages of the landmark 1998 book *Missional Church* as well as Sunquist and Young's 2015 edited volume of essays assessing Newbigin's work; Darrell L. Guder et al., eds., *Missional Church: A Vision for the Sending of the Church in North America*, The Gospel and Our Culture (Grand Rapids: Eerdmans, 1998), 3–5, 18–76; Scott W. Sunquist and Amos Yong, eds., *The Gospel and Pluralism Today: Reassessing Lesslie Newbigin in the 21st Century*, Missiological Engagements (Downers Grove, IL: InterVarsity Press, 2015).

120 Newbigin, *Mission in Christ's Way*; Newbigin, *Gospel in a Pluralist Society*.

121 Newbigin, *Gospel in a Pluralist Society*, 152.

122 Newbigin, *Gospel in a Pluralist Society*, 222–33.

123 E.g., Gibbs and Bolger, *Emerging Churches*, 47–64; Brian M. McLaughlin, "The Ecclesiology of the Emerging Church Movement," *Reformed Review* 61, no. 3 (2008): 105–8.

124 Escobar, "Evangelism and Man's Search."

125 Bielo, *Emerging Evangelicals*, 12.

126 Carson, *Becoming Conversant with the Emerging Church*, 14–25; Bielo, *Emerging Evangelicals*, 28–46; James, *Church Planting in Post-Christian Soil*, 122.

127 Bielo, *Emerging Evangelicals*, 45–46.

128 Carson, *Becoming Conversant with the Emerging Church*, 36–41; Bielo, *Emerging Evangelicals*; James, *Church Planting in Post-Christian Soil*, 113.

129 Bielo, *Emerging Evangelicals*, 40–42, 76–79; James, *Church Planting in Post-Christian Soil*, 119–21.

130 Craig Van Gelder and Dwight J. Zscheile, *Participating in God's Mission: A Theological Missiology for the Church in America*, The Gospel and Our Culture (Grand Rapids: Eerdmans, 2018), 188–222; Bielo, *Emerging Evangelicals*, 12.

131 Scot McKnight, *The King Jesus Gospel: The Original Good News Revisited* (Grand Rapids: Zondervan, 2011).

132 James, *Church Planting in Post-Christian Soil*, 119.

133 Hybels and Hybels, *Rediscovering Church*, 209.

134 Newbigin, *Gospel in a Pluralist Society*, 131.

135 James, *Church Planting in Post-Christian Soil*, 124–25.

136 Escobar, "Evangelism and Man's Search"; Stott, "Lausanne Covenant"; James, *Church Planting in Post-Christian Soil*, 122–25. The Lausanne Covenant is included on the Acts 29 Network website as part of their statement of faith; see "Lausanne Covenant Statement of Faith."

137 Newbigin, *Gospel in a Pluralist Society*, 134.

138 James, *Church Planting in Post-Christian Soil*, 113; Driscoll and Breshears, *Vintage Church*, 53; Driscoll, *Religion Saves*, 209–10.

139 Hoekendijk, "Call to Evangelism"; Hoekendijk, "Church in Missionary Thinking." Mark Driscoll accused some ECM leaders like Rob Bell of this problem, particularly when he felt that their theology had strayed from traditional Christian teaching; see Driscoll, *Religion Saves*, 209–42.
140 Van Engen, *Mission on the Way*, 155.
141 Van Engen, *Mission on the Way*, 155.
142 Bosch, *Transforming Mission*, 334; cf. 276, 334, 491–96, 401–2.
143 Webber, *Younger Evangelicals*, 107–23; Bielo, *Emerging Evangelicals*, 14–15, 70–117.
144 Bielo, *Emerging Evangelicals*, 15.
145 McLaughlin, "Ecclesiology of the Emerging Church Movement."
146 Bielo, *Emerging Evangelicals*, 14.
147 Bielo, *Emerging Evangelicals*, 82–97; James, *Church Planting in Post-Christian Soil*, 115–19.
148 Bielo, *Emerging Evangelicals*, 96.
149 Winfield Bevins, *Ever Ancient, Ever New: The Allure of Liturgy for a New Generation* (Grand Rapids: Zondervan, 2019); Bielo, *Emerging Evangelicals*, 41–42; James, *Church Planting in Post-Christian Soil*, 114–16.
150 McLaughlin, "Ecclesiology of the Emerging Church Movement," 102–3; Bielo, *Emerging Evangelicals*, 95.
151 McLaughlin, "Ecclesiology of the Emerging Church Movement," 102–3; Bielo, *Emerging Evangelicals*, 95.
152 Bielo, *Emerging Evangelicals*, 78–79, 95.
153 McLaughlin, "Ecclesiology of the Emerging Church Movement," 107–8.
154 Webber, *Younger Evangelicals*; McLaughlin, "Ecclesiology of the Emerging Church Movement"; Bielo, *Emerging Evangelicals*.
155 James, *Church Planting in Post-Christian Soil*, 122.
156 Gibbs and Bolger, *Emerging Churches*, 24.
157 Pritchard, *Willow Creek Seeker Services*, 25.
158 Warren, *Purpose Driven Church*, 80, 103, 239–49.
159 Wilford, *Sacred Subdivisions*, 1.
160 Bielo, *Emerging Evangelicals*, 47–69.
161 Gibbs and Bolger, *Emerging Churches*, 24. Cf. Fletcher, *Preaching to Convert*, 257–60.
162 Gibbs and Bolger, *Emerging Churches*, 24, 242–46.
163 Johnson, *Biblical Porn*, 6.
164 Driscoll and Breshears, *Vintage Church*, 247.
165 Driscoll and Breshears, *Vintage Church*, 247–48.
166 For example, the New Testament mentions multiple local leaders in Ephesus; see Acts 18:24–19:7; 20:17–38; 1 and 2 Timothy.
167 Driscoll and Breshears, *Vintage Church*, 247.

168 Johnson, *Biblical Porn*, 24.

169 Johnson, *Biblical Porn*, 24. Cf. Pritchard, *Willow Creek Seeker Services*, 25, 188–89.

170 Mike Cosper, host, *The Rise and Fall of Mars Hill*, podcast, "Episode 6: The Brand," *Christianity Today*, August 2, 2021, https://www.christianitytoday.com/ct/podcasts/rise-and-fall-of-mars-hill/rise-fall-mars-hill-podcast-mark-driscoll-brand.html.

171 E.g., Win Arn and Charles Arn, *The Master's Plan for Making Disciples: Every Christian an Effective Witness Through an Enabling Church*, 2nd ed. (Grand Rapids: Baker Books, 1998); Michael Moynagh, *Being Church, Doing Life: Creating Gospel Communities Where Life Happens* (Oxford: Lion Hudson, 2014), 180–236; Roy Moran, *Spent Matches: Igniting the Signal Fire for the Spiritually Dissatisfied* (Nashville: Thomas Nelson, 2015).

172 E.g., Arn and Arn, *Master's Plan*; Moynagh, *Being Church, Doing Life*, 180–236; Moran, *Spent Matches*.

173 Pritchard, *Willow Creek Seeker Services*, 223, 258–71; McKnight, *King Jesus Gospel*; Hawkins and Parkinson, *Reveal*.

174 Jeff Vanderstelt, *One Eighty: A Return to Disciple-Making* (Exponential, 2023), 29.

175 Vanderstelt, *One Eighty*, 78.

176 Bosch, *Transforming Mission*, 10, 232, 386, 436, 507; Newbigin, *Mission in Christ's Way*, 35–37.

177 This move also responds to critics of decision-based evangelism, which similarly focuses on numbers and "results"; McKnight, *King Jesus Gospel*.

178 E.g., Arn and Arn, *Master's Plan*. Moran describes one Kansas City, MO church's transition from a church plant inspired by Roland Allen and modeled after Willow Creek to a church focused on adopting DMM strategies, but still with an eye to numerical growth; Moran, *Spent Matches*, 97–119.

179 Arn and Arn, *Master's Plan*, 30.

180 McGavran, *Understanding Church Growth*, 216–32.

181 Arn and Arn, *Master's Plan*, 121–36.

182 E.g., Francis Chan, *Letters to the Church* (Colorado Springs: David C Cook, 2018). DMMs somewhat echo practices seen in the United Kingdom's Fresh Expressions of Church, though it is important to underscore that Fresh Expressions is a church planting movement whose literature explicitly articulates ways that new ecclesial communities might form, while DMM literature sometimes presumes that churches already exist and/or says little about them; see Moynagh, *Being Church, Doing Life*; Moynagh, *Church in Life*; cf. Arn and Arn, *Master's Plan*.

183 Vanderstelt, *One Eighty*, 101–2.

184 Christerson and Flory, *Rise of Network Christianity*, 158; Kirk Johnson, "Haggard's Church Discloses More on Sex Scandal," *New York Times*,

January 26, 2009, https://www.nytimes.com/2009/01/27/us/27haggard.html.

185 Craig Welch, "The Rise and Fall of Mars Hill Church," *Seattle Times*, September 12, 2014, updated February 4, 2016, https://www.seattletimes.com/seattle-news/the-rise-and-fall-of-mars-hill-church/.

186 Ruth Graham, "How a Megachurch Melts Down," *Atlantic*, November 7, 2014, https://www.theatlantic.com/national/archive/2014/11/houston-mark-driscoll-megachurch-meltdown/382487/.

187 Zylstra, "How Acts 29 Survived—and Thrived."

188 Kate Shellnutt, "Acts 29 Network CEO Removed amid 'Accusations of Abusive Leadership,'" *Christianity Today*, February 7, 2020, https://www.christianitytoday.com/news/2020/february/acts-29-ceo-steve-timmis-removed-spiritual-abuse-tch.html.

189 Jeff Coen and Manya Brachear Pashman, "After Years of Inquiries, Willow Creek Pastor Denies Misconduct Allegations," *Chicago Tribune*, March 23, 2018, https://www.chicagotribune.com/news/breaking/ct-met-willow-creek-pastor-20171220-story.html.

190 Emily McFarlan Miller, "Can Willow Creek Find Closure After Bill Hybels?" *Christianity Today*, July 24, 2019, https://www.christianitytoday.com/news/2019/july/willow-creek-bill-hybels-reconciliation-service.html.

191 Abby Perry, "Willow Creek and Harvest Struggle to Move On," *Christianity Today*, February 13, 2020, https://www.christianitytoday.com/ct/2020/february-web-only/willow-creek-harvest-after-hybels-macdonald-moving-on.html.

192 McFarlan Miller, "Can Willow Creek Find Closure?"

193 Russell Moore, "Southern Baptists Face Their #MeToo Moment," *New York Times*, February 13, 2019, https://www.nytimes.com/2019/02/13/opinion/southern-baptists-sexual-abuse.html.

194 Russell Moore, "This Is the Southern Baptist Apocalypse," *Christianity Today*, May 22, 2022, https://www.christianitytoday.com/ct/2022/may-web-only/southern-baptist-abuse-apocalypse-russell-moore.html; Kate Shellnutt, "Southern Baptists Refused to Act on Abuse, Despite Secret List of Pastors," *Christianity Today*, May 22, 2022, https://www.christianitytoday.com/news/2022/may/southern-baptist-abuse-investigation-sbc-ec-legal-survivors.html.

195 Peter Wehner, "The Evangelical Church Is Breaking Apart: Christians Must Reclaim Jesus from His Church," *Atlantic*, October 24, 2021, https://www.theatlantic.com/ideas/archive/2021/10/evangelical-trump-christians-politics/620469/.

196 Carl F. H. Henry, *The Uneasy Conscience of Modern Fundamentalism* (Grand Rapids: Eerdmans, 2003), 4; Pritchard, *Willow Creek Seeker Services*, 179–81; Emerson and Smith, *Divided by Faith*, 76–80; McKnight, *King Jesus Gospel*, 18, 26.

197 One reason why SBC problems became so overwhelming was precisely this structure, which conferred some legal protection on denominational oversight authorities. An attorney for the SBC's legal counsel reportedly told its Executive Committee that advising local congregations whom to hire, or not hire, might expose them to liability when problems surfaced; Shellnutt, "Southern Baptists."

198 Warren, *Purpose Driven Church.*

199 E.g., Van Engen, "Growth of the True Church"; Stetzer, *Planting Missional Churches*, 24.

200 Cosper, "Bonus Episode: Boca Raton's Church Planting O.G."

201 Van Engen, "Growth of the True Church."

202 Bielo, *Emerging Evangelicals*, 34–45.

203 James, *Church Planting in Post-Christian Soil*, 122.

204 Hybels and Hybels, *Rediscovering Church*, 208.

205 Mulder and Martí, *Glass Church*, 8.

206 Hybels and Hybels, *Rediscovering Church*, 169–75; Pritchard, *Willow Creek Seeker Services*, 23–26. DMMs are a notable exception to this pattern.

207 Hybels and Hybels, *Rediscovering Church*, 175–81.

208 Pritchard, *Willow Creek Seeker Services*, 27.

209 Warren, *Purpose Driven Church*, 129–34; Wilford, *Sacred Subdivisions*, 15.

210 Hybels and Hybels, *Rediscovering Church*, 210; Gibbs and Bolger, *Emerging Churches*, 142–59.

211 Perry, "Willow Creek and Harvest Struggle to Move On"; Graham, "How a Megachurch Melts Down."

212 This is the subtitle of Johnson, *Biblical Porn.*

213 Johnson, *Biblical Porn*, 14; Graham, "How a Megachurch Melts Down."

214 Perry, "Willow Creek and Harvest Struggle to Move On"; Johnson, *Biblical Porn*, 186; Graham, "How a Megachurch Melts Down"; Paas, *Church Planting*, 203.

215 Scott M. Gibson, *Should We Use Someone Else's Sermon? Preaching in a Cut-and-Paste World* (Grand Rapids: Zondervan, 2008).

216 Johnson, *Biblical Porn*, 35; Graham, "How a Megachurch Melts Down"; Ruth Graham, "'Sermongate' Prompts a Quandary: Should Pastors Borrow Words from One Another?" *New York Times*, July 6, 2021, https://www.nytimes.com/2021/07/06/us/sermongate-plagiarism-litton-greear.html.

217 Noll, *Protestants in America*, 137; Finke and Stark, *Churching of America*; Mulder and Martí, *Glass Church*, 20–24.

218 SBC-affiliated "Saddleback Community Church" is perhaps the best example of this omission, but it is far from alone; Wilford, *Sacred Subdivisions*, 10; Miller, *Reinventing American Protestantism*, 19, 35–37, 50–51.

219 Stetzer, *Planting Missional Churches*, 32; Paas, *Church Planting*, 181–241.
220 Cosper, "Bonus Episode: Boca Raton's Church Planting O.G."
221 Mulder and Martí, *Glass Church*, 20–24, 61–91; Cosper, "Episode 2: Boomers, the Big Sort."
222 Bob Smietana, "Saddleback Church Just Ordained Three Women as Pastors. The Southern Baptist Convention Says Only Men Should Be," *Washington Post*, May 11, 2021, https://www.washingtonpost.com/religion/2021/05/11/saddleback-ordain-women-sbc/.
223 Brandon Showalter, "SBC Committee to Consider Disaffiliating Saddleback Church for Ordaining Women Pastors," *Christian Post*, June 18, 2021, https://www.christianpost.com/news/sbc-committee-to-consider-disaffiliating-saddleback-church.html; SBC Executive Committee, *Annual of the 2021 Southern Baptist Convention*, 74; Kate Shellnutt, "Southern Baptist Convention Disfellowships Saddleback Church," *Christianity Today*, February 21, 2023, https://www.christianitytoday.com/news/2023/february/saddleback-church-southern-baptist-sbc-disfellowship-female.html.
224 Tim Morey, *Planting a Church Without Losing Your Soul: Nine Questions for the Spiritually Formed Pastor* (Downers Grove, IL: InterVarsity Press, 2020), 11.
225 Morey, *Planting a Church Without Losing Your Soul*, 11.
226 Morey, *Planting a Church Without Losing Your Soul*, 11–12.
227 Roxanne Stone, Emily McFarlan Miller, and Alejandra Molina, "Jarrid Wilson, a Megachurch Pastor Known Widely for His Mental Health Advocacy, Dies by Suicide," *Washington Post*, September 10, 2019, https://www.washingtonpost.com/religion/2019/09/10/jarrid-wilson-megachurch-pastor-known-widely-his-mental-health-advocacy-dies-by-suicide/.

3 Cultural Influences and American Church Planting Movements

1 Andrew F. Walls, *The Missionary Movement in Christian History: Studies in the Transmission of Faith* (Maryknoll, NY: Orbis, 1996), 8.
2 E.g., Walls, *Missionary Movement*, 3–15, 43–54, 221–40.
3 Osmer, *Practical Theology*, 4–7, 79–128.
4 Cahalan and Nieman, "Mapping the Field," 82.
5 Osmer, *Practical Theology*, 4–7, 79–128.
6 H. Richard Niebuhr, *Christ and Culture* (New York: Harper & Row, 1951).
7 Cahalan and Nieman, "Mapping the Field."
8 Cahalan and Nieman, "Mapping the Field," 84–85.
9 Cahalan and Nieman, "Mapping the Field," 83.
10 Swinton and Mowat, *Practical Theology and Qualitative Research*, 13; Ward, *Introducing Practical Theology*, 103–4.

11 William G. McLoughlin, *Revivals, Awakenings, and Reform: An Essay on Religion and Social Change in America, 1607–1977*, Chicago History of American Religion (Chicago: University of Chicago Press, 1978). Diana Butler Bass argues that there is a fourth Awakening in process, tied to contemporary modes of spirituality that are not necessarily church-based or even all Christian; Diana Butler Bass, *Christianity After Religion: The End of Church and the Beginning of a New Spiritual Awakening* (New York: HarperCollins, 2012).

12 McLoughlin, *Revivals, Awakenings, and Reform*, 45–96; Mark A. Noll, *The Rise of Evangelicalism: The Age of Edwards, Whitefield and the Wesleys*, A History of Evangelicalism: People, Movements and Ideas in the English-Speaking World (Downers Grove, IL: InterVarsity Press, 2003).

13 Iain Murray, "Charles Finney: How Theology Affects Understanding of Revival," in *Pentecost—Today? The Biblical Basis for Understanding Revival* (Edinburgh: Banner of Truth Trust, 1998).

14 McLoughlin, *Revivals, Awakenings, and Reform*, 122–31, 141–50; Murray, "Charles Finney."

15 McKnight, *King Jesus Gospel*, 73–93; Michael S. Hamilton, "From Desire to Decision: The Evangelistic Preaching of Billy Graham," in *Billy Graham: American Pilgrim*, ed. Andrew Finstuen, Anne Blue Wills, and Grant Wacker (Oxford: Oxford University Press, 2017), 54.

16 McKnight, *King Jesus Gospel*, 90.

17 Margaret Bendroth, "Afterword: Billy Graham's Legacy," in Finstuen, Wills, and Wacker, *Billy Graham: American Pilgrim*, 278; Grant Wacker, "Billy Graham's 1949 Los Angeles Revival," in Carter and Rominger Porter, *Turning Points in the History of American Evangelicalism*, 130.

18 Bendroth, "Afterword," 278.

19 Dochuk, "Lausanne '74"; William Martin, "God's Ambassador to the World," in Finstuen, Wills, and Wacker, *Billy Graham: American Pilgrim*, 108.

20 Gordon-Conwell Theological Seminary, "Our History," accessed December 10, 2021, https://www.gordonconwell.edu/about/history/; Mark A. Noll, *The Scandal of the Evangelical Mind* (Grand Rapids: Eerdmans, 1994), 219; Andrew Finstuen, "Professor Graham: Billy Graham's Missions to Colleges and Universities," in Finstuen, Wills, and Wacker, *Billy Graham: American Pilgrim*.

21 Rick Warren attended the Lausanne Convention of 1974, while Tim Keller, founding pastor of the City to City church planting movement, graduated from Gordon-Conwell in 1975. In the spirit of full disclosure, I am both a graduate of Gordon-Conwell and an adjunct instructor there.

22 Noll, *Scandal of the Evangelical Mind*, 213–14.

23 Andrew S. Finstuen, *Original Sin and Everyday Protestants: The Theology of Reinhold Niebuhr, Billy Graham, and Paul Tillich in an Age of Anxiety* (Chapel Hill: University of North Carolina Press, 2009), 132.

24 Finstuen, *Original Sin*, 132. Karl Barth similarly complained that Graham's preaching offered the "gospel at gunpoint," preaching "the law, not a message to make one happy"; Eberhard Busch, *Karl Barth: His Life from Letters and Autobiographical Texts*, trans. John Bowden (Philadelphia: Fortress, 1976), 446.

25 Perhaps most famously, Jonathan Edwards's eighteenth-century revival sermon "Sinners in the Hands of an Angry God."

26 William G. McLoughlin Jr., "Converts and Commercialism," in *Billy Graham: Revivalist in a Secular Age* (New York: Ronald Press, 1960), 177–78; Hamilton, "From Desire to Decision."

27 McLoughlin, "Converts and Commercialism," 175–77; Murray, "Charles Finney," 42–43.

28 McLoughlin, "Converts and Commercialism," 180.

29 Hamilton, "From Desire to Decision," 49.

30 Hybels and Hybels, *Rediscovering Church*, 174.

31 Hamilton, "From Desire to Decision," 49–50.

32 Anonymous Graham staffer, quoted in Sarah Lyall, "Billy Graham, Not Joel, Takes Long Island," *New York Times*, September 21, 1990, https://www.nytimes.com/1990/09/21/nyregion/billy-graham-not-joel-takes-long-island.html; quoted in Hamilton, "From Desire to Decision," 50.

33 Hybels and Hybels, *Rediscovering Church*, 69–70; Martí, *Hollywood Faith*, 1–2, 105–29; Hutchinson, "'Up the Windsor Road,'" 48; Martí, "Global Phenomenon of Hillsong Church," 382–83; Wagner, *Music, Branding, and Consumer Culture*, 48.

34 McLoughlin, "Converts and Commercialism," 184; Hamilton, "From Desire to Decision," 50. Wacker notes that photos of the 1949 Los Angeles revival indicate that people in attendance "mostly dressed as if they had just come from Sunday school," suggesting that Graham's encouragement fell largely on deaf ears; Wacker, "Billy Graham's 1949 Los Angeles Revival," 137. Cf. Warren, *Purpose Driven Church*, 273; Miller, *Reinventing American Protestantism*, 20.

35 Wacker, "Billy Graham's 1949 Los Angeles Revival," 134. Cf. Hybels and Hybels, *Rediscovering Church*, 57–59, 205; Warren, *Purpose Driven Church*, 197ff., 294–302.

36 Wacker, "Billy Graham's 1949 Los Angeles Revival," 135–36. Hillsong Church has most notably echoed this practice; Wagner, *Music, Branding, and Consumer Culture*, 63, 87.

37 Grant Wacker, "Introduction: An Overview," in Finstuen, Wills, and Wacker, *Billy Graham: American Pilgrim*, 2. During one of Graham's final crusades in my own hometown, I vividly recall a mentor saying that he had invited someone by arguing that Graham was a cultural icon and the opportunity to hear him in person was worth seizing.

38 Thumma, "Megachurch Phenomenon," 585.
39 Edith Blumhofer, "Singing to Save: Music in the Billy Graham Crusades," in Finstuen, Wills, and Wacker, *Billy Graham: American Pilgrim*. Cf. Pritchard, *Willow Creek Seeker Services*, 188–89.
40 McLoughlin, "Converts and Commercialism," 179, 182; Finstuen, *Original Sin*, 138–40.
41 Murray, "Charles Finney," 43–45.
42 McLoughlin, "Converts and Commercialism," 194–95.
43 McGavran, *Understanding Church Growth*.
44 McLoughlin, "Converts and Commercialism," 176.
45 McLoughlin, "Converts and Commercialism," 182–83.
46 See, for example, Grant Wacker's biography of Billy Graham; Grant Wacker, *America's Pastor: Billy Graham and the Shaping of a Nation* (Cambridge, MA: Belknap Press of Harvard University Press, 2014).
47 Elesha Coffman, "'You Cannot Fool the Electronic Eye': Billy Graham and Media," in Finstuen, Wills, and Wacker, *Billy Graham: American Pilgrim*, 200; Wacker, "Introduction: An Overview," 1–3.
48 Steven P. Miller, "Above Politics? Graham After Watergate," in *The Legacy of Billy Graham: Critical Reflections on America's Greatest Evangelist*, ed. Michael G. Long (Louisville: Westminster John Knox, 2008); Curtis J. Evans, "A Politics of Conversion: Billy Graham's Political and Social Vision," in Finstuen, Wills, and Wacker, *Billy Graham: American Pilgrim*, 150–51.
49 Miller, *Reinventing American Protestantism*, 134–56; Fletcher, *Preaching to Convert*, 254–55.
50 Hamilton, "From Desire to Decision," 54.
51 Carl F. H. Henry lamented that this was a common feature of evangelical preaching in the 1940s; Henry, *Uneasy Conscience*, 4; McKnight, *King Jesus Gospel*, 18.
52 Evans, "Politics of Conversion," 147; Hamilton, "From Desire to Decision," 57.
53 E.g., Karl Barth and Reinhold Niebuhr; Reinhold Niebuhr, "Literalism, Individualism, and Billy Graham," in *Essays in Applied Christianity*, ed. D. B. Robertson (New York: Meridian Books, 1959); Busch, *Karl Barth*, 446.
54 McKnight, *King Jesus Gospel*, 26. Cf. Pritchard, *Willow Creek Seeker Services*, 179–81.
55 N. T. Wright, foreword to McKnight, *King Jesus Gospel*, 13.
56 Emerson and Smith, *Divided by Faith*, 73–77.
57 Billy Graham, *Approaching Hoofbeats: The Four Horsemen of the Apocalypse* (Waco: Word, 1983). Graham later updated and republished much of this material; Billy Graham, *Storm Warning: Whether Global Recession, Terrorist Threats, or Devastating Natural Disasters, These Ominous Shadows Must Bring Us Back to the Gospel*, rev. ed. (Nashville: Thomas Nelson, 2010).

58 George M. Marsden, *Understanding Fundamentalism and Evangelicalism* (Grand Rapids: Eerdmans, 1991), 39–41, 66–71; Noll, *Scandal of the Evangelical Mind*, 126–41; Hamilton, "From Desire to Decision," 53.

59 Hamilton, "From Desire to Decision," 53.

60 Evans, "Politics of Conversion," 150.

61 Melvin L. Hodges, "A Pentecostal's View of Mission Strategy," *International Review of Missions* 57, no. 227 (1968): 310.

62 Bosch, *Transforming Mission*, 125–81, 320–34, 510–22; Bielo, *Emerging Evangelicals*, 138–56; Andrew F. Walls, "Eschatology and the Western Missionary Movement," *Studies in World Christianity* 22, no. 3 (2016).

63 Marsden, *Understanding Fundamentalism and Evangelicalism*, 66–67; Noll, *Scandal of the Evangelical Mind*, 132; Hamilton, "From Desire to Decision," 57.

64 David P. King, "Preaching Good News to the Poor: Billy Graham and Evangelical Humanitarianism," in Finstuen, Wills, and Wacker, *Billy Graham: American Pilgrim*, 127.

65 Jon Bialecki, "Eschatology, Ethics, and *Éthnos*: Ressentiment and Christian Nationalism in the Anthropology of Christianity," *Religion and Society: Advances in Research* 8, no. 1 (2017).

66 Martí, *Mosaic of Believers*, 79–85; Bielo, *Emerging Evangelicals*, 138–56.

67 Martí, *Mosaic of Believers*, 85.

68 Bielo, *Emerging Evangelicals*, 151–52.

69 Bielo, *Emerging Evangelicals*, 152.

70 Wacker, "Billy Graham's 1949 Los Angeles Revival," 133; Hamilton, "From Desire to Decision," 50.

71 Noll, *Rise of Evangelicalism*, 125–26.

72 McLoughlin, *Revivals, Awakenings, and Reform*, 63.

73 Evans, "Politics of Conversion," 146.

74 Evans, "Politics of Conversion," 144.

75 Evans, "Politics of Conversion," 144.

76 McLoughlin, "Converts and Commercialism," 186–88.

77 McLoughlin, "Converts and Commercialism," 193; Finstuen, *Original Sin*, 137.

78 Finstuen, *Original Sin*, 132.

79 McLoughlin, "Converts and Commercialism," 180–81.

80 C. Peter Wagner, *Frontiers in Missionary Strategy* (Chicago: Moody Press, 1972), 158.

81 Fletcher, *Preaching to Convert*, 252–55; Paas, *Church Planting*, 146–48. One recent study of megachurches, which admittedly are not all recently planted, found that no more than 6 percent of new members were previously "unchurched"; see Pitt, *Church Planters*, 242.

82 McKnight, *King Jesus Gospel*, 19–20. As evidence, McKnight cites prepublished findings of David Kinnaman's Barna study of young adults, which were subsequently published in David Kinnaman and Aly

Hawkins, *You Lost Me: Why Young Christians Are Leaving Church . . . and Rethinking Faith* (Grand Rapids: Baker Books, 2011). This study was repeated in 2019 using the same methodology, and the findings remained largely unchanged; David Kinnaman and Mark Matlock, *Faith for Exiles: 5 Proven Ways to Help a New Generation Follow Jesus and Thrive in Digital Babylon* (Grand Rapids: Baker Books, 2019).

83 McKnight, *King Jesus Gospel*, 19.

84 Pritchard, *Willow Creek Seeker Services*, 179–81; McKnight, *King Jesus Gospel*, 18.

85 R. Laurence Moore, *Selling God: American Religion in the Marketplace of Culture* (Oxford: Oxford University Press, 1994).

86 Moore, *Selling God*, 12–39; Matthew S. Hedstrom, "The Commodification of William James: The Book Business and the Rise of Liberal Spirituality in the Twentieth-Century United States," in *Religion and the Marketplace in the United States*, ed. Jan Stievermann, Philip Goff, and Detlef Junker (Oxford: Oxford University Press, 2015); Günter Leypoldt, "Literature and the Economy of the Sacred," in Stievermann, Goff, and Junker, *Religion and the Marketplace in the United States*.

87 Moore, *Selling God*, 40–66.

88 Moore, *Selling God*, 239–40.

89 Martí, *Hollywood Faith*, 49–51.

90 Moore, *Selling God*, 161; Martí, *Hollywood Faith*, 50–55.

91 Moore, *Selling God*, 161; Martí, *Hollywood Faith*, 50–55.

92 Martí, *Hollywood Faith*, 55.

93 Moore, *Selling God*, 220–31; Martí, *Hollywood Faith*, 43–59.

94 Hybels and Hybels, *Rediscovering Church*, 69–70; Martí, *Hollywood Faith*, 1–2, 105–29; Hutchinson, "'Up the Windsor Road,'" 48; Martí, "Global Phenomenon of Hillsong Church," 382–83; Wagner, *Music, Branding, and Consumer Culture*, 48.

95 Pitt, *Church Planters*, 32.

96 Martí, *Hollywood Faith*, 61–68; Stevenson, *Sensational Devotion*, 1–2.

97 Warren, *Purpose Driven Church*; Miller, *Reinventing American Protestantism*; Sargeant, *Seeker Churches*; Gibbs and Bolger, *Emerging Churches*, 242–46; Christerson and Flory, *Rise of Network Christianity*.

98 Martí, *Mosaic of Believers*, 88–116, 117–38; Martí, *Hollywood Faith*, 87–104, 177–92.

99 Niebuhr, *Christ and Culture*.

100 1 Cor 12.

101 Moore, *Selling God*, 41–43.

102 Paas, *Church Planting*, 224–41.

103 Martí, *Mosaic of Believers*; Martí, *Hollywood Faith*.

104 Jean-Claude Usunier and Jörg Stolz, eds., *Religions as Brands: New Perspectives on the Marketization of Religion and Spirituality*, Ashgate AHRC/ESRC Religion and Society (London: Ashgate, 2014), 8.

105 Pritchard, *Willow Creek Seeker Services*, 98–99.
106 Gibbs and Bolger, *Emerging Churches*, 24.
107 Pritchard, *Willow Creek Seeker Services*, 98–99.
108 Pritchard, *Willow Creek Seeker Services*, 98–99.
109 Pritchard, *Willow Creek Seeker Services*, 101–2, 209–11. Cf. Hybels and Hybels, *Rediscovering Church*, 211.
110 Pritchard, *Willow Creek Seeker Services*, 102.
111 Pritchard, *Willow Creek Seeker Services*, 102.
112 Josh Packard and George Sanders, "The Emerging Church as Corporatization's Line of Flight," *Journal of Contemporary Religion* 28, no. 3 (2013): 440.
113 Stevenson, *Sensational Devotion*, 182–83.
114 Driscoll and Breshears, *Vintage Church*, 247; Stevenson, *Sensational Devotion*, 184–91.
115 Hybels and Hybels, *Rediscovering Church*, 211; Pritchard, *Willow Creek Seeker Services*, 209–11; Stevenson, *Sensational Devotion*, 162–227.
116 Pete Ward, *Celebrity Worship*, Media, Religion and Culture (New York: Routledge, 2020), 139–55.
117 Coffman, "'You Cannot Fool the Electronic Eye,'" 207.
118 Seth Dowland, "Billy Graham's New Evangelical Manhood," in Finstuen, Wills, and Wacker, *Billy Graham: American Pilgrim*, 220.
119 Ward, *Celebrity Worship*, 8, 41.
120 Stevenson, *Sensational Devotion*, 187–88.
121 Fletcher, *Preaching to Convert*, 246.
122 Fletcher, *Preaching to Convert*, 224; Stevenson, *Sensational Devotion*, 24–49, 181–82.
123 Stevenson, *Sensational Devotion*, 191.
124 Fletcher, *Preaching to Convert*, 248.
125 Hybels and Hybels, *Rediscovering Church*, 209.
126 Driscoll and Breshears, *Vintage Church*, 247–48.
127 Francis Chan, *Forgotten God: Reversing Our Tragic Neglect of the Holy Spirit* (Colorado Springs: David C Cook, 2009), 143.
128 Fletcher, *Preaching to Convert*, 237–40; Packard and Sanders, "Emerging Church," 440–41.
129 Finke and Stark, *Churching of America*, 8–9.
130 Moore, *Selling God*, 214–15; Pritchard, *Willow Creek Seeker Services*, 50–79; Sargeant, *Seeker Churches*, 7–8.
131 Moore, *Selling God*, 214–15.
132 Fletcher, *Preaching to Convert*, 228; Stevenson, *Sensational Devotion*, 173–74.
133 Warren, *Purpose Driven Church*, 155–72; Pritchard, *Willow Creek Seeker Services*, 59–79; Packard and Sanders, "Emerging Church," 448–49.
134 Hybels and Hybels, *Rediscovering Church*, 57–58, 205.

135 Fletcher, *Preaching to Convert*, 220–22.
136 Fletcher, *Preaching to Convert*, 221; emphasis original.
137 Fletcher, *Preaching to Convert*, 222.
138 Stevenson, *Sensational Devotion*, 164–67; Wagner, *Music, Branding, and Consumer Culture*.
139 Packard and Sanders, "Emerging Church," 438.
140 Paas, "Church Renewal by Church Planting," 473.
141 Stevenson, *Sensational Devotion*, 172; Cosper, "Episode 6: The Brand."
142 Pritchard, *Willow Creek Seeker Services*, 208–22.
143 Finke and Stark, *Churching of America*, 8–9.
144 Adam Smith, *An Inquiry into the Nature and Causes of the Wealth of Nations*, Oxford World Classics (Oxford: Oxford University Press, 1998).
145 E.g., Smith, *Wealth of Nations*; Emerson and Smith, *Divided by Faith*, 126–33; Finke and Stark, *Churching of America*, 10–12.
146 Stark and Finke, *Acts of Faith*, 114–39.
147 Smith even argues that a cleric in an established state church, whose salary and living are secure, is likely to demonstrate much less "exertion," "zeal and industry" than pastors of independent churches, who rely on voluntary donations from members; Smith, *Wealth of Nations*, 437.
148 Stark and Finke, *Acts of Faith*, 201; Finke and Stark, *Churching of America*, 11–12.
149 Warren, *Purpose Driven Church*, 38–39.
150 Stark and Finke, *Acts of Faith*, 35–36.
151 Newbigin, *Household of God*, 165.
152 Newbigin, *Foolishness to the Greeks*, 114. Newbigin adds that similarly rapid growth "when it occurs in the human body is called cancer."
153 Newbigin, *Household of God*, 169.
154 Newbigin, *Open Secret*, 135–80.
155 Finke and Stark, *Churching of America*, 9.
156 Packard and Sanders, "Emerging Church," 450.
157 Packard and Sanders, "Emerging Church," 441.
158 Christerson and Flory, *Rise of Network Christianity*, 20–21. Cf. John Drane, *After McDonaldization: Mission, Ministry, and Christian Discipleship in an Age of Uncertainty*, Re:Lit Books (Grand Rapids: Baker Academic, 2008).
159 Christerson and Flory, *Rise of Network Christianity*, 21.
160 Packard and Sanders, "Emerging Church," 443.
161 Packard and Sanders, "Emerging Church," 446.
162 Packard and Sanders, "Emerging Church," 444.
163 Bob Smietana, "Americans Agree US Has Come Far in Race Relations, but Has a Long Way to Go," LifeWay Research, December 16, 2014, https://lifewayresearch.com/2014/12/16/americans-agree-u-s-has-come-far-in-race-relations-but-long-way-to-go/; Mark Chaves

and Alison Eagle, *Religious Congregations in 21st Century America*, National Congregations Study, November 2015, https://sites.duke.edu/ncsweb/files/2019/02/NCSIII_report_final.pdf.

164 Mark Chaves, *National Congregations Study: Machine-Readable File*, Department of Sociology, University of Arizona, 1999; quoted in Martí, *Mosaic of Believers*, 23.

165 Warren C. Bird and Scott Thumma, *Megachurch 2020: The Changing Reality in America's Largest Churches*, Hartford Institute for Religion Research/Evangelical Council for Financial Accountability, 2020, 4, https://hirr.hartfordinternational.edu/wp-content/uploads/2024/10/2020_megachurch_report.pdf

166 Thumma, *Twenty Years of Congregational Change*, 20–22.

167 Bird and Thumma, *Megachurch 2020*, 4.

168 McGavran, *Understanding Church Growth*, 198.

169 McGavran, *Understanding Church Growth*, 200, 215.

170 McGavran, *Understanding Church Growth*, 198–201, 215, 278–95.

171 McGavran, *Understanding Church Growth*, 215; emphasis original.

172 McGavran, *Bridges of God*, 10. Cf. Corwin, "From Roland Allen to Rick Warren," 71–72.

173 McGavran, *Bridges of God*, 10; Corwin, "From Roland Allen to Rick Warren," 71–72.

174 Emetuche, *Future of Church Planting*, 18.

175 Emetuche, *Future of Church Planting*, 13–26.

176 For a look at current regional confessional preferences, which broadly track with historic immigration patterns, see Olson, *American Church in Crisis*.

177 Dochuk, "Lausanne '74."

178 Jehu J. Hanciles, *Beyond Christendom: Globalization, African Migration, and the Transformation of the West* (Maryknoll, NY: Orbis, 2008).

179 Bonhoeffer, "Protestantism Without Reformation."

180 Bonhoeffer, "Protestantism Without Reformation."

181 Emerson and Smith, *Divided by Faith*, 135–52; Moynagh, *Church for Every Context*, 171–72; Bird and Thumma, *Megachurch 2020*, 5.

182 Emerson and Smith, *Divided by Faith*, 141–47; Michael O. Emerson, with Rodney M. Woo, *People of the Dream: Multiracial Congregations in the United States*, Course Book ed. (Princeton: Princeton University Press, 2006), 3.

183 Thumma, *Twenty Years of Congregational Change*, 20–22; Bird and Thumma, *Megachurch 2020*, 5.

184 Bob Smietana, "Sunday Morning in America Still Segregated—and That's OK with Worshipers," LifeWay Research, January 15, 2015, https://lifewayresearch.com/2015/01/15/sunday-morning-in-america-still-segregated-and-thats-ok-with-worshipers/.

185 Smietana, "Sunday Morning in America Still Segregated."

186 Emetuche, *Future of Church Planting*, 19.
187 Emerson, *People of the Dream*, 3.
188 Thumma, "Megachurch Phenomenon," 585.
189 Emerson and Smith, *Divided by Faith*, 147–51.
190 Warren, *Purpose Driven Church*, 173–84.
191 Wilford, *Sacred Subdivisions*, 71–88.
192 Hybels and Hybels, *Rediscovering Church*, 209; Warren, *Purpose Driven Church*, 325–27; Wilford, *Sacred Subdivisions*, 89–113.
193 Hozell C. Francis, *Church Planting in the African-American Context* (Grand Rapids: Zondervan, 1999), 102.
194 C. Peter Wagner, Win Arn, and Elmer L. Towns, *Church Growth: State of the Art* (Wheaton, IL: Tyndale House, 1986), 34; also cited in Francis, *Church Planting*, 101.
195 McGavran, *Understanding Church Growth*, 215; McGavran, "Essential Evangelism," 60–61.
196 McGavran, *Understanding Church Growth*, 215; emphasis original. Cf. McGavran, *Bridges of God*, 10–16.
197 Newbigin, *Mission in Christ's Way*, 35–37.
198 Bosch, *Transforming Mission*, 391, 408, 425. Having lived in South Africa under apartheid, Bosch had witnessed the damaging results of policies similar to the HUP; John Kevin Livingston, *A Missiology of the Road: Early Perspectives in David Bosch's Theology of Mission and Evangelism*, American Society of Missiology Scholarly Monograph Series (Cambridge: James Clarke, 2013), 42–58.
199 Emetuche, *Future of Church Planting*, 23–24.
200 Emetuche, *Future of Church Planting*, 19.
201 Pitt, *Church Planters*, 259. Pitt's research is the only formal study that I have encountered to include the COGIC in discussions of church planting.
202 "Attendance at religious services by race/ethnicity," Pew Research Center, 2014, https://www.pewforum.org/religious-landscape-study/compare/attendance-at-religious-services/by/racial-and-ethnic-composition/.
203 "Attendance at religious services by race/ethnicity."
204 C. Eric Lincoln and Lawrence H. Mamiya, *The Black Church in the African American Experience* (Durham, NC: Duke University Press, 1990), 382.
205 Lincoln and Mamiya, *Black Church*, 382.
206 Lincoln and Mamiya, *Black Church*, 382.
207 Lincoln and Mamiya, *Black Church*, 401.
208 Pitt, *Church Planters*, 197.
209 Lifeway Research, "Lifeway Research Shows 6 Keys to Success for African-American Church Plants," September 11, 2013, https://

lifewayresearch.com/2013/09/11/lifeway-research-shows-6-keys-to-success-for-african-american-church-plants/.

210 Tony Evans, *Oneness Embraced: Reconciliation, the Kingdom, and How We Are Stronger Together* (Chicago: Moody, 2011), 268.

211 Escobar, "Evangelism and Man's Search."

212 Spencer Perkins and Chris Rice, *More Than Equals: Racial Healing for the Sake of the Gospel* (Downers Grove, IL: InterVarsity Press, 1993); quoted in Emerson and Smith, *Divided by Faith*, 55.

213 James H. Cone, *Black Theology and Black Power* (Maryknoll, NY: Orbis, 1997/2018), 52.

214 Lincoln and Mamiya, *Black Church*, 13.

215 Escobar, "Evangelism and Man's Search."

216 Oak Cliff Bible Fellowship, "About Us: Our History," accessed December 7, 2021, https://www.ocbfchurch.org/about-us/our-history/.

217 "Tony Evans: The Urban Alternative," accessed December 7, 2021, https://tonyevans.org; "About Us: Our History"; "Tony Evans Shoots for the Goal," *DTS Voice*, July 7, 2006, accessed December 7, 2021, https://voice.dts.edu/article/tony-evans-shoots-for-the-goal-dallas-theological-seminary/.

218 For example, Conway Edwards of One Community Church near Dallas, the international church planter Jason Evans, and the founding of Dothan Community Church in Dothan, Alabama; One Community Church, "One Community Church Leadership Principles," accessed December 7, 2021; Jason E. Evans, "Who Will Go for Us?" Reconciliation Ministries Network, accessed December 7, 2021, https://www.rmni.org/files/afam/JasonEvansTeamFrance.pdf; Dothan Community Church, "About Us," accessed December 7, 2021. Evans identifies himself as a protégé of Sam Hart, who founded Grand Old Gospel Fellowship, a Black church planting network; Evans, *Oneness Embraced*, 228–29.

219 Evans, *Oneness Embraced*; Ryon J. Cobb, "Still Divided by Faith? Evangelical Religion and the Problem of Race in America, 1977–2010," in *Christians and the Color Line: Race and Religion After "Divided by Faith,"* ed. J Russell Hawkins and Phillip Luke Sinitiere (Oxford: Oxford University Press, 2013), 128; "Tony Evans Shoots for the Goal."

220 The Urban Alternative, "About The Urban Alternative," accessed December 13, 2021, http://tonyevans.org/about/the-urban-alternative.

221 Cf. Gerardo Martí, "Fluid Ethnicity and Ethnic Transcendence in Multiracial Churches," *Journal for the Scientific Study of Religion* 47, no. 1 (2008): 11.

222 Emerson, *People of the Dream*, 166.

223 Martí, *Hollywood Faith*; Korie L. Edwards, "Much Ado About Nothing? Rethinking the Efficacy of Multiracial Churches for Racial

Reconciliation," in Hawkins and Sinitiere, *Christians and the Color Line: Race and Religion After "Divided by Faith,"* 238.

224 Martí, *Mosaic of Believers*, 20–26; Emerson, *People of the Dream*, 29–46, 160; Thumma, *Twenty Years of Congregational Change*, 20–22.

225 Gibbs and Bolger, *Emerging Churches*, 30; Martí, *Mosaic of Believers*, 36–37; Bielo, *Emerging Evangelicals*, 115.

226 Martí, *Mosaic of Believers*, 29–32, 156–79.

227 Martí, *Mosaic of Believers*, 162.

228 Martí, *Mosaic of Believers*, 161.

229 Martí, *Mosaic of Believers*, 79–87. Cf. a recent ethnographic study of Calvary Chapel; Bialecki, "Eschatology, Ethics, and *Éthnos*."

230 Michael Lipka and Gregory A. Smith, "White Evangelical Approval of Trump Slips, but Eight-in-Ten Say They Would Vote for Him," Pew Research Center, July 1, 2020, https://www.pewresearch.org/fact-tank/2020/07/01/white-evangelical-approval-of-trump-slips-but-eight-in-ten-say-they-would-vote-for-him/

231 Justin Nortey, "Most White Americans Who Regularly Attend Worship Services Voted for Trump in 2020," Pew Research Center, August 30, 2021, https://www.pewresearch.org/fact-tank/2021/08/30/most-white-americans-who-regularly-attend-worship-services-voted-for-trump-in-2020/.

232 Lyman A. Kellstedt and John C. Green, "The Politics of the Willow Creek Association Pastors," *Journal for the Scientific Study of Religion* 42, no. 4 (2003): 550, 554.

233 Emerson and Smith, *Divided by Faith*, 97. Lincoln and Mamiya identified a similarly "wide gulf" separating Black and white cultures, which they argued had been "bolstered in large measure" by segregation; Lincoln and Mamiya, *Black Church*, 3.

234 Emerson and Smith, *Divided by Faith*, 173–82.

235 Emerson and Smith, *Divided by Faith*, 115–34.

236 Emerson and Smith, *Divided by Faith*, 76–80.

237 Emerson and Smith, *Divided by Faith*, 76–80.

238 Usunier and Stolz, *Religions as Brands*, 5.

239 Lincoln and Mamiya, *Black Church*, 5; Emerson and Smith, *Divided by Faith*, 173–82.

240 McGavran, *Bridges of God*, 45–46.

241 King, "Preaching Good News," 127.

242 Niebuhr, "Literalism, Individualism, and Billy Graham."

243 Niebuhr, "Literalism, Individualism, and Billy Graham."

244 Niebuhr, "Literalism, Individualism, and Billy Graham," 130.

245 Henry, *Uneasy Conscience*, 2.

246 Henry, *Uneasy Conscience*, 2.

247 King, "Preaching Good News," 127.

248 Pritchard, *Willow Creek Seeker Services*, 27.

249 King, "Preaching Good News," 121.
250 Emerson and Smith, *Divided by Faith*, 148–50.
251 Emerson and Smith, *Divided by Faith*, 148–50.
252 Emerson and Smith, *Divided by Faith*, 148–50.
253 Bird and Thumma, *Megachurch 2020*, 12.
254 Bird and Thumma, *Megachurch 2020*, 8–9, 12.
255 Cobb, "Still Divided by Faith?" 128–39.
256 Quoted in Wehner, "Evangelical Church."
257 Wehner, "Evangelical Church."
258 Wehner, "Evangelical Church." Bethlehem Baptist Church, though not itself a planted congregation, has experienced recent struggles that highlight challenges facing many planted congregations and training institutions; see Kate Shellnutt, "Bethlehem Baptist Leaders Clash over 'Coddling' and 'Cancel Culture,'" *Christianity Today*, August 20, 2021, https://www.christianitytoday.com/ct/2021/august-web-only/bethlehem-bcs-minneapolis-resign-meyer-empathy-rigney.html.
259 Jon Bialecki, *A Diagram for Fire: Miracles and Variation in an American Charismatic Movement*, The Anthropology of Christianity (Oakland: University of California Press, 2017), 193. Bialecki notes that the families that left were among the largest financial contributors to the church, and all were notably conservative politically, but there was still appreciable political diversity in the church after the split. This incident, though, suggests that planted churches risk losing both members and financial support if they do not project a sufficiently conservative perspective, something Wehner's reporting indicated was becoming a widespread concern; cf. Wehner, "Evangelical Church."
260 Gary Black Jr., "Finding Protoevangelical Faith: A Summary of Four Ethnographic Studies," *Ecclesial Practices* 2 (2015): 146.
261 Bialecki, "Eschatology, Ethics, and *Éthnos*," 49–51.
262 Black, "Finding Protoevangelical Faith," 146.
263 Timothy Keller, "The Decline and Renewal of the American Church: Part 2—The Decline of Evangelicalism," *Life in the Gospel* (Winter 2022), https://quarterly.gospelinlife.com/the-decline-of-evangelicalism/. Keller also argued that "liberal listeners" overattributed Mars Hill's struggles to theology, overlooking social and historical factors that shaped Mars Hill's expression of their theology. Keller's observation is important, but he fails to distinguish between operant and espoused theology. As Keller rightly notes, groups which espouse similar theologies in other parts of the world operate very differently due to different social and historical factors. Operant theology accounts for the expression of espoused theology, which social and historical factors indeed shape.
264 Bielo, *Emerging Evangelicals*.
265 As early as 2013, one blogger even wrote a "eulogy" for the movement; Morton, "Eulogizing the Emergent Church."

266 McLaughlin, "Ecclesiology of the Emerging Church Movement," 101; Packard and Sanders, "Emerging Church," 438–44; Black, "Finding Protoevangelical Faith," 142–43.

267 McLaughlin, "Ecclesiology of the Emerging Church Movement," 111–12; Bielo, *Emerging Evangelicals*, 13–14; Packard and Sanders, "Emerging Church," 448.

268 Jon Meacham, "Pastor Rob Bell: What if Hell Doesn't Exist?" *Time*, April 14, 2011, https://time.com/archive/6595616/pastor-rob-bell-what-if-hell-doesnt-exist/; Ed Thornton, "Heresy, Holiness, and Oprah: Rob Bell Interviewed," *Church Times*, June 14, 2018, https://www.churchtimes.co.uk/articles/2018/15-june/features/features/heresy-holiness-and-oprah-rob-bell-interviewed; Carson, *Becoming Conversant with the Emerging Church*, 157–87; Gerardo Martí and Gladys Ganiel, "Faith as Conversation," in *The Deconstructed Church: Understanding Emerging Christianity* (Oxford: Oxford University Press, 2014), 103–4; Johnson, *Biblical Porn*; Graham, "How a Megachurch Melts Down."

269 Carson, *Becoming Conversant with the Emerging Church*, 11–44; Bielo, *Emerging Evangelicals*, 5–10, 15–16; Black, "Finding Protoevangelical Faith."

270 Black, "Finding Protoevangelical Faith," 136–37. For example, Donald Miller, a popular author aligned with the Emerging church movement, delivered the benediction at the 2008 Democratic National Convention. LifeWay, a Christian bookstore operated by the SBC, eventually attached warning labels to Miller's books, alerting potential readers that some material within them was "inconsistent with historical evangelical theology" and advising readers to "read with discernment." Bob Smietana, "The Discerning Seller: LifeWay to Drop Warning Labels," *Christianity Today*, February 10, 2011, https://www.christianitytoday.com/ct/2011/february/discerningseller.html.

271 Keller, "Decline and Renewal."

272 Keller, "Decline and Renewal."

273 Stetzer, *Planting Missional Churches*, 166.

274 2 Cor 5:16–20.

275 Niebuhr, *Christ and Culture*.

4 Theological Interpretation of Church and the Revelation of the Word

1 Paul D. L. Avis, *The Church in the Theology of the Reformers* (Atlanta: John Knox, 1981), 81–94; Christoph Schwöbel, "The Creature of the Word: Recovering the Ecclesiology of the Reformers," in *On Being the Church: Essays on the Christian Community*, ed. Colin E. Gunton and Daniel W. Hardy (Edinburgh: T&T Clark, 1989).

2 Newbigin, *Gospel in a Pluralist Society*, 222–33.

3 Osmer, *Practical Theology*, 4, 8–9, 129–74.
4 Osmer, *Practical Theology*, 129–32, 139–47.
5 Cahalan and Nieman, "Mapping the Field," 84–85; Osmer, *Practical Theology*, 147; Ward, *Introducing Practical Theology*, 101–2.
6 Schwöbel, "Creature of the Word," 115.
7 Robert W. Jenson, *Systematic Theology*, vol. 1, *The Triune God* (Oxford: Oxford University Press, 1997); Robert W. Jenson, *Systematic Theology*, vol. 2, *The Works of God* (Oxford: Oxford University Press, 1999).
8 Karl Barth, *Evangelical Theology: An Introduction*, trans. Grover Foley (Edinburgh: T&T Clark, 1979); Karl Barth, *Church Dogmatics* I/2, ed. Geoffrey W. Bromiley and Thomas F. Torrance, trans. George T. Thomson and Harold Knight (Edinburgh: T&T Clark, 1956); Karl Barth, *Church Dogmatics* I/1, ed. Geoffrey Bromiley and Thomas Torrance, trans. Geoffrey Bromiley (Edinburgh: T&T Clark, 1975); Karl Barth, *Church Dogmatics* IV/1, ed. Geoffrey W. Bromiley and Thomas F. Torrance, trans. Geoffrey Bromiley (Edinburgh: T&T Clark, 1956/1988).
9 E.g., Dietrich Bonhoeffer, "The Visible Church in the New Testament," in *A Testament to Freedom: The Essential Writings of Dietrich Bonhoeffer*, ed. Geffrey B. Kelly and F. Burton Nelson (New York: HarperCollins, 1995), 153–54; Dietrich Bonhoeffer, "The Nature of the Church," in *Testament to Freedom*, 83–84; Dietrich Bonhoeffer, *Sanctorum Communio: A Theological Study of the Sociology of the Church*, ed. Clifford J. Green, trans. Reinhard Krauss and Nancy Lukens, vol. 1 of *Dietrich Bonhoeffer Works* (Minneapolis: Fortress, 2009), 225–29; Dietrich Bonhoeffer, *Discipleship*, ed. Geffrey B. Kelly and John D. Godsey, trans. Barbara Green and Reinhard Krauss, vol. 4 of *Dietrich Bonhoeffer Works* (Minneapolis: Fortress, 2001), 226.
10 Bonhoeffer, "Nature of the Church"; Bonhoeffer, "Visible Church in the New Testament"; Dietrich Bonhoeffer, *Life Together; Prayerbook of the Bible*, ed. Geffrey B. Kelly, trans. Daniel W. Bloesch and James H. Burtness, vol. 5 of *Dietrich Bonhoeffer Works* (Minneapolis: Fortress, 2005); Bonhoeffer, *Sanctorum Communio*; Bonhoeffer, *Discipleship*; Dietrich Bonhoeffer, *Letters and Papers from Prison*, ed. John W. de Gruchy, trans. Isabel Best et al., vol. 8 of *Dietrich Bonhoeffer Works* (Minneapolis: Fortress, 2010).
11 Avis, *Church in the Theology of the Reformers*, 81–94; Schwöbel, "Creature of the Word."
12 Quoted in Avis, *Church in the Theology of the Reformers*, 81.
13 Unless otherwise indicated, biblical quotations are from the ESV.
14 Jenson, *Systematic Theology*, 1:223; emphasis original.
15 Jenson, *Systematic Theology*, 2:270.
16 Jenson, *Systematic Theology*, 1:79.
17 Craig S. Keener, *The Gospel of John: A Commentary*, vol. 1 (Peabody, MA: Hendrickson, 2003), 346.

18 Jenson, *Systematic Theology*, 1:79–80.

19 Keener, *John*, 1:361. Cf. Martin Hengel, "The Prologue of the Gospel of John as the Gateway to Christological Truth," in *The Gospel of John and Christian Theology*, ed. Richard Bauckham and Carl Mosser (Grand Rapids: Eerdmans, 2008).

20 Keener, *John*, 1:361.

21 There is also one reference in John to "the *logos* that was written in the law" (15:25).

22 This same usage is consistent with the usage patterns seen in Philo's work describing a *logos*, which, much like the *logos* in John 1:1–18, describes a spoken word that creates the world according to a divine pattern. Philo also compares *logos* to a fast-moving stream, an image that Philo links to speech. See Philo, *On the Creation*, trans. F. H. Colson and G. H. Whitaker, Loeb Classical Library 226 (Cambridge, MA: Harvard University Press, 1929), 24–25; Philo, *The Sacrifices of Abel and Cain*, trans. F. H. Colson and G. H. Whitaker, Loeb Classical Library 227 (Cambridge, MA: Harvard University Press, 1929), 64–68; Philo, *On Dreams*, trans. F. H. Colson and G. H. Whitaker, Loeb Classical Library 275 (Cambridge, MA: Harvard University Press, 1934), 2:238–40. Cf. C. H. Dodd, *The Interpretation of the Fourth Gospel* (Cambridge: Cambridge University Press, 1953), 276–85; Raymond E. Brown, *The Gospel According to John I–XII*, Anchor Bible 29 (New Haven: Yale University Press, 2006), lvi; Hengel, "Prologue of the Gospel of John."

23 Cf. Brown, *Gospel According to John I–XII*, 523–24. Brown ultimately rejects this reading but calls it an "attractive hypothesis."

24 Barth, *Church Dogmatics* I/1.5, 33.

25 Barth, *Evangelical Theology*, 18–19.

26 Barth, *Church Dogmatics* I/1.5, 132–33.

27 Barth, *Church Dogmatics* I/1.5, 136. Cf. Eberhard Jüngel, *God as the Mystery of the World: On the Foundation of the Theology of the Crucified One in the Dispute Between Theism and Atheism*, trans. Darrell L. Guder (London: Bloomsbury T&T Clark, 2014), 11–12.

28 Barth, *Church Dogmatics* I/1.5, 135.

29 Jenson, *Systematic Theology*, 1:270.

30 Barth, *Evangelical Theology*, 18.

31 Barth, *Church Dogmatics*, I/1.5, 140.

32 Eberhard Jüngel, "My Theology—A Short Summary," in *Theological Essays II*, trans. Arnold Neufeldt-Fast and J. B. Webster (London: Bloomsbury Academic, 1995/2014), 6.

33 Martin Luther, *Sermons on the Gospel of St. John: Chapters 1–4*, ed. Jaroslav Pelikan, trans. Martin H. Bertram, vol. 22 of *Luther's Works*, ed. Jaroslav Pelikan and Helmut Lehmann (St. Louis: Concordia, 1957), 9.

34 Barth, *Church Dogmatics* I/2.19, 517.
35 Barth, *Church Dogmatics* I/1.5, 164.
36 Barth, *Church Dogmatics* I/1.5, 166.
37 Barth, *Church Dogmatics* I/1.5, 162–86.
38 Escobar, "Evangelism and Man's Search," 315.
39 Martin Luther, *Church and Ministry II*, ed. Conrad Bergendoff, trans. Helmut Lehmann, vol. 40 of *Luther's Works*, ed. Jaroslav Pelikan and Helmut Lehmann (St. Louis: Concordia, 1958), 37.
40 Luther, *Church and Ministry II*, 21–23.
41 Calvin, *Institutes* IV.8.2, 159f.; quoted in Schwöbel, "Creature of the Word," 145.
42 Calvin, *Institutes* IV.1.9, 21f.; quoted in Schwöbel, "Creature of the Word," 143. As Schwöbel rightly observes, in Calvin's understanding "everything else is excluded from the marks which distinguish the true church."
43 Questions occasionally arise about whether Matthew composed the pericope contained in 16:13–20 by adding the material in verses 17–19 from a separate tradition, which presumably included verses 17–19 in the context of different events. Such questions arise in part because verses 17–19 do not appear in parallel versions of the story recorded in Mark 8:27–30 or Luke 9:18–21. This analysis treats the final form of Matt 16:13–20 as a unified pericope because, in addition to the arguments Davies and Allison offer, manuscript evidence does not currently support omitting vv. 17–19. Furthermore, Tertullian, Origen, and Chrysostom all analyze the final form of the text, treating 16:17–19 with 16:13–20 as a single pericope. For a thorough examination of scholarly arguments about this text, see W. D. Davies and D. C. Allison, *Matthew 8–18*, International Critical Commentary (London: T&T Clark, 1991), 602–15.
44 The most natural reading of 16:18 is that the rock on which Jesus will build the church is Peter, the spokesperson of the disciples; cf. Davies and Allison, *Matthew 8–18*, 608–9, 627; Donald A. Hagner, *Matthew 14–28*, Word Biblical Commentary 33B (Dallas: Word, 1995), 470.
45 The only other appearances of the term *ekklesia* in the Gospels occur in Matt 18:17. The context is a discussion of church discipline (18:15–20), during which Jesus describes a series of conversations within the *ekklesia*. After addressing the possibility that a fallen Christian might not listen to the church (18:17), Jesus extends the same promise of authority that he previously gave to Peter (16:19) to include the entire church (18:18). Jesus also affirms his presence within the church (18:19–20). Matt 18:15–20 thus reinforces the idea that conversations, even in the face of different opinions, are an important means by which churches refine their identity.
46 Henry J. Cadbury, *The Making of Luke-Acts*, 2nd ed. (Peabody, MA: Hendrickson, 1999), 127–39; Craig S. Keener, *Acts*, ed. Ben

Witherington III, New Cambridge Bible Commentary (Cambridge: Cambridge University Press, 2020), 1–46.

47 Keener, *Acts*, 9–10.

48 E.g., Kenneth Duncan Litwak, *Echoes of Scripture in Luke-Acts: Telling the History of God's People Intertextually*, Journal for the Study of the New Testament Supplement Series (London: T&T Clark International, 2005), 168–73.

49 C. M. Blumhofer, "Luke's Alteration of Joel 3:1–5 in Acts 2:17–21," *New Testament Studies* 62, no. 4 (2016): 506. Cf. Litwak, *Echoes of Scripture*, 166–68; Craig S. Keener, *Acts: An Exegetical Commentary*, vol. 1, *An Introduction and 1:1–2:47* (Grand Rapids: Baker Academic, 2012), 872–73.

50 E.g., Allen, *Missionary Methods*; McGavran, *How Churches Grow*, 67–76; Gibbs, *Rebirth of the Church*.

51 Tom Greggs, "Sola Scriptura, the Community of the Church and a Pluralist Age: A Methodist Theologian Seeking to Read Scripture in and for the World," in *Theologians on Scripture*, ed. Angus Paddison (London: T&T Clark, 2016), 79–92.

52 Jack Barentsen and Léon van Ommen, "*Sola Scriptura* as Social Construction: A Practical Theological Approach," in *Sola Scriptura: Biblical and Theological Perspectives on Scripture, Authority, and Hermeneutics*, ed. Hans Burger, Arnold Huijgen, and Eric Peels, Studies in Reformed Theology 32 (Leiden: Brill, 2018), 290. Cf. Tom Greggs, *Dogmatic Ecclesiology*, vol. 1, *The Priestly Catholicity of the Church* (Grand Rapids: Baker Academic, 2019), 261.

53 Greggs, *Dogmatic Ecclesiology*, 1:262.

54 Greggs, *Dogmatic Ecclesiology*, 1:263.

55 This is particularly evident in Acts 15:22, which references "the whole church" deciding with the apostles and elders whom to send to Antioch. Luke also describes the Jerusalem "assembly" in 15:12 using the same Greek word (πλῆθος) that he uses in 15:30 to denote the full church gathering in Antioch to describe the complete, gathered congregation. See also Acts 4:32, 6:5.

56 Greggs, *Dogmatic Ecclesiology*, 1:263–64.

57 Greggs, *Dogmatic Ecclesiology*, 1:265.

58 Tom Greggs, "*Communio* Ecclesiology: The Spirit's Work of Salvation in the Life of the Church," in *Third Article Theology: A Pneumatological Dogmatics*, ed. Myk Habets (Minneapolis: Fortress, 2016), 357ff.

59 Jenson, *Systematic Theology*, 2:271.

60 Jenson, *Systematic Theology*, 1:121; emphasis original.

61 Martin Luther, *First Lectures on the Psalms II: Psalms 76–126*, ed. Hilton C. Oswald, trans. Herbert J. A. Bouman, vol. 11 of *Luther's Works*, ed. Jaroslav Pelikan and Helmut Lehmann (St. Louis: Concordia, 1976), 160.

62 Martin Luther, *Lectures on Titus, Philemon, and Hebrews*, ed. Jaroslav Pelikan and Walter Hansen, trans. Walter Hansen, vol. 29 of *Luther's Works*, ed. Jaroslav Pelikan and Helmut Lehmann (St. Louis: Concordia, 1968), 224.

63 Luther, *Lectures on Titus, Philemon, and Hebrews*, 224.

64 Timothy George, *Theology of the Reformers*, rev. ed. (Nashville: Broadman & Holman, 2013), 55. Cf. Jenson, *Systematic Theology*, 2:295; Willem van Vlastuin, "*Sola Scriptura*: The Relevance of Luther's Use of *Sola Scriptura* in *De Servo Arbitrio*," in Burger, Huijgen, and Peels, *Sola Scriptura*, 255.

65 According to Luther, this question had also worried Jerome; Martin Luther, *Lectures on Galatians: Chapters 5–6 (1535); Lectures on Galatians: Chapters 1–6 (1519)*, ed. Jaroslav Pelikan and Walter Hansen, trans. Richard Jungkuntz, vol. 27 of *Luther's Works*, ed. Jaroslav Pelikan and Helmut Lehmann (St. Louis: Concordia, 1964), 248–49. For a fuller assessment of the practical consequences of this reasoning for deaf Christians, see Rosamund Oates, "Speaking in Hands: Early Modern Preaching and Signed Languages for the Deaf," *Past and Present* 256, no. 1 (2021), https://doi.org/10.1093/pastj/gtab019.

66 Luther, *Lectures on Galatians*, 248–49.

67 Cf. Greggs, "Sola Scriptura," 81.

68 Augustine Thompson, "From Texts to Preaching: Retrieving the Medieval Sermon as an Event," in *Preacher, Sermon and Audience in the Middle Ages*, ed. Carolyn Muessig (Leiden: Brill, 2002), 16–18. The language used to preach medieval sermons is sometimes disputed, but the text of many vernacular medieval sermons has survived, some of which are examined in detail in various other essays in Muessig's edited volume. Cf. Van Vlastuin, "*Sola Scriptura*," 256.

69 Van Vlastuin, "*Sola Scriptura*," 255.

70 Greggs, "Sola Scriptura," 82.

71 Barth, *Church Dogmatics* I/1.4, 121.

72 Barth, *Church Dogmatics* I/1.4, 121.

73 Barth, *Church Dogmatics* I/1.4, 90.

74 Barth, *Church Dogmatics* I/2.19, 491.

75 Barth, *Church Dogmatics* I/2.19, 491.

76 Barth, *Evangelical Theology*, 17; emphasis original. Barth does give some possible scope for creative expression, saying, "Theology responds to the Logos of God . . . when it endeavors to hear and speak of him always anew on the basis of his self-disclosure in the Scriptures" (Barth, *Evangelical Theology*, 34). There is at least something "anew" in theology, though in Barth's conception it remains largely an echo or "response" to God, not a prayerful cry to God.

77 Barth, *Evangelical Theology*, 31.

78 Barth, *Church Dogmatics* I/1.5, 150.

79 Barth, *Evangelical Theology*, 38.
80 Barth, *Evangelical Theology*, 37–38. Cf. Barth, *Church Dogmatics* I/2.19, 490.
81 Jenson, *Systematic Theology*, 2:271.
82 Jenson, *Systematic Theology*, 1:80. Cf. Jüngel, "My Theology."
83 Jenson, *Systematic Theology*, 1:121.
84 Jenson, *Systematic Theology*, 2:16; emphasis original.
85 Jenson, *Systematic Theology*, 2:5–12.
86 Pritchard, *Willow Creek Seeker Services*, 25.
87 Blumhofer, "Luke's Alteration of Joel 3:1–5," 508.
88 C. K. Barrett, *A Critical and Exegetical Commentary on the Acts of the Apostles*, vol. 1, *Preliminary Introduction and Commentary on Acts I–XIV*, International Critical Commentaries (Edinburgh: T&T Clark, 1994), 137.
89 Keener, *Acts*, vol. 1, *An Introduction and 1:1–2:47*, 811.
90 Barth, *Church Dogmatics* I/1.4, 94.
91 Cf. Barth, *Church Dogmatics* I/2.19, 518.
92 Barth, *Church Dogmatics* I/1.4, 94.
93 Barth, *Church Dogmatics* I/2.19, 530.
94 Barth, *Church Dogmatics* I/2.19, 533.
95 Barth, *Evangelical Theology*, 39–40; emphasis original.
96 Martin Luther, *Lectures on Galatians: Chapters 1–4 (1535)*, ed. Jaroslav Pelikan and Walter Hansen, trans. Jaroslav Pelikan, vol. 26 of *Luther's Works*, ed. Jaroslav Pelikan and Helmut Lehmann (St. Louis: Concordia, 1963), 232–33; Luther, *Lectures on Galatians: Chapters 5–6 (1535); Lectures on Galatians: Chapters 1–6 (1519)*, 231.
97 Bonhoeffer, *Sanctorum Communio*, 145.
98 Bonhoeffer, *Sanctorum Communio*, 225.
99 Markus Barth, *The Broken Wall: A Study of the Epistle to the Ephesians* (London: Collins, 1960), 108; Jean-Noël Aletti, "Les difficultés ecclésiologiques de la lettre aux Éphésiens: Des quelques suggestions," *Biblica* 85, no. 4 (2004): 460.
100 Barth, *Broken Wall*, 90; Ernest Best, *A Critical and Exegetical Commentary on Ephesians*, International Critical Commentaries (Edinburgh: T&T Clark, 1998), 628.
101 Bonhoeffer, *Sanctorum Communio*, 229.
102 E.g., Schwöbel, "Creature of the Word."
103 Greggs, *Dogmatic Ecclesiology*, 1:12–15.
104 Edward Van't Slot, "Theonomy and Analogy in Ecclesiology: Sources in Barth and Bonhoeffer for a Dynamic Ecclesiology," *Zeitschrift für Dialektische Theologie*, Supplement Series 5 (2011): 51.
105 Bonhoeffer, "Nature of the Church," 84.
106 Greggs, *Dogmatic Ecclesiology*, 1:9.
107 Bonhoeffer, "Nature of the Church," 84.

108 Identifying "receptive populations" where churches might expect to grow quickly was a thread of McGavran's work which found wide resonance; McGavran, *Bridges of God*, 118–19; McGavran, *Understanding Church Growth*, 216–32, 282. Cities, for example, have long been cited as a particularly promising strategic location for planting churches; Allen, *Missionary Methods*, 12, 15; Roger S. Greenway, "Urbanization and Missions," in Glasser et al., *Crucial Dimensions in World Evangelization*; Roger S. Greenway and Timothy M. Monsma, *Cities: Missions' New Frontier*, 2nd ed. (Grand Rapids: Baker Academic, 2000); Timothy Keller, *Center Church: Doing Balanced, Gospel-Centered Ministry in Your City* (Grand Rapids: Zondervan, 2012), 181–249. David Olsen particularly critiqued this approach, concerned that it risked unduly aligning Christian churches with wealthy, educated, and influential urban populations and neglecting struggling rural communities; Olson, *American Church in Crisis*, 89–90. Lesslie Newbigin and Michael Green similarly worried about the potential for Western churches to develop a "Constantinian Captivity" to spheres of cultural and political influence; Newbigin, *Other Side of 1984*; Michael Green, *Evangelism in the Early Church: Lessons from the First Christians for the Church Today*, rev. ed. (Grand Rapids: Eerdmans, 2003), 364–65.

109 Thompson, *Church According to Paul*, 212.

110 Bonhoeffer, "Visible Church in the New Testament," 153–54.

111 Bonhoeffer, *Discipleship*, 226.

112 Bonhoeffer, "Nature of the Church," 83–84.

113 Bonhoeffer, *Sanctorum Communio*, 229.

114 Greggs, *Dogmatic Ecclesiology*, 1:4.

115 Tet-Lim N. Yee, *Jews, Gentiles and Ethnic Reconciliation: Paul's Jewish Identity and Ephesians*, Society for New Testament Studies Monograph Series 130 (Cambridge: Cambridge University Press, 2005); J. Albert Harrill, "Ethnic Fluidity in Ephesians," *New Testament Studies* 60, no. 3 (2014): 394; Thompson, *Church According to Paul*, 213.

116 Thompson, *Church According to Paul*, 19. Cf. Acts 2:44–47; 8:2; 15:20; Rom 14; 1 Cor 10:23–33.

117 Bonhoeffer, *Sanctorum Communio*.

118 Bonhoeffer, *Sanctorum Communio*, 93–94.

119 Bonhoeffer, *Sanctorum Communio*, 100–101. Cf. Warren, *Purpose Driven Church*.

120 For example, Mosaic Church in Hollywood, CA, has developed creative ministries to Christians navigating challenging dynamics in the modern entertainment industry. Professional networking and other related ministries within this planted church appear to be offered as pastoral care for their own members, many of whom work in entertainment industries; Martí, *Hollywood Faith*.

121 Bonhoeffer, *Sanctorum Communio*, 101.

122 Bonhoeffer, *Sanctorum Communio*, 173. Newbigin was wholly in agreement; cf. Newbigin, *Household of God*, 169.
123 Bonhoeffer, *Discipleship*, 238.
124 Bonhoeffer, "Nature of the Church," 85.
125 Bonhoeffer, *Discipleship*, 238.
126 Hoekendijk, "Call to Evangelism"; Hoekendijk, "Church in Missionary Thinking."
127 Bonhoeffer, *Discipleship*, 238.
128 Bonhoeffer, *Discipleship*, 233.
129 Dietrich Bonhoeffer, *Spiritual Care*, trans. Jay C. Rochelle (Minneapolis: Fortress, 1985), 71.
130 Barth, *Evangelical Theology*, 38.
131 Robert W. Jenson, *Visible Words: The Interpretation and Practice of the Christian Sacraments* (Philadelphia: Fortress, 1978).
132 Newbigin, *Gospel in a Pluralist Society*, 222–33.
133 Newbigin, *Gospel in a Pluralist Society*, 152.
134 Newbigin, *Gospel in a Pluralist Society*, 230. For a fuller discussion of how the church participates in Christ's priesthood on behalf of the world, see Greggs, *Dogmatic Ecclesiology*, 1:48–147.
135 Newbigin, *Gospel in a Pluralist Society*, 230.
136 Newbigin, *Gospel in a Pluralist Society*, 35.
137 Reggie L. Williams, *Bonhoeffer's Black Jesus: Harlem Renaissance Theology and an Ethic of Resistance* (Waco: Baylor University Press, 2014).
138 Williams, *Bonhoeffer's Black Jesus*, 4–5, 89–91.
139 Bonhoeffer, *Discipleship*, 248.
140 Bonhoeffer, *Discipleship*, 173.
141 Cf. Phil 2:3–11.
142 Bonhoeffer, *Letters and Papers from Prison*, 503–4.
143 Hoekendijk, "Church in Missionary Thinking"; Hoekendijk, "Call to Evangelism." David Platt, an American church planting advocate, helpfully reframes the act of church planting in terms of Christlike sacrifice; David Platt, *Radical Together: Unleashing the People of God for the Purpose of God* (Colorado Springs: Multnomah, 2011). See also Michael Jinkins, *The Church Faces Death: Ecclesiology in a Post-Modern Context* (Oxford: Oxford University Press, 1999).
144 Bonhoeffer, *Sanctorum Communio*, 152–53.
145 Bonhoeffer, *Sanctorum Communio*, 158. Cf. Bonhoeffer, *Sanctorum Communio*, 137–38, note 29.
146 Bonhoeffer, *Sanctorum Communio*, 158.
147 Dietrich Bonhoeffer, "The Question of the Boundaries of the Church and Church Union," in *Testament to Freedom*, 166.
148 Bonhoeffer, *Sanctorum Communio*, 141–42. Cf. Eph 4:13.
149 Bonhoeffer, *Sanctorum Communio*, 208–16.
150 Bonhoeffer, *Life Together*, 36.

151 Nicholas M. Healy, *Church, World and the Christian Life: Practical-Prophetic Ecclesiology* (Cambridge: Cambridge University Press, 2004), 25–51; Moynagh, *Church for Every Context*, 111; Moynagh, *Church in Life*, 241–42.

5 Practical Ways Forward for American Church Planting Movements

1 Moynagh, *Church for Every Context*, 105–7, 112, 118; Moynagh, *Church in Life*, 242, 247.

2 Moynagh, *Church for Every Context*; Moynagh, *Church in Life*; John A. Williams, "In Search of 'Fresh Expressions of Believing' for a Mission-Shaped Church," *Ecclesiology* 12, no. 3 (2016): 288–89.

3 Moynagh, *Church for Every Context*, 105–7, 112, 118; Moynagh, *Church in Life*, 242, 247.

4 To date, Moynagh has only briefly mentioned the four Nicene marks, and only to argue that they are too "performative" and fail to capture the "essence" of ecclesial relationships as fully as his model does; Moynagh, *Church for Every Context*, 109, 106–8. A forthcoming book by Moynagh, developed independently of this research, addresses the four Nicene marks more fully, albeit with a slightly different focus than this book has chosen; see Michael Moynagh, *Giving the Church: The Christian Community Through the Looking Glass of Generosity* (London: SCM, 2024), chap. 3, "An Attractive Gift? The Four Marks."

5 Osmer, *Practical Theology*, 175–218.

6 Osmer, *Practical Theology*, 175–218.

7 Ward, *Introducing Practical Theology*, 100. Cf. Osmer, *Practical Theology*, 21–24, 43, 148.

8 Ward, *Introducing Practical Theology*, 100.

9 Osmer, *Practical Theology*, 175–218.

10 Mission and Public Affairs Council, Church of England, *Mission-Shaped Church: Church Planting and Fresh Expressions of Church in a Changing Context* (London: Church House Publishing, 2004); Steven Croft, "What Counts as a Fresh Expression of Church and Who Decides?" in *Evaluating Fresh Expressions: Explorations in Emerging Church*, ed. Louise Nelstrop and Martyn Percy (London: Canterbury Press Norwich, 2008), 3.

11 Mission and Public Affairs Council, *Mission-Shaped Church*; Croft, "What Counts as a Fresh Expression," 3.

12 Croft, "What Counts as a Fresh Expression," 10.

13 Warren, *Purpose Driven Church*, 38–39; Pritchard, *Willow Creek Seeker Services*, 27; Sargeant, *Seeker Churches*, 2; Wilford, *Sacred Subdivisions*, 14.

14 Croft, "What Counts as a Fresh Expression," 4, 5–6. Cf. Mission and Public Affairs Council, *Mission-Shaped Church*, 33–34.

15 Michael Moynagh, *Emergingchurch.Intro* (Oxford: Monarch Books, 2004); Moynagh, *Church for Every Context*, 51–72; Gibbs and Bolger, *Emerging Churches*, 15–26; Cory E. Labanow, *Evangelicalism and the Emerging Church: A Congregational Study of a Vineyard Church*, Explorations in Practical, Pastoral and Empirical Theology (London: Routledge, 2016).

16 Martyn Percy, "Old Tricks for New Dogs? A Critique of Fresh Expressions," in Nelstrop and Percy, *Evaluating Fresh Expressions*, 27.

17 Books "introducing" Fresh Expressions to American audiences appeared only in the mid- to late 2010s; e.g., Travis Collins, *Fresh Expressions of Church* (Franklin, TN: Seedbed, 2015); Kenneth H. Carter and Audrey Warren, *Fresh Expressions: A New Kind of Methodist Church for People Not in Church* (Nashville: Abingdon, 2017). As the latter title indicates, Fresh Expressions in the United States have found the most traction within the United Methodist Church.

18 Mission and Public Affairs Council, *Mission-Shaped Church*, 91.

19 Percy, "Old Tricks for New Dogs," 35–36. Cf. Mission and Public Affairs Council, *Mission-Shaped Church*, 34.

20 Patricia Shaw, *Changing Conversations in Organizations: A Complexity Approach to Change*, Complexity and Emergence in Organizations (London: Routledge, 2002).

21 Moynagh, *Church for Every Context*, 106–7.

22 Moynagh, *Church for Every Context*, 118; emphasis added.

23 Moynagh, *Church in Life*, 247.

24 Moynagh, *Church for Every Context*, 118.

25 Mission and Public Affairs Council, *Mission-Shaped Church*, 105–6; Croft, "What Counts as a Fresh Expression," 3.

26 Moynagh, *Church for Every Context*, 208.

27 Moynagh, *Church for Every Context*, 197–221.

28 Moynagh, *Church for Every Context*, 208–11.

29 Moynagh, *Church for Every Context*, 208–9.

30 Moynagh, *Church for Every Context*, 209–13.

31 Pitt, *Church Planters*, 93–99, 121–27.

32 E.g., Hybels and Hybels, *Rediscovering Church*, 172–75; Pitt, *Church Planters*, 27–33. ECMs espoused a similar missional emphasis on relationships, but in practice sometimes operated more similarly to Seeker Sensitive churches; Gibbs and Bolger, *Emerging Churches*, 24; Bielo, *Emerging Evangelicals*, 12; Fletcher, *Preaching to Convert*, 257–60; James, *Church Planting in Post-Christian Soil*, 122.

33 Croft, "What Counts as a Fresh Expression," 10.

34 Barth, *Evangelical Theology*, 38; Bonhoeffer, "Nature of the Church," 84; Bonhoeffer, *Discipleship*, 226, 233, 238; Bonhoeffer, *Letters and Papers from Prison*, 503–4.

35 Moynagh, *Church for Every Context*, 105.

36 Newbigin, *Household of God*, 168–69; Bonhoeffer, *Sanctorum Communio*, 93–101.
37 Barth, *Church Dogmatics* I/1.4, 121; Barth, *Evangelical Theology*, 37–38.
38 Moynagh, *Church for Every Context*, 111; Moynagh, *Church in Life*, 241–42.
39 Barth, *Church Dogmatics* I/2.19, 530; Barth, *Church Dogmatics* I/1.4, 94; Bonhoeffer, "Visible Church in the New Testament," 153–54; Bonhoeffer, *Life Together*, 36; Bonhoeffer, *Discipleship*, 226.
40 Luther, *Lectures on Galatians: Chapters 5–6 (1535); Lectures on Galatians: Chapters 1–6 (1519)*, 248–49; Luther, *Lectures on Titus, Philemon, and Hebrews*, 224; Luther, *First Lectures on the Psalms II: Psalms 76–126*, 160; Oates, "Speaking in Hands."
41 Moynagh, *Church for Every Context*, 112.
42 Jenson, *Visible Words.*
43 John M. Hull, *Mission-Shaped Church: A Theological Response* (London: SCM, 2006).
44 Bonhoeffer, "Question of the Boundaries," 166; Bonhoeffer, *Sanctorum Communio*, 137–38, 152–53, 158.
45 Snyder, "Church as God's Agent in Evangelism"; Van Engen, *Mission on the Way*, 154–55; Tennent, "Lausanne and Global Evangelicalism," 50.
46 Hoekendijk, "Call to Evangelism"; Hoekendijk, "Church in Missionary Thinking."
47 Henry Blackaby, Richard Blackaby, and Claude King, *Experiencing God: Knowing and Doing the Will of God*, rev. ed. (Nashville: B&H, 2008); Henry Blackaby and Avery Willis Jr., "On Mission with God," in *Perspectives on the World Christian Movement: A Reader*, 4th ed., ed. Ralph D. Winter et al. (Pasadena: William Carey, 2013).
48 Moynagh, *Church for Every Context*, 118.
49 This type of problem was arguably best documented in Mars Hill Church in Seattle; Johnson, *Biblical Porn*, 76–110. Johnson also found that online forums created spaces that disrupted Driscoll's control over the church's conversations; Johnson, "Fall of Mars Hill."
50 E.g., Robert Mai and Alan Akerson, *The Leader as Communicator: Strategies and Tactics to Build Loyalty, Focus Effort, and Spark Creativity* (New York: AMACOM, 2003). Cf. Mark 10:42–45; 1 Tim 3:1–13; Titus 1:7–9; Jas 3:1; 1 Pet 5:1–4.
51 Moynagh, *Church in Life*, 242.
52 Charges of spiritual abuse arose at Mars Hill Church in Seattle and within the Acts 29 Network that emerged from Mars Hill; Johnson, *Biblical Porn*; Shellnutt, "Acts 29 Network CEO Removed."
53 Moynagh, *Church in Life*, 242.
54 Moynagh, *Church for Every Context*, 112.
55 Mission and Public Affairs Council, *Mission-Shaped Church*, 96–99.
56 Mission and Public Affairs Council, *Mission-Shaped Church*, 99.

57 Mission and Public Affairs Council, *Mission-Shaped Church*, 96–99.

58 Paul B. Coulter, "Church and Mission in Four Aspects: Church Planting Within a Missionary Ecclesiology for the One, Holy, Catholic and Apostolic Church in Contemporary Northern Ireland" (PhD diss., University of Aberdeen, 2016).

59 E.g., Stephen Pattison, "Some Straw for the Bricks: A Basic Introduction to Theological Reflection," in *The Blackwell Reader in Pastoral and Practical Theology*, ed. James Woodward and Stephen Pattison (Malden, MA: Blackwell, 2000); Shaw, *Changing Conversations*; Christoph Schwöbel, "A Theological Ontology of Communicative Relations," in *Theology and Conversation: Towards a Relational Theology*, ed. J. Haers and P. De Mey, Bibliotheca Ephemeridum Theologicarum Lovaniensium 172 (Leuven: Leuven University Press; Leuven: Peeters, 2003); Bruce L. McCormack and Kimlyn J. Bender, eds., *Theology as Conversation: The Significance of Dialogue in Historical and Contemporary Theology; A Festschrift for Daniel L. Migliore* (Grand Rapids: Eerdmans, 2009); Jeff Astley, "Ordinary Theology and the Learning Conversation with Academic Theology," in Astley and Francis, *Exploring Ordinary Theology*, 45–54; Martí and Ganiel, "Faith as Conversation"; Stephen B. Bevans, "A Prophetic Dialogue Approach," in *The Mission of the Church: Five Views in Conversation*, ed. Craig Ott (Grand Rapids: Baker Academic, 2016); Stephen B. Bevans and Roger P. Schroeder, *Prophetic Dialogue: Reflections on Christian Mission Today* (Maryknoll, NY: Orbis, 2011); Clare Watkins, *Disclosing Church: An Ecclesiology Learned from Conversations in Practice*, Explorations in Practical, Pastoral and Empirical Theology (London: Routledge, 2020).

60 Moynagh, *Church in Life*, 237.

61 Rom 12:4–8; 1 Cor 12; Eph 4, 5:21–6:9.

62 Eph 2:11–22; Yee, *Jews, Gentiles and Ethnic Reconciliation*; Harrill, "Ethnic Fluidity in Ephesians," 394; Thompson, *Church According to Paul*, 213.

63 Dietrich Bonhoeffer, *Barcelona, Berlin, New York: 1928–1931*, ed. Clifford J. Green, trans. Douglas W. Stott, vol. 10 of *Dietrich Bonhoeffer Works* (Minneapolis: Fortress, 2008), 581.

64 Bonhoeffer, *Discipleship*, 220.

65 Pattison, "Some Straw for the Bricks," 140.

66 Pattison, "Some Straw for the Bricks," 140.

67 Bonhoeffer, *Life Together*, 95.

68 E.g., Warren, *Purpose Driven Church*, 325–27.

69 Bonhoeffer, *Sanctorum Communio*, 245.

70 Bonhoeffer, *Sanctorum Communio*, 245. See also Peter Berger, "Sociology and Ecclesiology," in *The Place of Bonhoeffer: Essays on the Problems and Possibilities in His Thought*, ed. Martin E. Marty (Eugene, OR: Wipf and Stock, 1962), 72–73; Bruce Hindmarsh, "Is Evangelical

Ecclesiology an Oxymoron? A Historical Perspective," in *Evangelical Ecclesiology: Reality or Illusion?* ed. John G. Stackhouse Jr. (Grand Rapids: Baker Academic, 2003), 26–27.

71 Hybels and Hybels, *Rediscovering Church*, 209; Warren, *Purpose Driven Church*, 325–27; Wilford, *Sacred Subdivisions*, 89–113.

72 Barth, *Church Dogmatics* IV/1.62, 675.

73 This has been one of the most trenchant and persistent critiques of Fresh Expressions of Church, which applies the HUP when starting new Fresh Expressions. The basis of commonality is generally a shared interest, not a shared demographic. Nonetheless, the effect is often similar to churches built on shared demographics, particularly if an interest group becomes its own "niche" church that does not engage with any wider ecclesial community; Percy, "Old Tricks for New Dogs," 27, 36–38; Andrew Davison and Alison Milbank, *For the Parish: A Critique of Fresh Expressions* (London: SCM, 2010), 75–81.

74 Hybels and Hybels, *Rediscovering Church*, 69–70; Driscoll and Breshears, *Vintage Church*, 247; Martí, *Hollywood Faith*, 1–2, 105–29; Stevenson, *Sensational Devotion*, 184–91; Hutchinson, "'Up the Windsor Road,'" 48; Martí, "Global Phenomenon of Hillsong Church," 382–83; Wagner, *Music, Branding, and Consumer Culture*, 48.

75 Allen, *Spontaneous Expansion*; McGavran, *Understanding Church Growth*, 198, 278–95; Hybels and Hybels, *Rediscovering Church*, 57–58; Warren, *Purpose Driven Church*, 15–16, 251–55.

76 Warren, *Purpose Driven Church*, 273; Pritchard, *Willow Creek Seeker Services*, 28, 116–21; Miller, *Reinventing American Protestantism*, 13, 20, 22.

77 Rick Warren and Kay Warren, "Rick and Kay Warren on Navigating the Pain of Loss, Building Resiliency and Rebuilding in the Post-Pandemic World," in Leadership Conference (Holy Trinity Church Brompton, London, UK, May 4–5, 2021), accessed March 1, 2022, https://alpha.org/leadership-conversations-with-nicky-gumbel-podcast-rick-kay-warren/.

78 Warren and Warren, "Navigating the Pain of Loss."

79 Warren and Warren, "Navigating the Pain of Loss."

80 Warren and Warren, "Navigating the Pain of Loss."

81 Bonhoeffer, *Spiritual Care*, 71.

82 Barth, *Church Dogmatics* IV/1.62, 668–85, 712.

83 Bonhoeffer, "Nature of the Church," 84.

84 Bonhoeffer, "Nature of the Church," 84.

85 McGavran, *Bridges of God*, 118–19; McGavran, *Understanding Church Growth*, 216–32, 82.

86 Allen, *Missionary Methods*, 12, 15; Greenway, "Urbanization and Missions"; Greenway and Monsma, *Cities: Missions' New Frontier*; Keller, *Center Church*.

87 Olson, *American Church in Crisis*, 89–90.
88 Newbigin, *Other Side of 1984*; Green, *Evangelism in the Early Church*, 364–65.
89 Cf. Bonhoeffer, "Nature of the Church," 84.
90 Newbigin, *Mission in Christ's Way*, 14. Cf. 1 Cor 3:5–9
91 Pritchard, *Willow Creek Seeker Services*, 25.
92 Cf. Jenson, *Systematic Theology* 1; Jüngel, "My Theology."
93 Jenson, *Systematic Theology*, 2:235.
94 Cf. Jenson, *Systematic Theology*, 1:234–36; Jenson, *Systematic Theology*, 2:38–41. Jenson explicitly borrows from Jonathan Edwards, but we might also recall C. S. Lewis's image of Aslan singing creation into being; C. S. Lewis, *The Magician's Nephew*, The Chronicles of Narnia (New York: HarperCollins, 1983), 103–13, 119–21.
95 Jenson, *Systematic Theology*, 1:235.
96 Warren, *Purpose Driven Church*, 239–42.
97 McLaughlin, "Ecclesiology of the Emerging Church Movement," 102–3; Bielo, *Emerging Evangelicals*, 95.
98 Bonhoeffer, *Sanctorum Communio*, 161–62.
99 Bonhoeffer, *Life Together*, 82.
100 Erin Crider, *Writing Spiritual Autobiography: Discerning God in Your Personal Story*, Grove Spirituality Series 155 (Cambridge: Grove Books, 2020), 17–18, 23–24.
101 Bonhoeffer, *Life Together*, 82.
102 Acts 10:1–23; 15:1–35.
103 Driscoll and Breshears, *Vintage Church*, 247; Stevenson, *Sensational Devotion*, 184–91.
104 Driscoll and Breshears, *Vintage Church*, 247–48; Molly Worthen, "Who Would Jesus Smack Down?" *New York Times Magazine*, January 6, 2009, https://www.nytimes.com/2009/01/11/magazine/11punk-t.html.
105 Pritchard, *Willow Creek Seeker Services*, 188–89; Blumhofer, "Singing to Save"; Hamilton, "From Desire to Decision."
106 Barth, *Evangelical Theology*, 38; Greggs, "Sola Scriptura," 81.
107 Newbigin, *Mission in Christ's Way*, 30.
108 Heb 4:6.
109 Dan 9:1–19; cf. Dan 10:1–3, 12–14.
110 Jer 29:5–8.
111 Barth, *Church Dogmatics* IV/1.62, 701–12.
112 Bonhoeffer, "Protestantism Without Reformation," 95.
113 Bonhoeffer, "Protestantism Without Reformation," 95.
114 Hybels and Hybels, *Rediscovering Church*, 57–58, 205.
115 Allen, *Spontaneous Expansion*; McGavran, *How Churches Grow*; McGavran, *Understanding Church Growth*; Warren, *Purpose Driven Church*, 16, 30; Sargeant, *Seeker Churches*, 4.

116 Similarly, some Fresh Expressions have seen "a strong feeling of disenfranchisement, even disconnect" between their own congregations and existing parish churches; Davison and Milbank, *For the Parish*, x.

117 Stark and Finke, *Acts of Faith*, 114–39, 201; Finke and Stark, *Churching of America*, 8–9, 11–12.

118 Warren, *Purpose Driven Church*, 38–39.

119 Pitt, *Church Planters*, 81–93; Hybels and Hybels, *Rediscovering Church*, 46–55; Christerson and Flory, *Rise of Network Christianity*, 21. The limited literature that focuses on church planting in Black congregations acknowledges this problem with refreshing frankness; see Willie McPherson, "Planting Churches in the Black Community," in *Church Planting in the Black Community*, ed. Sid Smith (Nashville: Black Church Development Section, Sunday School Board of the Southern Baptist Convention, 1989), 123–24; Francis, *Church Planting*, 23–34.

120 Pitt, *Church Planters*, 81.

121 Utuk, "From Wheaton to Lausanne," 211–13; Jooseop Keum, "Beyond Dichotomy: Towards a Convergence Between the Ecumenical and Evangelical Understanding of Mission in Changing Landscapes," in Dahle, Dahle, and Jørgensen, *Lausanne Movement*; Tennent, "Lausanne and Global Evangelicalism," 49.

122 Zylstra, "How Acts 29 Survived—and Thrived."

123 E.g., Keller, "Why Plant Churches?" 2–4, 6.

124 Olson, *American Church in Crisis*, 145–46; Emetuche, *Future of Church Planting*, 15; Christerson and Flory, *Rise of Network Christianity*; North American Mission Board, Southern Baptist Convention, *2021 North American Mission Board Ministry Report*, July 2021, https://www.namb.net/wp-content/uploads/2021/07/2021_Annual_Ministry_Report.pdf.

125 Tormod Engelsviken, "The Role of the Lausanne Movement in Modern Christian Mission," in Dahle, Dahle, and Jørgensen, *Lausanne Movement*. The researcher recently spoke with someone involved in planning one such regional meeting.

126 Sargeant, *Seeker Churches*, 7–8.

127 Cosper, "Bonus Episode: Boca Raton's Church Planting O.G."

128 "Leadership Conference from Alpha," accessed March 1, 2022, https://www.leadershipconference.org.uk.

129 Martí and Ganiel, "Faith as Conversation," 79.

130 Reggie L. Williams, "Dietrich Bonhoeffer, the Harlem Renaissance and the Black Christ," in *Bonhoeffer, Christ and Culture*, ed. Keith L. Johnson and Timothy Larsen (Downers Grove, IL: InterVarsity Press, 2013); Williams, *Bonhoeffer's Black Jesus*, 4–5, 89–91. Cf. Bonhoeffer, *Discipleship*, 173, 248; Bonhoeffer, *Letters and Papers from Prison*, 503–4.

131 Evans, *Oneness Embraced*, 268.

132 Moynagh, *Church in Life*, 253.

133 Keller, *Center Church*, 360–62; Paas, *Church Planting*, 224–40.

134 Barth, *Church Dogmatics* IV/1.62, 714.
135 Barth, *Church Dogmatics* IV/1.62, 715–16.
136 Michael Frost and Alan Hirsch, *The Shaping of Things to Come: Innovation and Mission for the 21st-Century Church* (Grand Rapids: Baker Books, 2013), 273, 205–24.
137 See especially Frost and Hirsch, *Shaping of Things to Come*, 273, 5–24.
138 Bonhoeffer, *Discipleship*, 238.
139 Bonhoeffer, *Discipleship*, 238.
140 Moynagh, *Church for Every Context*, 208.
141 Moynagh, *Church for Every Context*, 211.
142 Moynagh, *Church in Life*, 149–50.
143 Emmanuel Levinas, *Totality and Infinity: An Essay on Exteriority*, trans. Alphonso Lingis (Pittsburgh: Duquesne University Press, 1992), 51; emphasis original.
144 Levinas, *Totality and Infinity*, 72–77.
145 For one of the clearest accounts of this stream of missional ecclesiology, see Guder, *Be My Witnesses*.
146 Bonhoeffer, *Spiritual Care*, 71; Bonhoeffer, *Sanctorum Communio*, 229; Bonhoeffer, *Discipleship*, 238.
147 Jay Pathak and Dave Runyon, *The Art of Neighboring: Building Genuine Relationships Right Outside Your Door* (Grand Rapids: Baker Books, 2012).
148 James, *Church Planting in Post-Christian Soil*, 125–26.
149 James, *Church Planting in Post-Christian Soil*, 125–36.
150 Moynagh, *Church for Every Context*, 215–16.
151 Bonhoeffer, "Nature of the Church," 85; Bonhoeffer, *Discipleship*, 238. Note especially the subtitle of Moynagh's 2014 book *Being Church, Doing Life*, which reads "Creating Gospel Communities Where Life Happens."
152 Marsden, *Understanding Fundamentalism and Evangelicalism*, 66–67; Bosch, *Transforming Mission*, 132; Martí, *Mosaic of Believers*, 79–85; Bielo, *Emerging Evangelicals*, 138–56; Evans, "Politics of Conversion," 150; Hamilton, "From Desire to Decision," 57; Hodges, "A Pentecostal's View of Mission Strategy," 310.
153 Keller, "Decline and Renewal." Cf. Stetzer, *Planting Missional Churches*, 166; Moynagh, *Church for Every Context*, 206–9.
154 Percy, "Old Tricks for New Dogs," 33.
155 Mission and Public Affairs Council, *Mission-Shaped Church*, 87. See also Moynagh, *Church in Life*, 254.
156 Moynagh, *Church for Every Context*, 101; emphasis original.
157 Moynagh, *Church for Every Context*, 101.
158 Matt 16:13–20; Acts 2:1–47; Acts 10:1–11:18; Acts 15:1–35.
159 Niebuhr, *Christ and Culture*; Percy, "Old Tricks for New Dogs," 35.
160 Moynagh, *Church for Every Context*, 102.

161 Newbigin, *Mission in Christ's Way*.
162 Newbigin, *Mission in Christ's Way*, 27.
163 Bevans and Schroeder, *Prophetic Dialogue*; Bevans, "Prophetic Dialogue Approach."
164 Moynagh, *Church in Life*, 252–53.
165 Stott, "Lausanne Covenant."
166 Hoekendijk, "Call to Evangelism"; Stetzer, *Planting Missional Churches*, 166; Keller, "Decline and Renewal." Such a posture resembles what Tom Greggs helpfully called the *ecclesia incurvata in se*, a church that embodies Augustine's description of sin: the soul turned in on itself; Greggs, *Dogmatic Ecclesiology*, 1:115.
167 E.g., Stark and Finke, *Acts of Faith*; Finke and Stark, *Churching of America*; Thumma, "Megachurch Phenomenon"; Mulder and Martí, *Glass Church*.

Conclusion

1 Newbigin, *Mission in Christ's Way*, 38.
2 Newbigin, *Mission in Christ's Way*, 38.
3 Newbigin, *Mission in Christ's Way*, 39.
4 Newbigin, *Mission in Christ's Way*, 16, 33–38.
5 Newbigin, *Mission in Christ's Way*, 13.
6 Matt 13:57; Mark 6:4; Luke 4:6, cf. Isa 53:3.
7 Bonhoeffer, *Discipleship*, 173.
8 Newbigin, *Mission in Christ's Way*, 20.
9 Bonhoeffer, *Spiritual Care*, 71; Bonhoeffer, *Sanctorum Communio*, 229; Bonhoeffer, *Discipleship*, 238.
10 Bonhoeffer, *Letters and Papers from Prison*, 503–4. Cf. Matt 18:19–20.
11 I recall here a personal testimony of a friend, once a nominal member of another faith, whose experiences gave her cause to be suspicious of Christians, now serving in full-time Christian ministry. The turning point for her was experiencing a church ministering to her family during her late father's terminal illness. As she said, in that experience she "saw a very different side of the church."
12 Bonhoeffer, *Spiritual Care*, 71.
13 Cahalan and Nieman, "Mapping the Field," 84.
14 Cahalan and Nieman, "Mapping the Field," 84.

Bibliography

Akomiah-Conteh, Sheila. "The Changing Landscape of the Church in Post-Christendom Britain: New Churches in Glasgow, 2000–2016." PhD diss., University of Aberdeen, 2019.

Aletti, Jean-Noël. "Les difficultés ecclésiologiques de la lettre aux Éphésiens: Des quelques suggestions." *Biblica* 85, no. 4 (2004): 457–74.

Allen, Roland. *Missionary Methods: St. Paul's or Ours?* Cambridge: Lutterworth Press, 2006.

Allen, Roland. *The Spontaneous Expansion of the Church—and the Causes Which Hinder It*. Cambridge: Lutterworth Press, 2006.

Arn, Win, and Charles Arn. *The Master's Plan for Making Disciples: Every Christian an Effective Witness Through an Enabling Church*. 2nd ed. Grand Rapids: Baker Books, 1998.

Astley, Jeff. "The Analysis, Investigation, and Application of Ordinary Theology." In *Exploring Ordinary Theology: Everyday Christian Believing and the Church*, edited by Jeff Astley and Leslie J. Francis, 1–9. Explorations in Practical, Pastoral and Empirical Theology. London: Routledge; New York: Taylor & Francis, 2016.

Astley, Jeff. "Ordinary Theology and the Learning Conversation with Academic Theology." In *Exploring Ordinary Theology: Everyday Christian Believing and the Church*, edited by Jeff Astley and Leslie J. Francis, 45–54. Explorations in Practical, Pastoral and Empirical Theology. London: Routledge; New York: Taylor & Francis, 2016.

Astley, Jeff. *Ordinary Theology: Looking, Listening and Learning in Theology*. Explorations in Practical, Pastoral and Empirical Theology. London: Ashgate; New York: Routledge, 2017.

"Attendance at religious services by race/ethnicity." Pew Research Center, 2014. https://www.pewresearch.org/religious-landscape-study/racial-and-ethnic-composition.

Avis, Paul D. L. *The Church in the Theology of the Reformers*. Atlanta: John Knox, 1981.

Barentsen, Jack, and Léon van Ommen. "*Sola Scriptura* as Social Construction: A Practical Theological Approach." In *Sola Scriptura: Biblical and Theological Perspectives on Scripture, Authority, and Hermeneutics*, edited by Hans Burger, Arnold Huijgen, and Eric Peels, 279–93. Studies in Reformed Theology 32. Leiden: Brill, 2018.

Barrett, C. K. *A Critical and Exegetical Commentary on the Acts of the Apostles*. International Critical Commentaries. Vol. 1, *Preliminary Introduction and Commentary on Acts I–XIV*. Edinburgh: T&T Clark, 1994.

Barth, Karl. *Church Dogmatics* I/1. Edited by Geoffrey W. Bromiley and Thomas F. Torrance. Translated by Geoffrey W. Bromiley. Edinburgh: T&T Clark, 1975.

Barth, Karl. *Church Dogmatics* I/2. Edited by Geoffrey W. Bromiley and Thomas F. Torrance. Translated by George T. Thomson and Harold Knight. Edinburgh: T&T Clark, 1956.

Barth, Karl. *Church Dogmatics* IV/1. Edited by Geoffrey W. Bromiley and Thomas F. Torrance. Translated by Geoffrey Bromiley. Edinburgh: T&T Clark, 1988.

Barth, Karl. *Evangelical Theology: An Introduction*. Translated by Grover Foley. Edinburgh: T&T Clark, 1979.

Barth, Markus. *The Broken Wall: A Study of the Epistle to the Ephesians*. London: Collins, 1960.

Bass, Diana Butler. *Christianity After Religion: The End of Church and the Beginning of a New Spiritual Awakening*. New York: HarperCollins, 2012.

Bendroth, Margaret. "Afterword: Billy Graham's Legacy." In *Billy Graham: American Pilgrim*, edited by Andrew Finstuen, Anne Blue Wills, and Grant Wacker, 278–91. Oxford: Oxford University Press, 2017.

Berger, Peter. "Sociology and Ecclesiology." In *The Place of Bonhoeffer: Essays on the Problems and Possibilities in His Thought*, edited by Martin E. Marty, 51–80. Eugene, OR: Wipf and Stock, 1962.

Best, Ernest. *A Critical and Exegetical Commentary on Ephesians*. International Critical Commentaries. Edinburgh: T&T Clark, 1998.

Bevans, Stephen B. "A Prophetic Dialogue Approach." In *The Mission of the Church: Five Views in Conversation*, edited by Craig Ott, 3–20. Grand Rapids: Baker Academic, 2016.

Bevans, Stephen B., and Roger P. Schroeder. *Prophetic Dialogue: Reflections on Christian Mission Today*. Maryknoll, NY: Orbis, 2011.

Bevins, Winfield. *Ever Ancient, Ever New: The Allure of Liturgy for a New Generation*. Grand Rapids: Zondervan, 2019.

Bialecki, Jon. *A Diagram for Fire: Miracles and Variation in an American Charismatic Movement.* The Anthropology of Christianity. Oakland: University of California Press, 2017.

Bialecki, Jon. "Eschatology, Ethics, and *Éthnos*: Ressentiment and Christian Nationalism in the Anthropology of Christianity." *Religion and Society: Advances in Research* 8, no. 1 (2017): 42–61.

Bielo, James S. *Emerging Evangelicals: Faith, Modernity, and the Desire for Authenticity.* New York: New York University Press, 2011.

Bird, Warren C., and Scott Thumma. *Megachurch 2020: The Changing Reality in America's Largest Churches.* Hartford Institute for Religion Research/Evangelical Council for Financial Accountability, 2020. https://hirr.hartfordinternational.edu/wp-content/uploads/2024/10/2020_megachurch_report.pdf.

Bishop, Jordan. "Numerical Growth—An Adequate Criterion of Mission?" *International Review of Missions* 57, no. 227 (1968): 284–90.

Black, Gary, Jr. "Finding Protoevangelical Faith: A Summary of Four Ethnographic Studies." *Ecclesial Practices* 2 (2015): 129–55.

Blackaby, Henry, Richard Blackaby, and Claude King. *Experiencing God: Knowing and Doing the Will of God.* Rev. ed. Nashville: B&H, 2008.

Blackaby, Henry, and Avery Willis Jr. "On Mission with God." In *Perspectives on the World Christian Movement: A Reader*, 4th ed., edited by Ralph D. Winter, Steven C. Hawthorne, Darrell R. Dorr, D. Bruce Graham, and Bruce A. Koch, 74–77. Pasadena: William Carey, 2013.

Blumhofer, C. M. "Luke's Alteration of Joel 3:1–5 in Acts 2:17–21." *New Testament Studies* 62, no. 4 (2016): 499–516.

Blumhofer, Edith. "Singing to Save: Music in the Billy Graham Crusades." In *Billy Graham: American Pilgrim*, edited by Andrew Finstuen, Anne Blue Wills, and Grant Wacker, 64–79. Oxford: Oxford University Press, 2017.

Bonhoeffer, Dietrich. *Barcelona, Berlin, New York: 1928–1931.* Edited by Clifford J. Green. Translated by Douglas W. Stott. Vol. 10 of *Dietrich Bonhoeffer Works.* Minneapolis: Fortress, 2008.

Bonhoeffer, Dietrich. *Discipleship.* Edited by Geffrey B. Kelly and John D. Godsey. Translated by Barbara Green and Reinhard Krauss. Vol. 4 of *Dietrich Bonhoeffer Works.* Minneapolis: Fortress, 2001.

Bonhoeffer, Dietrich. *Letters and Papers from Prison.* Edited by John W. de Gruchy. Translated by Isabel Best, Lisa E. Dahill, Reinhard Krauss, and Nancy Lukens. Vol. 8 of *Dietrich Bonhoeffer Works.* Minneapolis: Fortress, 2010.

Bonhoeffer, Dietrich. *Life Together; Prayerbook of the Bible.* Edited by Geffrey B. Kelly. Translated by Daniel W. Bloesch and James H. Burtness. Vol. 5 of *Dietrich Bonhoeffer Works.* Minneapolis: Fortress, 2005.

Bonhoeffer, Dietrich. "The Nature of the Church." In *A Testament to Freedom: The Essential Writings of Dietrich Bonhoeffer*, edited by Geffrey B. Kelly and F. Burton Nelson, 82–87. New York: HarperCollins, 1995.

Bonhoeffer, Dietrich. "Protestantism Without Reformation." In *Theological Education Underground, 1937–1940*, edited by Victoria J. Barnett, translated by Victoria J. Barnett, Claudia D. Bergmann, Peter Frick, and Scott A. Moore, 438–62. Vol. 15 of *Dietrich Bonhoeffer Works*. Minneapolis: Fortress, 2012.

Bonhoeffer, Dietrich. "The Question of the Boundaries of the Church and Church Union." In *A Testament to Freedom: The Essential Writings of Dietrich Bonhoeffer*, edited by Geffrey B. Kelly and F. Burton Nelson, 158–67. New York: HarperCollins, 1995.

Bonhoeffer, Dietrich. *Sanctorum Communio: A Theological Study of the Sociology of the Church*. Edited by Clifford J. Green. Translated by Reinhard Krauss and Nancy Lukens. Vol. 1 of *Dietrich Bonhoeffer Works*. Minneapolis: Fortress, 2009.

Bonhoeffer, Dietrich. *Spiritual Care*. Translated by Jay C. Rochelle. Minneapolis: Fortress, 1985.

Bonhoeffer, Dietrich. "The Visible Church in the New Testament." In *A Testament to Freedom: The Essential Writings of Dietrich Bonhoeffer*, edited by Geffrey B. Kelly and F. Burton Nelson, 153–57. New York: HarperCollins, 1995.

Bosch, David J. *Transforming Mission: Paradigm Shifts in the Theology of Mission*. Twentieth anniversary ed. American Society of Missiology Series 16. Maryknoll, NY: Orbis, 2011.

Brown, Raymond E. *The Gospel According to John I–XII*. Anchor Bible 29. New Haven: Yale University Press, 2006.

Bruce, Steve. *Choice and Religion: A Critique of Rational Choice Theory*. Oxford: Oxford University Press, 1999.

Bruce, Steve. "The Pervasive World-View: Religion in Pre-Modern Britain." *British Journal of Sociology* 48, no. 4 (1997): 667–80.

Bruce, Steve. "Religion and Rational Choice: A Critique of Economic Explanations of Religious Behavior." *Sociology of Religion* 54, no. 2 (1993): 193–205.

Bruce, Steve, and Roy Wallis. "Homage to Ozymandias: A Rejoinder to Bainbridge and Stark." *Sociological Analysis* 46, no. 1 (1985): 73–76.

Busch, Eberhard. *Karl Barth: His Life from Letters and Autobiographical Texts*. Translated by John Bowden. Philadelphia: Fortress, 1976.

Cadbury, Henry J. *The Making of Luke-Acts*. 2nd ed. Peabody, MA: Hendrickson, 1999.

Cahalan, Kathleen A., and James Nieman. "Mapping the Field of Practical Theology." In *For Life Abundant: Practical Theology, Theological Education, and Christian Ministry*, edited by Dorothy C. Bass and Craig Dykstra, 62–85. Grand Rapids: Eerdmans, 2008.

Calvin, John. *Institutes of the Christian Religion*. Translated by Henry Beveridge. Vol. 4. Edinburgh: Calvin Translation Society, 1846.

Cameron, Helen, Deborah Bhatti, Catherine Duce, James Sweeney, and Clare Watkins. *Talking About God in Practice: Theological Action Research and Practical Theology*. London: SCM, 2010.

Carson, D. A. *Becoming Conversant with the Emerging Church: Understanding a Movement and Its Implications*. Grand Rapids: Zondervan, 2005.

Carter, Kenneth H., Jr., and Audrey Warren. *Fresh Expressions: A New Kind of Methodist Church for People Not in Church*. Nashville: Abingdon, 2017.

Chamberlain, Dale. "Hillsong Atlanta Pastor Sam Collier Announces Resignation, Cites Recent Scandals as Reason." *Church Leaders*, March 23, 2022. https://churchleaders.com/news/420312-sam-collier-resignation-hillsong-atlanta.html.

Chan, Francis. *Forgotten God: Reversing Our Tragic Neglect of the Holy Spirit*. Colorado Springs: David C Cook, 2009.

Chan, Francis. *Letters to the Church*. Colorado Springs: David C Cook, 2018.

Chaves, Mark, and Alison Eagle. *Religious Congregations in 21st Century America*. National Congregations Study, November 2015. https://sites.duke.edu/ncsweb/files/2019/02/NCSIII_report_final.pdf.

Christerson, Brad, and Richard Flory. *The Rise of Network Christianity: How Independent Leaders Are Changing the Religious Landscape*. Global Pentecostal and Charismatic Christianity. New York: Oxford University Press, 2017.

Christianity Today. "*Christianity Today*'s New Hit Podcast, 'The Rise and Fall of Mars Hill,' Stirs Evangelical Soul-Searching." News release, August 13, 2021. https://www.christianitytoday.org/media-room/news/2021/christianity-todays-new-hit-podcast-rise-and-fall-of-mars-h.html.

Cobb, Ryon J. "Still Divided by Faith? Evangelical Religion and the Problem of Race in America, 1977–2010." In *Christians and the Color Line: Race and Religion After "Divided by Faith,"* edited by J. Russell Hawkins and Phillip Luke Sinitiere, 128–39. Oxford: Oxford University Press, 2013.

Coen, Jeff, and Manya Brachear Pashman. "After Years of Inquiries, Willow Creek Pastor Denies Misconduct Allegations." *Chicago Tribune*, March 23, 2018. https://www.chicagotribune.com/news/breaking/ct-met-willow-creek-pastor-20171220-story.html.

Coffman, Elesha. "'You Cannot Fool the Electronic Eye': Billy Graham and Media." In *Billy Graham: American Pilgrim*, edited by Andrew Finstuen, Anne Blue Wills, and Grant Wacker, 197–212. Oxford: Oxford University Press, 2017.

Collins, Travis. *Fresh Expressions of Church*. Franklin, TN: Seedbed, 2015.

Cone, James H. *Black Theology and Black Power*. Twentieth Century Religious Thought. Maryknoll, NY: Orbis, 2018.

Corwin, Gary. "From Roland Allen to Rick Warren: Sources of Inspiration Guiding North American Evangelical Missions Methodology, 1912–2012." In *Missionary Methods: Research, Reflections, and Realities*, edited by Craig Ott and J. D. Payne, 63–91. Evangelical Missiological Society Series 21. Pasadena: William Carey Library, 2013.

Cosper, Mike, host. *The Rise and Fall of Mars Hill*. Podcast. "Episode 1: Who Killed Mars Hill?" *Christianity Today*, June 22, 2021. https://www.christianitytoday.com/ct/podcasts/rise-and-fall-of-mars-hill/who-killed-mars-hill-church-mark-driscoll-rise-fall.html.

Cosper, Mike, host. *The Rise and Fall of Mars Hill*. Podcast. "Episode 2: Boomers, the Big Sort, and Really, Really Big Churches." *Christianity Today*, June 28, 2021. https://www.christianitytoday.com/ct/podcasts/rise-and-fall-of-mars-hill/mars-hill-podcast-boomers-big-sort-hybels-warren-driscoll.html.

Cosper, Mike, host. *The Rise and Fall of Mars Hill*. Podcast. "Episode 6: The Brand." *Christianity Today*, August 2, 2021. https://www.christianitytoday.com/ct/podcasts/rise-and-fall-of-mars-hill/rise-fall-mars-hill-podcast-mark-driscoll-brand.html.

Cosper, Mike, host. *The Rise and Fall of Mars Hill*. Podcast. "Bonus Episode: Boca Raton's Church Planting O.G." *Christianity Today*, October 19, 2021. https://www.christianitytoday.com/ct/podcasts/rise-and-fall-of-mars-hill/mars-hill-podcast-driscoll-david-nicholas.html.

Coulter, Paul B. "Church and Mission in Four Aspects: Church Planting Within a Missionary Ecclesiology for the One, Holy, Catholic and Apostolic Church in Contemporary Northern Ireland." PhD diss., University of Aberdeen, 2016.

Crider, Erin. *Writing Spiritual Autobiography: Discerning God in Your Personal Story*. Grove Spirituality Series 155. Cambridge: Grove Books, 2020.

Croft, Steven. "What Counts as a Fresh Expression of Church and Who Decides?" In *Evaluating Fresh Expressions: Explorations in Emerging Church*, edited by Louise Nelstrop and Martyn Percy, 3–14. London: Canterbury Press Norwich, 2008.

Davies, W. D., and D. C. Allison. *Matthew 8–18*. International Critical Commentary. London: T&T Clark, 1991.

Davison, Andrew, and Alison Milbank. *For the Parish: A Critique of Fresh Expressions*. London: SCM Press, 2010.

Dochuk, Darren. "Lausanne '74 and American Evangelicalism's Latin Turn." In *Turning Points in the History of American Evangelicalism*, edited by Heath W. Carter and Laura Rominger Porter. Grand Rapids: Eerdmans, 2017.

Dodd, C. H. *The Interpretation of the Fourth Gospel*. Cambridge: Cambridge University Press, 1953.

Dothan Community Church. "About Us." Accessed December 7, 2021.

Dowland, Seth. "Billy Graham's New Evangelical Manhood." In *Billy Graham: American Pilgrim*, edited by Andrew Finstuen, Anne Blue Wills, and Grant Wacker, 216–30. Oxford: Oxford University Press, 2017.

Drane, John. *After McDonaldization: Mission, Ministry, and Christian Discipleship in an Age of Uncertainty*. Grand Rapids: Baker Academic, 2008.

Driscoll, Mark. "Born Again to Follow Jesus." In video sermon series Follow Me: What It Means to Be a Disciple of Jesus. Saddleback Church, June 9, 2013. https://saddleback.com/watch/follow-me/born-again-to-follow-jesus?autoplay=true.

Driscoll, Mark. *Religion Saves + Nine Other Misconceptions*. Wheaton, IL: Crossway, 2009.

Driscoll, Mark, and Gerry Breshears. *Vintage Church: Timeless Truths and Timely Methods*. Re:Lit Books. Wheaton, IL: Crossway, 2008.

Dulles, Avery. "The Changing Nature of Mission." In *Eye of the Storm: The Great Debate in Mission*, edited by Donald McGavran, 87–94. Waco: Word, 1972.

Edwards, Korie L. "Much Ado About Nothing? Rethinking the Efficacy of Multiracial Churches for Racial Reconciliation." In *Christians and the Color Line: Race and Religion After "Divided by Faith,"* edited by J. Russell Hawkins and Phillip Luke Sinitiere, 231–50. Oxford: Oxford University Press, 2013.

Emerson, Michael O., with Rodney M. Woo. *People of the Dream: Multiracial Congregations in the United States*. Course Book ed. Princeton: Princeton University Press, 2006.

Emerson, Michael O., and Christian Smith. *Divided by Faith: Evangelical Religion and the Problem of Race in America*. Oxford: Oxford University Press, 2000.

Emetuche, Damian O. *The Future of Church Planting in North America*. American University Studies, Series VII, Theology and Religion 342. New York: Peter Lang, 2014.

Engelsviken, Tormod. "The Role of the Lausanne Movement in Modern Christian Mission." In *The Lausanne Movement: A Range of Perspectives*, edited by Margunn Serigstad Dahle, Lars Dahle, and Knud Jørgensen, 26–44. Regnum Edinburgh Centenary Series 22. Oxford: Regnum Books International, 2014.

Escobar, Samuel. "Evangelism and Man's Search for Freedom, Justice, and Fulfillment." In *Let the Earth Hear His Voice: Official Reference Volume, Papers and Responses*, edited by J. D. Douglas, 303–26. Minneapolis: World Wide Publications, 1975.

Evans, Curtis J. "A Politics of Conversion: Billy Graham's Political and Social Vision." In *Billy Graham: American Pilgrim*, edited by Andrew Finstuen, Anne Blue Wills, and Grant Wacker, 143–58. Oxford: Oxford University Press, 2017.

Evans, Jason E. "Who Will Go for Us?" Reconciliation Ministries Network. Accessed December 7, 2021. https://www.rmni.org/files/afam/JasonEvansTeamFrance.pdf.

Evans, Tony. *Oneness Embraced: Reconciliation, the Kingdom, and How We Are Stronger Together*. Chicago: Moody, 2011.

Fife, Eric S., and Arthur F. Glasser. *Missions in Crisis: Rethinking Missionary Strategy*. Chicago: InterVarsity Press, 1961.

Finke, Roger, and Rodney Stark. *The Churching of America, 1776–2005: Winners and Losers in Our Religious Economy*. Rev. ed. New Brunswick, NJ: Rutgers University Press, 2005.

Finstuen, Andrew S. *Original Sin and Everyday Protestants: The Theology of Reinhold Niebuhr, Billy Graham, and Paul Tillich in an Age of Anxiety*. Chapel Hill: University of North Carolina Press, 2009.

Finstuen, Andrew S. "Professor Graham: Billy Graham's Missions to Colleges and Universities." In *Billy Graham: American Pilgrim*, edited by Andrew Finstuen, Anne Blue Wills, and Grant Wacker, 23–38. Oxford: Oxford University Press, 2017.

Fletcher, John. *Preaching to Convert: Evangelical Outreach and Performance Activism in a Secular Age*. Ann Arbor: University of Michigan Press, 2013.

Francis, Hozell C. *Church Planting in the African-American Context*. Grand Rapids: Zondervan, 1999.

Frost, Michael, and Alan Hirsch. *The Shaping of Things to Come: Innovation and Mission for the 21st-Century Church*. Rev. ed. Grand Rapids: Baker Books, 2013.

Gallagher, Robert L. "Missionary Methods: St. Paul's, St. Roland's, or Ours?" In *Missionary Methods: Research, Reflections, and Realities*, edited by Craig Ott and J. D. Payne, 3–22. Evangelical Missiological Society Series 21. Pasadena: William Carey Library, 2013.

Garrison, David V. *Church Planting Movements: How God Is Redeeming a Lost World*. Monument, CO: WIGTake Resources, 2004.

George, Timothy. *Theology of the Reformers*. Rev. ed. Nashville: Broadman & Holman, 2013.

Gibbs, Eddie. *The Rebirth of the Church: Applying Paul's Vision for Ministry in Our Post-Christian World*. Grand Rapids: Baker Academic, 2013.

Gibbs, Eddie, and Ryan K. Bolger. *Emerging Churches: Creating Christian Community in Postmodern Cultures*. Grand Rapids: Baker Academic, 2005.

Gibson, Scott M. *Should We Use Someone Else's Sermon? Preaching in a Cut-and-Paste World*. Grand Rapids: Zondervan, 2008.

Global Leadership Network. "Who We Are." Accessed November 1, 2021. https://globalleadership.org/who-we-are/.

Godon, Henri, Yvan Daniel, and Georges Guérin. *La France, pays de mission?* Lyon: Les Éditions de l'Abeille, 1943.

Gordon-Conwell Theological Seminary. "Our History." Accessed December 10, 2021. https://www.gordonconwell.edu/about/history/.

Graham, Billy. *Approaching Hoofbeats: The Four Horsemen of the Apocalypse*. Waco: Word, 1983.

Graham, Billy. *Storm Warning: Whether Global Recession, Terrorist Threats, or Devastating Natural Disasters, These Ominous Shadows Must Bring Us Back to the Gospel*. Rev. ed. Nashville: Thomas Nelson, 2010.

Graham, Ruth. "How a Megachurch Melts Down." *Atlantic*, November 7, 2014. https://www.theatlantic.com/national/archive/2014/11/houston-mark-driscoll-megachurch-meltdown/382487/.

Graham, Ruth. "'Sermongate' Prompts a Quandary: Should Pastors Borrow Words from One Another?" *New York Times*, July 6, 2021. https://www.nytimes.com/2021/07/06/us/sermongate-plagiarism-litton-greear.html.

Green, Michael. *Evangelism in the Early Church: Lessons from the First Christians for the Church Today*. Rev. ed. Grand Rapids: Eerdmans, 2003.

Greenway, Roger S. "Urbanization and Missions." In *Crucial Dimensions in World Evangelization*, edited by Arthur F. Glasser, Paul G. Hiebert, C. Peter Wagner, and Ralph D. Winter, 215–32. Pasadena: William Carey Library, 1976.

Greenway, Roger S., and Timothy M. Monsma. *Cities: Missions' New Frontier*. 2nd ed. Grand Rapids: Baker Academic, 2000.

Greggs, Tom. "*Communio* Ecclesiology: The Spirit's Work of Salvation in the Life of the Church." In *Third Article Theology: A Pneumatological Dogmatics*, edited by Myk Habets, 347–65. Minneapolis: Fortress, 2016.

Greggs, Tom. *Dogmatic Ecclesiology*. Vol. 1, *The Priestly Catholicity of the Church*. Grand Rapids: Baker Academic, 2019.

Greggs, Tom. "Sola Scriptura, the Community of the Church and a Pluralist Age: A Methodist Theologian Seeking to Read Scripture in and for the World." In *Theologians on Scripture*, edited by Angus Paddison, 79–92. London: T&T Clark, 2016.

Guder, Darrell L. *Be My Witnesses: The Church's Mission, Message, and Messengers*. Grand Rapids: Eerdmans, 1985.

Guder, Darrell L. "Ecclesiology and Witness." In *The T&T Clark Handbook of Ecclesiology*, edited by Kimlyn J. Bender and D. Stephen Long, 449–62. New York: T&T Clark, 2020.

Guder, Darrell L., Lois Barrett, Inagrace T. Dietterich, George R. Hunsberger, Alan J. Roxburgh, and Craig Van Gelder, eds. *Missional Church: A Vision for the Sending of the Church in North America*. The Gospel and Our Culture. Grand Rapids: Eerdmans, 1998.

Hagner, Donald A. *Matthew 14–28*. Word Biblical Commentary 33B. Dallas: Word, 1995.

Hamilton, Michael S. "From Desire to Decision: The Evangelistic Preaching of Billy Graham." In *Billy Graham: American Pilgrim*, edited by Andrew Finstuen, Anne Blue Wills, and Grant Wacker, 43–60. Oxford: Oxford University Press, 2017.

Hanciles, Jehu J. *Beyond Christendom: Globalization, African Migration, and the Transformation of the West*. Maryknoll, NY: Orbis, 2008.

Harrill, J. Albert. "Ethnic Fluidity in Ephesians." *New Testament Studies* 60, no. 3 (2014): 379–402.

Hawkins, Greg, and Cally Parkinson. *Reveal: Where Are You?* Barrington, IL: Willow Creek Resources, 2007.

Healy, Nicholas M. *Church, World and the Christian Life: Practical-Prophetic Ecclesiology*. Cambridge Studies in Christian Doctrine. Cambridge: Cambridge University Press, 2004.

Hedstrom, Matthew S. "The Commodification of William James: The Book Business and the Rise of Liberal Spirituality in the Twentieth-Century United States." In *Religion and the Marketplace in the United States*, edited by Jan Stievermann, Philip Goff and Detlef Junker, 125–40. Oxford: Oxford University Press, 2015.

Hengel, Martin. "The Prologue of the Gospel of John as the Gateway to Christological Truth." In *The Gospel of John and Christian Theology*, edited by Richard Bauckham and Carl Mosser, 265–94. Grand Rapids: Eerdmans, 2008.

Henry, Carl F. H. *The Uneasy Conscience of Modern Fundamentalism*. Grand Rapids: Eerdmans, 2003.

Hindmarsh, Bruce. "Is Evangelical Ecclesiology an Oxymoron? A Historical Perspective." In *Evangelical Ecclesiology: Reality or Illusion?* edited by John G. Stackhouse Jr., 15–37. Grand Rapids: Baker Academic, 2003.

Hodges, Melvin L. "A Pentecostal's View of Mission Strategy." *International Review of Missions* 57, no. 227 (1968): 304–10.

Hoekendijk, Johannes C. "The Call to Evangelism." *International Review of Mission* 39, no. 154 (1950): 162–75.

Hoekendijk, Johannes C. "The Church in Missionary Thinking." *International Review of Mission* 41, no. 3 (1952): 324–36.

Hoffman, Ronan. "Conversion and the Mission of the Church." *Journal of Ecumenical Studies* 5, no. 1 (1968): 1–20.

Hughes, Rob S. "Roland Allen's Understanding of the Spirit's Centrality in Mission." In *Missionary Methods: Research, Reflections, and Realities*, edited by Craig Ott and J. D. Payne, 23–37. Evangelical Missiological Society Series 21. Pasadena: William Carey Library, 2013.

Hull, John M. *Mission-Shaped Church: A Theological Response*. London: SCM Press, 2006.

Hutchinson, Mark. "'Up the Windsor Road': Social Complexity, Geographies of Emotion, and the Rise of Hillsong." In *The Hillsong Movement Examined: You Call Me Out upon the Waters*, edited by Tom Wagner and Tanya Riches, 39–62. Cham, Switzerland: Palgrave Macmillan, 2017.

Hybels, Lynne, and Bill Hybels. *Rediscovering Church: The Story and Vision of Willow Creek Community Church*. Grand Rapids: Zondervan, 1995.

Irvin, Dale T. "For the Sake of the World: Stephen B. Bevans and Johannes C. Hoekendijk in Dialogue." *International Bulletin of Mission Research* 44, no. 1 (2020): 20–32. https://doi.org/10.1177/2396939319839291.

James, Christopher. *Church Planting in Post-Christian Soil: Theology and Practice*. Oxford: Oxford University Press, 2017.

Jenson, Robert W. *Systematic Theology*. Vol. 1, *The Triune God*. Oxford: Oxford University Press, 1997.

Jenson, Robert W. *Systematic Theology*. Vol. 2, *The Works of God*. Oxford: Oxford University Press, 1999.

Jenson, Robert W. *Visible Words: The Interpretation and Practice of the Christian Sacraments*. Philadelphia: Fortress, 1978.

Jinkins, Michael. *The Church Faces Death: Ecclesiology in a Post-Modern Context*. Oxford: Oxford University Press, 1999.

John, Matthew. "Evangelism and the Growth of the Church." *International Review of Missions* 57, no. 227 (1968): 278–83.

Johnson, Jessica. *Biblical Porn: Affect, Labor, and Pastor Mark Driscoll's Evangelical Empire*. Durham, NC: Duke University Press, 2018.

Johnson, Jessica. "The Fall of Mars Hill Church in Seattle: How Online Counter-Narratives Catalyzed Change." In *The Demise of Religion: How Religions End, Die, or Dissipate*, edited by Michael Stausberg, Stuart A. Wright, and Carole M. Cusack, 119–34. London: Bloomsbury Academic, 2020.

Johnson, Kirk. "Haggard's Church Discloses More on Sex Scandal." *New York Times*, January 26, 2009. https://www.nytimes.com/2009/01/27/us/27haggard.html.

Jüngel, Eberhard. *God as the Mystery of the World: On the Foundation of the Theology of the Crucified One in the Dispute Between Theism and Atheism*. Translated by Darrell L. Guder. London: Bloomsbury T&T Clark, 2014.

Jüngel, Eberhard. "My Theology—A Short Summary." In *Theological Essays II*, translated by Arnold Neufeldt-Fast and J. B. Webster, 1–19. London: Bloomsbury T&T Clark, 2014.

Keener, Craig S. *Acts*. New Cambridge Bible Commentary. Edited by Ben Witherington III. Cambridge: Cambridge University Press, 2020.

Keener, Craig S. *Acts: An Exegetical Commentary*. Vol. 1, *An Introduction and 1:1–2:47*. Grand Rapids: Baker Academic, 2012.

Keener, Craig S. *The Gospel of John: A Commentary*. Vol. 1. Peabody, MA: Hendrickson, 2003.

Keller, Timothy. *Center Church: Doing Balanced, Gospel-Centered Ministry in Your City*. Grand Rapids: Zondervan, 2012.

Keller, Timothy. "The Decline and Renewal of the American Church: Part 2—The Decline of Evangelicalism." *Life in the Gospel* (Winter 2022). https://quarterly.gospelinlife.com/the-decline-of-evangelicalism/.

Keller, Timothy. "How Do You Reach Cities?" Paper presented at the Third Lausanne Congress on World Evangelization, Cape Town, South Africa, October 22, 2010. https://lausanne.org/content/how-reach-cities.

Keller, Timothy. "Why Church Planting?" Acts 29. January 9, 2012. https://www.acts29.com/why-church-planting/.

Keller, Timothy. "Why Cities?" Paper presented at the Third Lausanne Congress on World Evangelization, Cape Town, South Africa, October 20, 2010. Accessed November 4, 2021. https://lausanne.org/content/world-faiths-what-is-gods-global-urban-mission-tim-keller.

Keller, Timothy. "Why Plant Churches?" 2009. https://gospelinlife.com/manual-paper/why-plant-churches/.

Kellstedt, Lyman A., and John C. Green. "The Politics of the Willow Creek Association Pastors." *Journal for the Scientific Study of Religion* 42, no. 4 (2003): 547–61.

Keum, Jooseop. "Beyond Dichotomy: Towards a Convergence Between the Ecumenical and Evangelical Understanding of Mission in Changing Landscapes." In *The Lausanne Movement: A Range of Perspectives*, edited by Margunn Serigstad Dahle, Lars Dahle, and Knud Jørgensen, 383–98. Regnum Edinburgh Centenary Series 22. Oxford: Regnum Books, 2014.

King, David P. "Preaching Good News to the Poor: Billy Graham and Evangelical Humanitarianism." In *Billy Graham: American Pilgrim*, edited by Andrew Finstuen, Anne Blue Wills, and Grant Wacker, 119–37. Oxford: Oxford University Press, 2017.

Kinnaman, David, and Aly Hawkins. *You Lost Me: Why Young Christians Are Leaving Church . . . and Rethinking Faith*. Grand Rapids: Baker Books, 2011.

Kinnaman, David, and Mark Matlock. *Faith for Exiles: 5 Proven Ways to Help a New Generation Follow Jesus and Thrive in Digital Babylon*. Grand Rapids: Baker Books, 2019.

Labanow, Cory E. *Evangelicalism and the Emerging Church: A Congregational Study of a Vineyard Church*. Explorations in Practical, Pastoral and Empirical Theology. London: Routledge, 2016.

"The Lausanne Covenant Statement of Faith." Acts 29. Accessed November 4, 2021. https://www.acts29.com/the-lausanne-covenant-statement-of-faith/.

Lausanne Movement. "Movement Day and Lausanne: Increasing the Impact of the Gospel in Cities Globally." Accessed November 4, 2021. https://lausanne.org/content/lga/2016-05/movement-day-and-lausanne.

Lausanne Movement. "What Global Leaders Were Saying About Cape Town 2010." Accessed November 5, 2021. https://lausanne.org/gatherings/related/what-global-leaders-were-saying-about-cape-town-2010.

"Leadership Conference from Alpha." Accessed March 1, 2022. https://www.leadershipconference.org.uk.

Levinas, Emmanuel. *Totality and Infinity: An Essay on Exteriority*. Translated by Alphonso Lingis. Pittsburgh: Duquesne University Press, 1992.

Lewis, C. S. *The Magician's Nephew*. The Chronicles of Narnia. New York: HarperCollins, 1983.

Leypoldt, Günter. "Literature and the Economy of the Sacred." In *Religion and the Marketplace in the United States*, edited by Jan Stievermann, Philip Goff, and Detlef Junker, 145–57. Oxford: Oxford University Press, 2015.

LifeWay Research. "Lifeway Research Shows 6 Keys to Success for African-American Church Plants." September 11, 2013. https://lifewayresearch.com/2013/09/11/lifeway-research-shows-6-keys-to-success-for-african-american-church-plants/.

Lincoln, C. Eric, and Lawrence H. Mamiya. *The Black Church in the African American Experience*. Durham, NC: Duke University Press, 1990.

Lipka, Michael, and Gregory A. Smith. "White Evangelical Approval of Trump Slips, but Eight-in-Ten Say They Would Vote for Him." Pew Research Center, July 1, 2020. https://www.pewresearch.org/fact-tank/2020/07/01/white-evangelical-approval-of-trump-slips-but-eight-in-ten-say-they-would-vote-for-him/.

Litwak, Kenneth Duncan. *Echoes of Scripture in Luke-Acts: Telling the History of God's People Intertextually*. Journal for the Study of the New Testament Supplement Series. London: T&T Clark International, 2005.

Livingston, John Kevin. *A Missiology of the Road: Early Perspectives in David Bosch's Theology of Mission and Evangelism*. American Society of Missiology Scholarly Monograph Series. Cambridge: James Clarke, 2013.

Luther, Martin. *Church and Ministry II*. Edited by Conrad Bergendoff. Translated by Helmut Lehmann. Vol. 40 of *Luther's Works*, edited by Jaroslav Pelikan and Helmut Lehmann. St. Louis: Concordia, 1958.

Luther, Martin. *First Lectures on the Psalms II: Psalms 76–126*. Edited by Hilton C. Oswald. Translated by Herbert J. A. Bouman. Vol. 11 of *Luther's Works*, edited by Jaroslav Pelikan and Helmut Lehmann. St. Louis: Concordia, 1976.

Luther, Martin. *Lectures on Galatians: Chapters 1–4 (1535)*. Edited by Jaroslav Pelikan and Walter Hansen. Translated by Jaroslav Pelikan. Vol. 26 of *Luther's Works*, edited by Jaroslav Pelikan and Helmut Lehmann. St. Louis: Concordia, 1963.

Luther, Martin. *Lectures on Galatians: Chapters 5–6 (1535); Lectures on Galatians: Chapters 1–6 (1519)*. Edited by Jaroslav Pelikan and Walter Hansen. Translated by Richard Jungkuntz. Vol. 27 of *Luther's Works*, edited by Jaroslav Pelikan and Helmut Lehmann. St. Louis: Concordia, 1964.

Luther, Martin. *Lectures on Titus, Philemon, and Hebrews*. Edited by Jaroslav Pelikan and Walter Hansen. Translated by Walter Hansen. Vol. 20 of *Luther's Works*, edited by Jaroslav Pelikan and Helmut Lehmann. St. Louis: Concordia, 1968.

Luther, Martin. *Sermons on the Gospel of St. John: Chapters 1–4*. Edited by Jaroslav Pelikan. Translated by Martin H. Bertram. Vol. 22 of *Luther's Works*, edited by Jaroslav Pelikan and Helmut Lehmann. St. Louis: Concordia, 1957.

Lyall, Sarah. "Billy Graham, Not Joel, Takes Long Island." *New York Times*, September 21, 1990. https://www.nytimes.com/1990/09/21/nyregion/billy-graham-not-joel-takes-long-island.html.

Mai, Robert, and Alan Akerson. *The Leader as Communicator: Strategies and Tactics to Build Loyalty, Focus Effort, and Spark Creativity*. New York: AMACOM, 2003.

Marsden, George M. *Understanding Fundamentalism and Evangelicalism*. Grand Rapids: Eerdmans, 1991.

Martí, Gerardo. "Fluid Ethnicity and Ethnic Transcendence in Multiracial Churches." *Journal for the Scientific Study of Religion* 47, no. 1 (2008): 11–16.

Martí, Gerardo. "The Global Phenomenon of Hillsong Church: An Initial Assessment." *Sociology of Religion: A Quarterly Review* 78, no. 4 (2017): 377–86.

Martí, Gerardo. *Hollywood Faith: Holiness, Prosperity, and Ambition in a Los Angeles Church*. New Brunswick, NJ: Rutgers University Press, 2008.

Martí, Gerardo. *A Mosaic of Believers: Diversity and Innovation in a Multiethnic Church*. Bloomington: Indiana University Press, 2005.

Martí, Gerardo, and Gladys Ganiel. "Faith as Conversation." In *The Deconstructed Church: Understanding Emerging Christianity*, 78–108. Oxford: Oxford University Press, 2014.

Martin, Marie-Louise. "Does the World Need Fantastically Growing Churches?" *International Review of Missions* 57, no. 227 (1968): 311–17.

Martin, William. "God's Ambassador to the World." In *Billy Graham: American Pilgrim*, edited by Andrew Finstuen, Anne Blue Wills, and Grant Wacker, 83–110. Oxford: Oxford University Press, 2017.

McCormack, Bruce L., and Kimlyn J. Bender, eds. *Theology as Conversation: The Significance of Dialogue in Historical and Contemporary Theology; A Festschrift for Daniel L. Migliore*. Grand Rapids: Eerdmans, 2009.

McFarlan Miller, Emily. "Can Willow Creek Find Closure After Bill Hybels?" *Christianity Today*, July 24, 2019. https://www.christianitytoday.com/news/2019/july/willow-creek-bill-hybels-reconciliation-service.html.

McGavran, Donald Anderson. *The Bridges of God: A Study in the Strategy of Missions*. London: World Dominion Press; New York: Friendship Press, 1955.

McGavran, Donald Anderson. "The Dimensions of World Evangelization." In *Let the Earth Hear His Voice: Official Reference Volume, Papers and Responses*, edited by J. D. Douglas, 94–115. Minneapolis: World Wide Publications, 1975.

McGavran, Donald Anderson. "Essential Evangelism." In *Eye of the Storm: The Great Debate in Mission*, edited by Donald McGavran, 55–66. Waco: Word, 1972.

McGavran, Donald Anderson, ed. *Eye of the Storm: The Great Debate in Mission*. Waco: Word, 1972.

McGavran, Donald Anderson. *How Churches Grow: The New Frontiers of Mission*. London: World Dominion Press, 1959.

McGavran, Donald Anderson. *Understanding Church Growth*. Grand Rapids: Eerdmans, 1970.

McGavran, Donald Anderson. "Will Uppsala Betray the Two Billion?" In *Eye of the Storm: The Great Debate in Mission*, edited by Donald McGavran, 233–41. Waco: Word, 1972.

McIntosh, Gary L. "Donald McGavran: Life, Influence and Legacy in Mission." In *The State of Missiology Today: Global Innovations in Christian Witness*, edited by Charles E. Van Engen, 19–37. Missiological Engagements. Downers Grove, IL: InterVarsity Press, 2016.

McKnight, Scot. *The King Jesus Gospel: The Original Good News Revisited*. Grand Rapids: Zondervan, 2011.

McLaughlin, Brian M. "The Ecclesiology of the Emerging Church Movement." *Reformed Review* 61, no. 3 (2008): 101–18.

McLoughlin, William G., Jr. "Converts and Commercialism." In *Billy Graham: Revivalist in a Secular Age*, 174–203. New York: Ronald Press, 1960.

McLoughlin, William G., Jr. *Revivals, Awakenings, and Reform: An Essay on Religion and Social Change in America, 1607–1977*. Chicago History of American Religion. Chicago: University of Chicago Press, 1978.

McPherson, Willie. "Planting Churches in the Black Community." In *Church Planting in the Black Community*, edited by Sid Smith, 122–33. Nashville: Black Church Development Section, Sunday School Board of the Southern Baptist Convention, 1989.

Meacham, Jon. "Pastor Rob Bell: What if Hell Doesn't Exist?" *Time*, April 14, 2011. https://time.com/archive/6595616/pastor-rob-bell-what-if-hell-doesnt-exist/.

Miller, Donald E. *Reinventing American Protestantism: Christianity in the New Millennium*. Berkeley: University of California Press, 1997.

Miller, Steven P. "Above Politics? Graham After Watergate." In *The Legacy of Billy Graham: Critical Reflections on America's Greatest Evangelist*, edited by Michael G. Long, 179–94. Louisville: Westminster John Knox, 2008.

Mission and Public Affairs Council, Church of England. *Mission-Shaped Church: Church Planting and Fresh Expressions of Church in a Changing Context*. London: Church House Publishing, 2004.

Moore, R. Laurence. *Selling God: American Religion in the Marketplace of Culture*. Oxford: Oxford University Press, 1994.

Moore, Russell. "Southern Baptists Face Their #MeToo Moment." *New York Times*, February 13, 2019. https://www.nytimes.com/2019/02/13/opinion/southern-baptists-sexual-abuse.html.

Moore, Russell. "This Is the Southern Baptist Apocalypse." *Christianity Today*, May 22, 2022. https://www.christianitytoday.com/ct/2022/may-web-only/southern-baptist-abuse-apocalypse-russell-moore.html.

Moran, Roy. *Spent Matches: Igniting the Signal Fire for the Spiritually Dissatisfied*. Nashville: Thomas Nelson, 2015.

Moreton, Bethany. *To Serve God and Wal-Mart: The Making of Christian Free Enterprise*. Cambridge, MA: Harvard University Press, 2009.

Morey, Tim. *Planting a Church Without Losing Your Soul: Nine Questions for the Spiritually Formed Pastor*. Downers Grove, IL: InterVarsity Press, 2020.

Morton, Chris. "Eulogizing the Emergent Church and Defining a Missional Movement." *Growth and Mission*, February 21, 2013.

Moynagh, Michael. *Being Church, Doing Life: Creating Gospel Communities Where Life Happens*. Oxford: Lion Hudson, 2014.

Moynagh, Michael. *Church for Every Context*. London: SCM, 2012.

Moynagh, Michael. *Church in Life: Innovation, Mission and Ecclesiology*. London: SCM, 2017.

Moynagh, Michael. *Emergingchurch.Intro*. Oxford: Monarch Books, 2004.

Moynagh, Michael. *Giving the Church: The Christian Community Through the Looking Glass of Generosity*. London: SCM, 2024.

Mulder, Mark T., and Gerardo Martí. *The Glass Church: Robert H. Schuller, the Crystal Cathedral, and the Strain of Megachurch Ministry*. New Brunswick, NJ: Rutgers University Press, 2020.

Murray, Iain. "Charles Finney: How Theology Affects Understanding of Revival." In *Pentecost—Today? The Biblical Basis for Understanding Revival*, 33–54. Edinburgh: Banner of Truth Trust, 1998.

Murray, Stuart. *Church Planting: Laying Foundations*. Scottsdale, PA: Herald Press, 2001.

Newbigin, Lesslie. *Foolishness to the Greeks: The Gospel and Western Culture*. Grand Rapids: Eerdmans, 1988.

Newbigin, Lesslie. *The Gospel in a Pluralist Society*. Grand Rapids: Eerdmans, 1989.

Newbigin, Lesslie. *The Household of God: Lectures on the Nature of the Church*. London: SCM, 1953; New York: Friendship Press, 1954.

Newbigin, Lesslie. *Mission in Christ's Way: Bible Studies*. Geneva: World Council of Churches Publications, 1987. Accessed June 21, 2021. https://newbiginresources.org/wp-content/uploads/2016/12/87mcw.pdf.

Newbigin, Lesslie. *The Open Secret: An Introduction to the Theology of Mission*. Rev. ed. Grand Rapids: Eerdmans, 1995.

Newbigin, Lesslie. *The Other Side of 1984: Questions for the Churches*. Geneva: World Council of Churches Publications, 1983. https://newbiginresources.org/1983-the-other-side-of-1984-questions-for-the-churches-with-a-postscript-by-s-wesley-ariarajah/.

Niebuhr, H. Richard. *Christ and Culture*. New York: Harper & Row, 1951.

Niebuhr, Reinhold. "Literalism, Individualism, and Billy Graham." In *Essays in Applied Christianity*, edited by D. B. Robertson, 123–31. New York: Meridian Books, 1959.

Noll, Mark A. *The New Shape of World Christianity: How American Experience Reflects Global Faith*. Downers Grove, IL: InterVarsity Press, 2009.

Noll, Mark A. *Protestants in America*. Religion in American Life. Oxford: Oxford University Press, 2000.

Noll, Mark A. *The Rise of Evangelicalism: The Age of Edwards, Whitefield and the Wesleys*. A History of Evangelicalism: People, Movements and Ideas in the English-Speaking World. Downers Grove, IL: InterVarsity Press, 2003.

Noll, Mark A. *The Scandal of the Evangelical Mind*. Grand Rapids: Eerdmans, 1994.

Nortey, Justin. "Most White Americans Who Regularly Attend Worship Services Voted for Trump in 2020." Pew Research Center, August 30, 2021. https://www.pewresearch.org/fact-tank/2021/08/30/most-white-americans-who-regularly-attend-worship-services-voted-for-trump-in-2020/.

North American Mission Board, Southern Baptist Convention. *2021 North American Mission Board Ministry Report*. July 2021. https://www.namb.net/wp-content/uploads/2021/07/2021_Annual_Ministry_Report.pdf.

Oak Cliff Bible Fellowship. "About Us: Our History." Accessed December 7, 2021. https://www.ocbfchurch.org/about-us/our-history/.

Oates, Rosamund. "Speaking in Hands: Early Modern Preaching and Signed Languages for the Deaf." *Past and Present* 256, no. 1 (2021): 49–85. https://doi.org/10.1093/pastj/gtab019.

Olson, David T. *The American Church in Crisis*. Grand Rapids: Zondervan, 2008.

One Community Church. "One Community Church Leadership Principles." Accessed December 7, 2021.

Osmer, Richard R. *Practical Theology: An Introduction*. Grand Rapids: Eerdmans, 2008.

Ott, Craig, and J. D. Payne, eds. *Missionary Methods: Research, Reflections, and Realities*. Evangelical Missiological Society Series 21. Pasadena: William Carey Library, 2013.

Paas, Stefan. *Church Planting in the Secular West: Learning from the European Experience*. The Gospel and Our Culture. Grand Rapids: Eerdmans, 2016.

Paas, Stefan. "Church Renewal by Church Planting: The Significance of Church Planting for the Future of Christianity in Europe." *Theology Today* 68, no. 4 (2012): 467–77. https://doi.org/10.1177/0040573611424326.

Packard, Josh, and George Sanders. "The Emerging Church as Corporatization's Line of Flight." *Journal of Contemporary Religion* 28, no. 3 (2013): 437–55.

Pathak, Jay, and Dave Runyon. *The Art of Neighboring: Building Genuine Relationships Right Outside Your Door*. Grand Rapids: Baker Books, 2012.

Pattison, Stephen. “Some Straw for the Bricks: A Basic Introduction to Theological Reflection.” In *The Blackwell Reader in Pastoral and Practical Theology*, edited by James Woodward and Stephen Pattison, 135–45. Malden, MA: Blackwell, 2000.

Percy, Martyn. “Old Tricks for New Dogs? A Critique of Fresh Expressions.” In *Evaluating Fresh Expressions: Explorations in Emerging Church*, edited by Louise Nelstrop and Martyn Percy, 27–39. London: Canterbury Press Norwich, 2008.

Perkins, Spencer, and Chris Rice. *More Than Equals: Racial Healing for the Sake of the Gospel*. Downers Grove, IL: InterVarsity Press, 1993.

Perry, Abby. “Willow Creek and Harvest Struggle to Move On.” *Christianity Today*, February 13, 2020. https://www.christianitytoday.com/ct/2020/february-web-only/willow-creek-harvest-after-hybels-macdonald-moving-on.html.

Philo. *On Dreams*. Translated by F. H. Colson and G. H. Whitaker. Loeb Classical Library 275. Cambridge, MA: Harvard University Press, 1934.

Philo. *On the Creation*. Translated by F. H. Colson and G. H. Whitaker. Loeb Classical Library 226. Cambridge, MA: Harvard University Press, 1929.

Philo. *The Sacrifices of Abel and Cain*. Translated by F. H. Colson and G. H. Whitaker. Loeb Classical Library 227. Cambridge, MA: Harvard University Press, 1929.

Pitt, Richard N. *Church Planters: Inside the World of Religion Entrepreneurs*. New York: Oxford University Press, 2022.

Platt, David. *Radical Together: Unleashing the People of God for the Purpose of God*. Colorado Springs: Multnomah, 2011.

Pritchard, G. A. *Willow Creek Seeker Services: Evaluating a New Way of Doing Church*. Grand Rapids: Baker Books, 1996.

Purpose Driven Church. “Where Healthy Churches Are Built.” Accessed November 1, 2021.

Robert, Dana L. “Historiographic Foundations from Latourette and Van Dusen to Andrew F. Walls.” In *Understanding World Christianity: The Vision and Work of Andrew F. Walls*, edited by William R. Burrows, Mark R. Gornik, and Janice A. McLean, 141–54. Maryknoll, NY: Orbis, 2011.

Saddleback Church. “Connect.” Accessed November 7, 2021. https://saddleback.com/connect.

Saddleback Church. “Made New.” Accessed November 24, 2021.

Sargeant, Kimon Howland. *Seeker Churches: Promoting Traditional Religion in a Nontraditional Way*. New Brunswick, NJ: Rutgers University Press, 2000.

SBC Executive Committee. *Annual of the 2021 Southern Baptist Convention*. Southern Baptist Convention. Nashville, TN: Southern Baptist Convention, 2021. Accessed March 28, 2021. https://www.sbc.net/wp-content/uploads/2021/09/2021-SBC-Annual.pdf.

Schaller, Lyle E. *44 Questions for Church Planters*. Nashville: Abingdon, 1991.

Schnabel, Eckhard J. *Paul the Missionary: Realities, Strategies and Methods*. Downers Grove, IL: InterVarsity Press, 2008.

Schuster, Jürgen. "Karl Hartenstein: Mission with a Focus on the End." *Mission Studies* 19, no. 1 (2002): 53–81.

Schwöbel, Christoph. "The Creature of the Word: Recovering the Ecclesiology of the Reformers." In *On Being the Church: Essays on the Christian Community*, edited by Colin E. Gunton and Daniel W. Hardy, 110–55. Edinburgh: T&T Clark, 1989.

Schwöbel, Christoph. "A Theological Ontology of Communicative Relations." In *Theology and Conversation: Towards a Relational Theology*, edited by J. Haers and P. De Mey, 43–67. Bibliotheca Ephemeridum Theologicarum Lovaniensium 152. Leuven: Leuven University Press; Leuven: Peeters, 2003.

Shaw, Patricia. *Changing Conversations in Organizations: A Complexity Approach to Change*. Complexity and Emergence in Organizations. London: Routledge, 2002.

Shellnutt, Kate. "Acts 29 Network CEO Removed amid 'Accusations of Abusive Leadership.'" *Christianity Today*, February 7, 2020. https://www.christianitytoday.com/news/2020/february/acts-29-ceo-steve-timmis-removed-spiritual-abuse-tch.html.

Shellnutt, Kate. "Bethlehem Baptist Leaders Clash over 'Coddling' and 'Cancel Culture.'" *Christianity Today*, August 20, 2021. https://www.christianitytoday.com/ct/2021/august-web-only/bethlehem-bcs-minneapolis-resign-meyer-empathy-rigney.html.

Shellnutt, Kate. "Southern Baptist Convention Disfellowships Saddleback Church." *Christianity Today*, February 21, 2023. https://www.christianitytoday.com/news/2023/february/saddleback-church-southern-baptist-sbc-disfellowship-female.html.

Shellnutt, Kate. "Southern Baptists Refused to Act on Abuse, Despite Secret List of Pastors." *Christianity Today*, May 22, 2022. https://www.christianitytoday.com/news/2022/may/southern-baptist-abuse-investigation-sbc-ec-legal-survivors.html.

Showalter, Brandon. "SBC Committee to Consider Disaffiliating Saddleback Church for Ordaining Women Pastors." *Christian Post*, June 18, 2021. https://www.christianpost.com/news/sbc-committee-to-consider-disaffiliating-saddleback-church.html.

Smietana, Bob. "Americans Agree US Has Come Far in Race Relations, but Has a Long Way to Go." LifeWay Research, December 16, 2014. https://lifewayresearch.com/2014/12/16/americans-agree-u-s-has-come-far-in-race-relations-but-long-way-to-go/.

Smietana, Bob. "The Discerning Seller: LifeWay to Drop Warning Labels." *Christianity Today*, February 2011. https://www.christianitytoday.com/ct/2011/february/discerningseller.html.

Smietana, Bob. "Saddleback Church Just Ordained Three Women as Pastors. The Southern Baptist Convention Says Only Men Should Be." *Washington Post*, May 11, 2021. https://www.washingtonpost.com/religion/2021/05/11/saddleback-ordain-women-sbc/.

Smietana, Bob. "Sunday Morning in America Still Segregated—and That's OK with Worshipers." LifeWay Research, January 15, 2015. https://lifewayresearch.com/2015/01/15/sunday-morning-in-america-still-segregated-and-thats-ok-with-worshipers/.

Smith, Adam. *An Inquiry into the Nature and Causes of the Wealth of Nations*. Oxford World Classics. Oxford: Oxford University Press, 1998.

Snyder, Howard. "The Church as God's Agent in Evangelism." In *Let the Earth Hear His Voice: Official Reference Volume, Papers and Responses*, edited by J. D. Douglas, 327–51. Minneapolis: World Wide Publications, 1975.

Stark, Rodney, and Roger Finke. *Acts of Faith: Explaining the Human Side of Religion*. Berkeley: University of California Press, 2000.

Stetzer, Ed. *Planting Missional Churches*. Nashville: Broadman & Holman, 2006.

Stetzer, Edward, and Warren Bird. "The State of Church Planting in the United States: Research Overview and Qualitative Study of Primary Church Planting Entities." *Journal of the American Society for Church Growth* 19, no. 2 (2008): 1–42. https://place.asburyseminary.edu/jascg/vol19/iss2/2/.

Stevenson, Jill. *Sensational Devotion: Evangelical Performance in Twenty-First-Century America*. Ann Arbor: University of Michigan Press, 2013.

Stone, Roxanne. "A Pair of Hillsong Docuseries Planned, Examining the Megachurch's Culture, the Fall of Carl Lentz." Church Leaders, June 25, 2021. https://churchleaders.com/news/400260-a-pair-of-hillsong-docuseries-planned-examining-the-megachurchs-culture-the-fall-of-carl-lentz.html.

Stone, Roxanne, Emily McFarlan Miller, and Alejandra Molina. "Jarrid Wilson, a Megachurch Pastor Known Widely for His Mental Health Advocacy, Dies by Suicide." *Washington Post*, September 10, 2019. https://www.washingtonpost.com/religion/2019/09/10/jarrid-wilson-megachurch-pastor-known-widely-his-mental-health-advocacy-dies-by-suicide/.

Stott, John. "Does Section Two Provide Sufficient Emphasis on Evangelism?" In *Eye of the Storm: The Great Debate in Mission*, edited by Donald McGavran, 266–68. Waco: Word, 1972.

Stott, John. "The Lausanne Covenant: An Exposition and Commentary." Lausanne Movement, Lausanne Occasional Papers 3, 1975. https://lausanne.org/occasional-paper/lop-3.

Sunquist, Scott W., and Amos Yong, eds. *The Gospel and Pluralism Today: Reassessing Lesslie Newbigin in the 21st Century*. Missiological Engagements. Downers Grove, IL: InterVarsity Press, 2015.

Swinton, John, and Harriet Mowat. *Practical Theology and Qualitative Research*. 2nd ed. London: SCM, 2016.

Tennent, Timothy C. "Lausanne and Global Evangelicalism: Theological Distinctives and Missiological Impact." In *The Lausanne Movement: A Range of Perspectives*, edited by Margunn Serigstad Dahle, Lars Dahle, and Knud Jørgensen, 45–60. Regnum Edinburgh Centenary Series 22. Oxford: Regnum Books International, 2014.

Thompson, Augustine. "From Texts to Preaching: Retrieving the Medieval Sermon as an Event." In *Preacher, Sermon and Audience in the Middle Ages*, edited by Carolyn Muessig, 13–37. Leiden: Brill, 2002.

Thompson, James W. *The Church According to Paul: Rediscovering the Community Conformed to Christ*. Grand Rapids: Baker Academic, 2014.

Thornton, Ed. "Heresy, Holiness, and Oprah: Rob Bell Interviewed." *Church Times*, June 14, 2018. https://www.churchtimes.co.uk/articles/2018/15-june/features/features/heresy-holiness-and-oprah-rob-bell-interviewed.

Thumma, Scott. "The Megachurch Phenomenon: Reshaping Church and Faith for the Twenty-First Century." In *The Cambridge History of Religions in America*, vol. 3, edited by Stephen Stein, 575–94. Cambridge: Cambridge University Press, 2012.

Thumma, Scott. *Twenty Years of Congregational Change: The 2020 Faith Communities Today Overview*. Hartford, CT: Hartford Institute for Religion Research/Faith Communities Today, 2021. https://faithcommunitiestoday.org/fact-2020-survey/.

Tippett, Alan. "For Uppsala to Consider." In *Eye of the Storm: The Great Debate in Mission*, edited by Donald McGavran, 246–48. Waco: Word, 1972.

"Tony Evans Shoots for the Goal." *DTS Voice*, July 7, 2006. https://voice.dts.edu/article/tony-evans-shoots-for-the-goal-dallas-theological-seminary/.

"Tony Evans: The Urban Alternative." Accessed December 7, 2021. https://tonyevans.org.

The Urban Alternative. "About The Urban Alternative." Accessed December 13, 2021. http://tonyevans.org/about/the-urban-alternative.

Usunier, Jean-Claude, and Jörg Stolz, eds. *Religions as Brands: New Perspectives on the Marketization of Religion and Spirituality*. Ashgate AHRC/ESRC Religion and Society Series. London: Routledge, 2016.

Utuk, Efiong S. "From Wheaton to Lausanne: The Road to Modification of Contemporary Evangelical Mission Theology." *Missiology: An International Review* 14, no. 2 (1986): 205–20.

Vanderstelt, Jeff. *One Eighty: A Return to Disciple-Making*. Exponential, 2023.

Van Engen, Charles. "The Growth of the True Church: An Analysis of the Ecclesiology of Church Growth Theory." Doctoral thesis, Vrije Universiteit, Amsterdam, 1981.

Van Engen, Charles E. "Innovating Mission: Retrospect and Prospect in the Field of Missiology." In *The State of Missiology Today: Global Innovations in Christian Witness*, edited by Charles E. Van Engen, 1–15. Missiological Engagements. Downers Grove, IL: InterVarsity Press, 2016.

Van Engen, Charles E. *Mission on the Way: Issues in Mission Theology*. Grand Rapids: Baker Books, 1996.

Van Gelder, Craig. *The Ministry of the Missional Church: A Community Led by the Spirit*. Grand Rapids: Baker Books, 2007.

Van Gelder, Craig, and Dwight J. Zscheile. *Participating in God's Mission: A Theological Missiology for the Church in America*. The Gospel and Our Culture. Grand Rapids: Eerdmans, 2018.

Van't Slot, Edward. "Theonomy and Analogy in Ecclesiology: Sources in Barth and Bonhoeffer for a Dynamic Ecclesiology." *Zeitschrift für Dialektische Theologie*, Supplement Series 5 (2011): 45–58.

Van Vlastuin, Willem. "*Sola Scriptura*: The Relevance of Luther's Use of *Sola Scriptura* in *De Servo Arbitrio*." In *Sola Scriptura: Biblical and Theological Perspectives on Scripture, Authority, and Hermeneutics*, edited by Hans Burger, Arnold Huijgen, and Eric Peels, 243–59. Studies in Reformed Theology 32. Leiden: Brill, 2018.

Wacker, Grant. *America's Pastor: Billy Graham and the Shaping of a Nation*. Cambridge, MA: Belknap Press of Harvard University Press, 2014.

Wacker, Grant. "Billy Graham's 1949 Los Angeles Revival." In *Turning Points in the History of American Evangelicalism*, edited by Heath W. Carter and Laura Rominger Porter. Grand Rapids: Eerdmans, 2017.

Wacker, Grant. "Introduction: An Overview." In *Billy Graham: American Pilgrim*, edited by Andrew Finstuen, Anne Blue Wills, and Grant Wacker, 1–19. Oxford: Oxford University Press, 2017.

Wagner, C. Peter. *Apostles Today: Biblical Government for Biblical Power*. Ventura, CA: Regal, 2006.

Wagner, C. Peter. *Church Planting for a Greater Harvest: A Comprehensive Guide*. Ventura, CA: Regal, 1990.

Wagner, C. Peter. *Frontiers in Missionary Strategy*. Chicago: Moody Press, 1972.

Wagner, C. Peter. "Mission and Church in Four Worlds." In *Crucial Dimensions in World Evangelization*, edited by Arthur F. Glasser, Paul G. Hiebert, C. Peter Wagner, and Ralph D. Winter, 275–92. Pasadena: William Carey Library, 1976.

Wagner, C. Peter, Win Arn, and Elmer L. Towns. *Church Growth: State of the Art*. Wheaton, IL: Tyndale House, 1986.

Wagner, Herwig. "Hartensteins Beitrag zum Aufbruch in der Missionstheologie 1945–1960." In *Karl Hartenstein—Leben in weltweitem Horizont Beitrage zu seinem 100 Geburtstag*, edited by Fritz Lamparter, 128–40. Bonn: Verlag für Kultur und Wissenschaft, 1995.

Wagner, Thomas. "Branding, Music, and Religion: Standardization and Adaptation in the Experience of the 'Hillsong Sound.'" In *Religions as Brands: New Perspectives on the Marketization of Religion and Spirituality*, edited by Jean-Claude Usunier and Jörg Stolz, 59–74. Ashgate AHRC/ESRC Religion and Society Series. London: Routledge, 2016.

Wagner, Tom. *Music, Branding, and Consumer Culture in Church: Hillsong in Focus*. Routledge Studies in Religion. London: Routledge, 2020.

Wallis, Roy, and Steve Bruce. "The Stark-Bainbridge Theory of Religion: A Critical Analysis and Counter Proposals." *Sociological Analysis* 45, no. 1 (1984): 11–28.

Walls, Andrew F. "Eschatology and the Western Missionary Movement." *Studies in World Christianity* 22, no. 3 (2016): 182–200.

Walls, Andrew F. *The Missionary Movement in Christian History: Studies in the Transmission of Faith*. Maryknoll, NY: Orbis, 1996.

Ward, Pete. *Celebrity Worship*. Media, Religion and Culture. New York: Routledge, 2020.

Ward, Pete. *Introducing Practical Theology: Mission, Ministry, and the Life of the Church*. Grand Rapids: Baker Academic, 2017.

Warren, Rick. *The Purpose Driven Church: Growth Without Compromising Your Message and Mission*. Grand Rapids: Zondervan, 1995.

Warren, Rick, and Kay Warren. "Rick and Kay Warren on Navigating the Pain of Loss, Building Resiliency and Rebuilding in the Post-Pandemic World." In Leadership Conference, Holy Trinity Church Brompton, London, UK, May 4–5, 2021, accessed March 1, 2022, https://alpha.org/leadership-conversations-with-nicky-gumbel-podcast-rick-kay-warren/.

Watkins, Clare. *Disclosing Church: An Ecclesiology Learned from Conversations in Practice*. Explorations in Practical, Pastoral and Empirical Theology. London: Routledge, 2020.

Webber, Robert E., ed. *Listening to the Beliefs of Emerging Churches: Five Perspectives*. Grand Rapids: Zondervan, 2007.

Webber, Robert E. *The Younger Evangelicals: Facing the Challenges of the New World*. Grand Rapids: Baker Books, 2002.

Wehner, Peter. "The Evangelical Church Is Breaking Apart: Christians Must Reclaim Jesus from His Church." *Atlantic*, October 24, 2021. https://www.theatlantic.com/ideas/archive/2021/10/evangelical-trump-christians-politics/620469/.

Welch, Craig. "The Rise and Fall of Mars Hill Church." *Seattle Times*, September 13, 2014, updated February 4, 2016. https://www.seattletimes.com/seattle-news/the-rise-and-fall-of-mars-hill-church/.

Wilford, Justin. *Sacred Subdivisions: The Posturban Transformation of American Evangelicalism*. New York: New York University Press, 2012.

Williams, John A. "In Search of 'Fresh Expressions of Believing' for a Mission-Shaped Church." *Ecclesiology* 12, no. 3 (2016): 279–97.

Williams, Reggie L. *Bonhoeffer's Black Jesus: Harlem Renaissance Theology and an Ethic of Resistance*. Waco: Baylor University Press, 2014.

Williams, Reggie L. "Dietrich Bonhoeffer, the Harlem Renaissance and the Black Christ." In *Bonhoeffer, Christ and Culture*, edited by Keith L. Johnson and Timothy Larsen, 59–72. Downers Grove, IL: InterVarsity Press, 2013.

Wingfield, Mark. "Acts 29 Ups the Ante by Offering Church Planters $50,000 Apiece." *Baptist News Global*, January 14, 2022. https://baptistnews.com/article/acts-29-ups-the-ante-by-offering-church-planters-50000-apiece/.

Winner, Lauren. *The Dangers of Christian Practice: On Wayward Gifts, Characteristic Damage, and Sin*. New Haven: Yale University Press, 2018.

Winter, Gibson. *The Suburban Captivity of the Churches: An Analysis of Protestant Responsibility in the Expanding Metropolis*. New York: Macmillan, 1962.

Winter, Ralph. "Further Comment on 'Drafts for Sections.'" In *Eye of the Storm: The Great Debate in Mission*, edited by Donald McGavran, 242–45. Waco: Word, 1972.

Winter, Ralph. "The Highest Priority: Cross-Cultural Evangelism." In *Let the Earth Hear His Voice: Official Reference Volume, Papers and Responses*, edited by J. D. Douglas, 213–25. Minneapolis: World Wide Publications, 1974.

Worthen, Molly. "Who Would Jesus Smack Down?" *New York Times Magazine*, January 6, 2009. https://www.nytimes.com/2009/01/11/magazine/11punk-t.html.

Yee, Tet-Lim N. *Jews, Gentiles and Ethnic Reconciliation: Paul's Jewish Identity and Ephesians*. Society for New Testament Studies Monograph Series 130. Cambridge: Cambridge University Press, 2005.

Zylstra, Sarah Eekhoff. "How Acts 29 Survived—and Thrived—After the Collapse of Mars Hill." The Gospel Coalition, December 5, 2017. https://www.thegospelcoalition.org/article/how-acts-29-survived-and-thrived-after-the-collapse-of-mars-hill/.

Index

www.ingramcontent.com/pod-product-compliance
Lightning Source LLC
Chambersburg PA
CBHW022347300825
31889CB00002B/2

* 9 7 8 1 4 8 1 3 2 2 8 7 4 *